THE WORLD OF CANADIAN WINE

D0789784

JOHN SCHREINER

THE WORLD OF CANADIAN WINE

Douglas & McIntyre
Vancouver/Toronto

To Marlene, who denies she had to drive me home

© 1984 by John Schreiner
First paperback edition, 1985

All rights reserved. No part of this book may be reproduced or transmitted in any form by any means without permission in writing from the publisher, except by a reviewer, who may quote brief passages in a review.

Douglas & McIntyre Ltd., 1615 Venables Street, Vancouver, British Columbia V5L 2H1

Canadian Cataloguing in Publication Data

Schreiner, John.
  The world of Canadian wine

ISBN 0-88894-440-3 (hardcover)
ISBN 0-88894-468-3 (paperback)

1. Wine and wine making– Canada. 2. Viticulture– Canada. I. Title.
TP559.C3S37 1984   663'.22'0971   C84-091226-9

Cover photograph by Derik Murray
Cover design by Barbara Hodgson
Design by Heather Griblin
Maps by David Gay
Typesetting by Vancouver Typesetting Co. Ltd.
Printed in Canada by Imprimerie Gagné Ltée.

CONTENTS

PART III

PART IV

ACKNOWLEDGEMENTS

Gratitude is due to a great many people whose help and co-operation have enabled me to write this book. The executives and the winemakers at wineries across Canada all have given generously of their time and have been rightfully proud to lead tastings of their wines. Some have invited criticism as well as encouragement and I trust they will find useful elements of both in this book.

Special recognition goes to two individuals whose foresight has resulted in their wineries maintaining some archival material: Noah Torno, whose family was long associated with Jordan Wines, and Jan Van Der Ree, the controller at Chateau-Gai Wines Ltd. Others filled in history with long and generous interviews, among them M. F. Jones, in his eighty-fifth year still a valued director of Bright's; George Hostetter, long-time director of research at Bright's; Brian Roberts, retired general manager of Growers Wines; Evans Lougheed, the founder of Casabello Wines; Andrew Peller, the founder of Andrés; O. A. Bradt, retired grape specialist at Vineland and his successor, Dr. Helen Fisher; Dr. Donald Fisher (no relation), the retired superintendent of the Summerland Research Station in B.C., and John Vielvoye, the B.C. Ministry of Agriculture's grape specialist.

Others whose help has been crucial include R. A. Wallace, the general manager of the Liquor Distribution Branch of B.C.; Daniel Werminlinger, retired president of the Société des Alcools; J. K. Couillard and Peter Galichon of the Liquor Control Board of Ontario, and retired LCBO Commissioner Maj.-Gen. George Kitching, who had the courage to license new wineries for the first time in fifty years. The logistic support of Brian Leyden and the Ontario Editorial Bureau was most valuable.

Finally, I would like to thank my colleagues at *The Financial Post* for their support: Neville Nankivell, editor-in-chief, and Jim Lyon in the Vancouver bureau, a fellow author who provided sound advice.

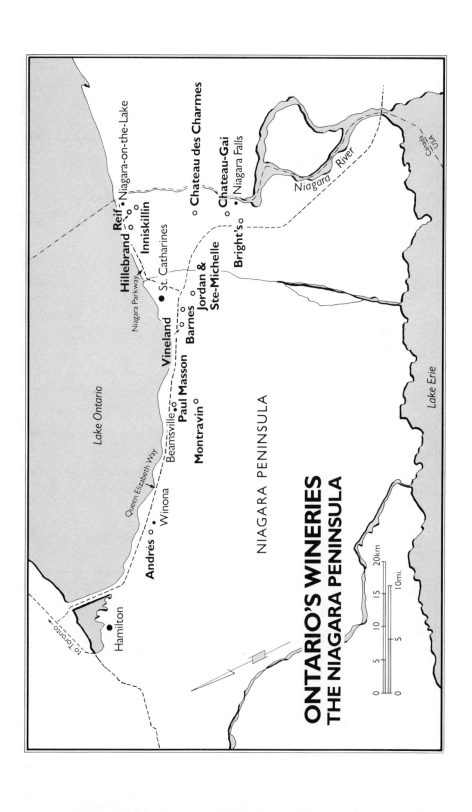

ONTARIO'S WINERIES
THE NIAGARA PENINSULA

Lake Ontario

Lake Erie

NIAGARA PENINSULA

Niagara River

Niagara Falls

Canada
USA

Niagara-on-the-Lake

Chateau des Charmes

Chateau-Gai

Hillebrand Reif

Inniskillin

Bright's

St. Catharines

Jordan &
Ste-Michelle

Barnes

Vineland

Paul Masson

Montravin

Beamsville

Winona

Andrés

Queen Elizabeth Way

Niagara Parkway

to Toronto

Hamilton

20km

15

10

10mi.

5

5

0

0

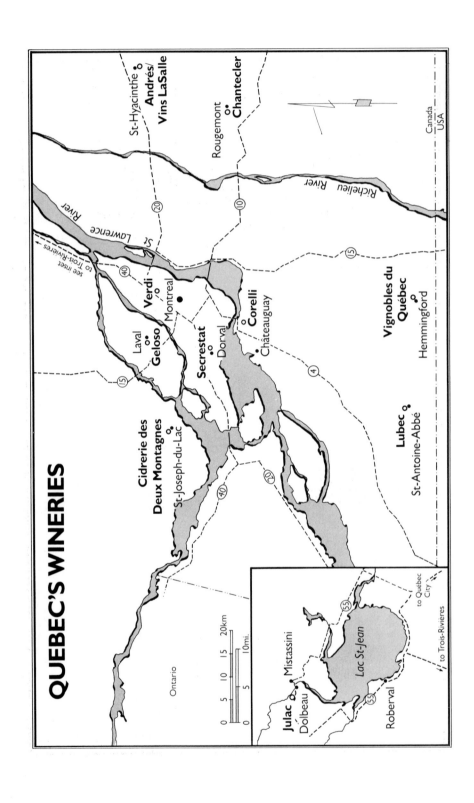

QUEBEC'S WINERIES

St-Hyacinthe
Andrès/
Vins LaSalle

Rougemont
Chantecler

Canada
USA

Richelieu River

St Lawrence River

see inset
to Trois-Rivières

Verdi
Montreal

Laval
Geloso

Secrestat

Dorval

Corelli
Châteauguay

Vignobles du
Québec
Hemmingford

Cidrerie des
Deux Montagnes
St-Joseph-du-Lac

Lubec
St-Antoine-Abbé

Ontario

20km
15
10
10mi.
5
5
0
0

Julac
Dolbeau
Mistassini

Lac St-Jean

Roberval

to Quebec
City

to Trois-Rivières

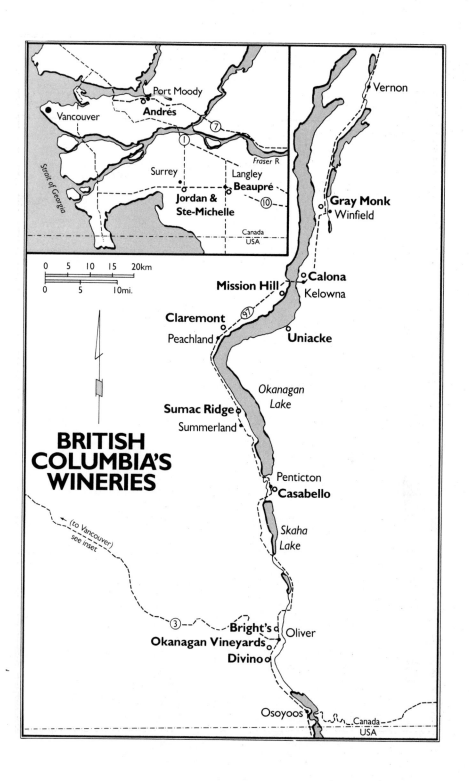

BRITISH COLUMBIA'S WINERIES

Port Moody
Andrés
Vancouver
Strait of Georgia
Surrey
Langley
Beaupré
Jordan & Ste-Michelle
Fraser R
⑦
①
⑩
Canada
USA

Vernon

Gray Monk
• Winfield

○**Calona**
Kelowna

Mission Hill○

Claremont○
Peachland
㊞
Uniacke

Sumac Ridge○
Summerland
Okanagan Lake

Penticton
○**Casabello**

Skaha Lake

(to Vancouver)
see inset

③
Bright's○
Oliver
Okanagan Vineyards○
Divino○

Osoyoos
Canada
USA

0 5 10 15 20km
0 5 10mi.

PART I

CHALLENGE
OF THE EIGHTIES

The year 1979 was a benchmark in the acceptance of Canadian wines. For it was in this year, for the first time, that the influential Opimian Society, a national body based in Montreal and dedicated to the importing and tasting of wines, included Canadian vintages in offerings to its twelve thousand members. The society had in the previous six years of its existence explored all the wine world but Canada, even acquiring a California winery. The Canadian offerings began with private-label bottlings by Chateau-Gai of Ontario, followed in 1981 by Calona of British Columbia, in 1982 by Chateau des Charmes of Ontario, and in 1984 by British Columbia's Mission Hill. Knowledgeable Canadians were now being invited to discover the products of their own wine industry as it broke from a history of sweet and fortified wines to produce quality table wines.

Wine has been made commercially in Canada since at least 1860. The wines featured by the Opimian Society, however, have come from vineyards and, for the most part, wineries that are less than a decade old. Few wines and trade names from the industry's first century have survived into its second. The durable survivors are typically fortified and sparkling wines, while the new products are table wines bearing little or no resemblance to the wines of the past. As the Opimian Society's selections suggest, Canadian table wines are reaching world standard. This is happening for three reasons: conversion to premium grape varieties in the vineyards, a dramatic increase in the technical competence of the winemakers, and a marked, relatively recent consumer preference for table wines over fortified and sweet novelty wines.

Good wine begins in the vineyard. The greatest deterrent to high-quality Canadian table wine has been the domination of our vineyards by varieties ill suited for table wine production. We had been warned:

as early as 1622, the Virginia colonists sent to Britain some wines made from similar native grapes that grew in wild abundance there, only to have them judged "a scandal." European grape varieties planted in early Virginia failed, however, as did virtually all vinifera plantings in eastern North America during the next three centuries, the vines succumbing to disease and cold winters. American horticulturists concentrated on developing productive varieties based on crosses with native varieties such as the labrusca. The most successful was the concord, a hardy, blue-skinned grape bred in 1843 in Concord, Massachusetts, which soon became the most widely grown grape in eastern Canada and the United States. Other varieties based on native crosses that became important included the niagara, the elvira and the agawam. None is suitable for dry table wine.

The unsuitability of these grapes was irrelevant during the first hundred years of commercial winemaking in Canada. Those Canadians who did drink wine preferred it sweet, in the style of ports and sherries. The native grapes were adequate for making such wines, since added sugar and barrel-aging masked flavour defects that otherwise emerged in stark relief. When consumer tastes began shifting in the sixties, there was a brief but enormous popularity for flavoured novelty wines and then sparkling blends. The concord and its stable-mates were so ideal for these wines that additional acreages were planted. In Ontario in 1956, there were 3.6 million concord vines, 670 000 niagara vines and 271 000 agawam. Twenty years later, just as the novelty wine fad was passing its peak, the figures were 4.7 million, 1.6 million and 720 000.

The growers had alternatives. In 1946 the T. G. Bright winery and the research station at Vineland, Ontario, began importing cuttings of hybrid varieties developed in France that were significantly more disease-resistant than the noble, or vinifera, European varieties. Adhémar de Chaunac, Bright's French-born winemaker, had convinced his employers as early as 1934 that he could produce competent table wines and better fortified wines from French hybrid grapes. However, only three of the hybrids – de chaunac, maréchal foch and chelois, all red-skinned – had achieved commercially significant plantings by 1976. Of the vinifera varieties imported in 1946, only the chardonnay had been propagated extensively.

It is not surprising that the growers should have been slow to respond. A potato farmer can change varieties in one season, providing he can obtain the seed, but when a grape grower replants a vineyard, it is four years before a new vine has a worthwhile yield. The Canadian growers have also enjoyed the institutional protection of marketing boards which, until the mid-seventies, resisted winery-imposed quality standards for grapes, but were able to negotiate satisfactory prices and reliable markets for their crop. In return for these privileges, the boards could be counted on to join the wineries in attacking any critic – and critics had grown numerous – of Canadian table wines. More to the point, consumer attitudes by the mid-seventies were harmfully negative. For example, Canadian wines were available on Air Canada, the national airline, but so seldom requested that cabin attendants had begun to call the bottles ''million milers.'' The president of a Canadian winery once asked for one of his products and the stewardess, who did not recognize him, gave him six bottles with the comment: ''You may as well have them all. No one else wants them.''

There was a basis for defending the maligned wines. In the mid-sixties, Canadian wines were outselling imports three to one in Canada, apparent confirmation that the wineries were producing what Canadians wanted. Demand had begun to change dramatically, however, and in a manner profoundly disturbing to Canadian wineries. In 1970, when Canadian wines still held a two-to-one edge in sales, imported wine sales increased by a third, while domestic wine sales rose by only 13 per cent. As liquor boards across Canada began listing ever-greater numbers of imports, the gap narrowed until, in 1977, imported wines outsold domestic ones for the first time.

Since then, the wineries of Canada have been able to hold slightly less than half the 47.5-million-gallon Canadian wine market. While liquor boards, under consumer pressure, allowed many more imported wines into the Canadian market, they have marked up those prices more aggressively than for Canadian wines. This critical measure of protection, which is under legal challenge and may not always be there, gave Canadian wineries a chance to respond to the enormous change in national wine tastes. There are practical limits to the protection which liquor boards can offer, however. When the French franc was devalued in 1983, French wine prices tumbled and those wines were able to grab major market share from Canadian wines.

The earliest response to changing Canadian preferences was the release of drier blends of table wines bearing labels which, for the most part, suggested an association with European classics. The most successful was Schloss Laderheim from Calona Wines, a white modelled consciously after such successful German brands as Blue Nun and Black Tower. The use of pseudolabels is hardly new in the

wine world – wines called burgundy, chablis and chianti are also produced in the United States and Australia – but the practice was taken to the extreme as the beleaguered Canadians battled for market share during the past decade. The current trend is away from such labels: the names of grape varieties or such local place names as Bright's Vaseaux Cellars in British Columbia are now being featured. This is happening because both wineries and consumers are increasingly confident, even proud, of the distinctively Canadian wines behind those labels.

The growing acceptance of better Canadian wines can be credited to immense changes that have swept the industry in the past few years. The vineyards are finally being replanted: the concord vine population of Ontario in 1981, for example, was 3.5 million, a decrease of 1.2 million in only five years. Replacing the native varieties have been premium French hybrids such as seyval blanc, up from 51 000 vines in 1976 to 670 000 in 1981, and such vinifera as chardonnay and johannisberg riesling. The latter variety, the great grape behind many classic German whites, has now become the most widely planted vinifera in Canada.

The technical change in the wineries has been equally important. Wines no longer referment in the bottle and explode on liquor store shelves as they did in the early years of both Andrés and Calona. Today's winemakers are likely to have graduated from Geisenheim in Germany or the University of California's Davis campus – or in chemistry and microbiology from a Canadian university, since there is no school of enology in this country. They have equipment ranging from temperature-controlled stainless steel tanks to sterile bottling lines. Under such conditions, there is no reason why wines should not be clean, fresh and free of technical faults. There are times when the technical winemaking is massaged too much: Canadian wineries are allowed to add water, sugar and grain alcohol in varying quantities in various provinces, with the result that the cheapest wines have been stretched to the point where quality suffers. In addition, provinces without commercial vineyards allow the import of raw materials ranging from grape concentrate to bulk wines. While these processed wines are generally acceptable, they are seldom examples of the best Canada has to offer.

The emergence of estate wineries, beginning with Inniskillin in 1975, has been profoundly positive. The Canadian wine industry had been stifled for a long time. After World War One, all provinces but Quebec kept prohibition: in Ontario, however, the grape growers, who even then had political leverage, got an exemption for wine. The result was an undisciplined expansion of wine production and consumption, followed by a dramatic collapse of the industry after Prohibition ended and during the depression of the thirties. Neither British Columbia nor Ontario was prepared to license new wineries, because the industry was financially unsound and because persistent puritanism militated against any official encouragement for the industry. It was an absurd time when wines were not sold with meals in many public dining rooms and women were not admitted to public drinking places. In the sixties, however, under pressure from immigrants and a newly travelled generation of Canadians, liquor laws became more realistic. First British Columbia and then Ontario began licensing new wineries for the first time since the depression.

The new wineries have created excitement with the novelty and quality of their products, drawing attention to Canadian wines generally and making it easier for established wineries to win recognition for their quality products. None of the large, established wineries own commercial vineyards today, but every estate winery has sprouted on its own soil. All have nurtured grape varieties not widely grown and produced distinctive and often distinguished wines from these varieties. Winemakers being proud people, the big wineries have responded with their own varietals. The acceptance of these wines in the market and their evident quality has made it much easier for growers to understand why concords must be uprooted and replaced.

The wines of Canada have chosen a difficult decade for their entry on to the world stage. All the older wine-growing nations have surplus production, available at bargain prices to the affluent consumers of North America. Nor are Canadian wines alone in clamouring for the recognition they deserve, for new vineyards are being planted from Texas to Japan, and noble grapes are replacing coarse ones in places as widely separated as New Zealand and Bulgaria. Winemaking technology has improved everywhere; even trained winemakers are in surplus supply. It is a tough, competitive environment. Just as vines produce some of the best vintages from barely hospitable soils, however, the best wines of Canada will be made in this time of challenge.

CHAMPAGNE AND THE ART OF LABEL WRITING

In 1955 Chateau-Gai mounted in a Paris store window a large display that featured the first bottles of Canadian champagne shown to the French public. The strategy worked, generating substantial publicity in Canada: a major article in the Toronto *Globe and Mail Magazine* was entitled, "He Sells Ontario's Wines in the Very Heart of France." It also triggered legal and political challenges to the Canadian wine industry's use of champagne and other offshore appellations. The controversy has played in the courts or the political arena ever since.

The Canadian wine industry has adopted foreign-sounding brand names with singular enthusiasm. A mythical German castle called Schloss Laderheim helped Calona's product become for several years the largest-selling domestic white, and start a fashion that includes Alpenweiss (Chateau-Gai), Hochtaler (Andrés), Liebesheim (Bright's), Falkenberg (Jordan), and a grandiloquent trio from Mission Hill – Tollercranz, Sonnenwein and Schloss Weinberg. Italian and French names have appeared with similar profusion. Canadian wineries in the past have also proposed to release wines simply called Beaujolais, Chianti and Liebfraumilch, only to be driven off by threats of legal action. The central thrust of these threats and of the champagne suit is that the use of foreign place names is deceptive. Deceptive or not, these labelling practices reflect the nature of the Canadian table wine market. The foreign-sounding labels are a clear attempt by Canadian wineries to attach to their products some of the sophisticated image of the imports. They also suggest to consumers what style of wine they will find in the bottle.

Under French law, no wine can be called "champagne" unless the grapes are harvested and the wine produced entirely in that district of France. When the French moved against Canadians, they had already been successful in arguing their point, in this case against Spanish "champagne," before a British court. In 1964 fifteen producers acting through the French government Institut National des Appellations d'Origine applied in a Quebec court for an injunction against the use of "champagne" on Chateau-Gai labels. The Niagara Falls company was singled out for two simple reasons, one being that the

1955 publicity stunt had attracted French attention, and the other the firm's relative isolation in the sixties. Alexander Sampson, who was running Chateau-Gai and who perennially quarrelled with others in the industry, had attacked the trendy pop-wine excesses of the day as degrading to the image of Canadian wine: when the Canadian Wine Institute failed to take a stand against them, he had resigned from that body in 1963.

Arguing that Canada had bound itself by a 1933 trade agreement to respect appellations such as "champagne," the French won in the Quebec High Court. In a decision later upheld by the provincial appeal court, Chateau-Gai was ordered to stop using the word on its labels in Quebec and pay $5,000 in damages to each of the producers who had launched the action. Chateau-Gai had now rejoined the

Canadian Wine Institute and, with that body's backing, took the champagne case to the Exchequer Court of Canada and ultimately to the Supreme Court, where, in 1974, the Quebec decision was again upheld. In the latter court, however, Chateau-Gai's argument that the term "champagne" had passed into common usage, like the brand name Aspirin, managed to impress one dissenting judge, Bora Laskin, who wrote that "the delay, the slumbering on their rights by the respondents, has been for an unconscionably long time." The French, despite the 1933 trade treaty, had not protested to Canada until 1958.

Chateau-Gai decided to call its bubbly "mousseux" in Quebec, but without much enthusiasm. "Our product won't be called champagne," president Thomas Comery, who has succeeded Sampson, told a Toronto paper. "Therefore, people will expect to pay less for it." Although the decision did not apply to the rest of Canada, the whole industry reacted with defiance. As for the French, they decided to press their attack in Ontario, bringing one action in 1975 against eight Ontario wineries, another in 1976 against Podamer, and yet another against London in 1980 when that winery reintroduced its brand of bubbly. And to make things worse, the federal authorities then circulated draft wine-labelling regulations that proposed to designate 250 foreign place names as trademarks unavailable to Canadian wineries. It was a sweeping list, including not just champagne but sauterne and burgundy as well. The Canadian industry then began

to lobby furiously. The Ontario Grape Growers Marketing Board angrily demanded that the provincial liquor board consider a retaliatory ban on French champagnes. Maj.-Gen. George Kitching, the board's commissioner, responded: "The implications of denying champagne – true champagne – to the people of Ontario are certainly serious. We have many consumers who would insist that it be available and I know many of them feel that the name 'champagne' should never have been used by the domestic wineries."

The Canadian wineries managed to sideline the federal draft regulations, and their attack on the 1933 trade agreement also succeeded, though for a reason that had nothing to do with wine. Ottawa sensitivities were inflamed when in 1977, a year after being elected, Quebec Premier René Lévesque was given head-of-state treatment in Paris. Near the end of a federal cabinet meeting late that year, discussion turned to how Canada could show its anger to France without creating an open diplomatic breach. Donald Jamieson, the minister of industry, trade and commerce, told his colleagues he knew precisely how, and the Canada-France treaty was declared to be null and void, effective the following March. Canadian wineries were free once again to label their bubblies as Canadian champagne.

The legal basis for the subsequent suits against Canadians using the term "champagne" is the one which the French established in Britain in 1960 against the Spanish: that the imitations cannot be passed off as the real thing. Canadian producers appear to have given their opponents some ammunition through the proliferation of proprietary labels in German, French and Italian, which can be confused with import labels. Italian authorities, for example, have convinced the federal government to ask one Canadian winery not to use the word "Asti," an Italian appellation of origin, as a domestic brand. The controversy arises, of course, because of the very success of such labels. While Schloss Laderheim rocketed to national prominence, sales of another Calona brand bearing the name of a British Columbia vineyard, Monashee Estate, remained marginal even in its home province. The problem was not a wide difference in quality but rather a difference in credibility. Bright's, with no Calona past to live down, has succeeded with a generic group of reds and whites sold simply as House Wine, the success a sign that consumers do respond to commonsense labels.

PART II

THE BIG SIX

ANDRES

ESTABLISHED 1961

COOPERAGE 11.2 million gallons at six wineries

TOURS & TASTINGS at the Ontario winery are available Monday through Saturday, 10 A.M. to 10 P.M. Tel. (416) 643-4131. The winery's barrels and tanks are visible beside the Queen Elizabeth Way at Kelson Avenue, Winona.

At the British Columbia winery tour times vary. Tel. (604) 937-3411. The winery store is open from 1 to 9 P.M., Monday through Friday. The winery is on Vintner Street at the western edge of the Vancouver suburb of Port Moody.

For tour arrangements in Quebec call the winery on Picard Street, St-Hyacinthe. Tel. (514) 773-7468.

For tour arrangements in Nova Scotia call the winery in Truro. Tel. (902) 895-2874.

There are no tours at the Alberta winery, but the retail store is open at 7530 Blackfoot Trail at the western edge of Calgary.

TASTER'S CHOICE features some outstanding varietals: the ♼♼1982 and ♼♼♼1983 scheurebes, fleshy, aromatic whites, and the 1982 and 1983 ehrenfelsers (both ♼♼♼), all British Columbia products. Excellent are the ♼British Columbia verdelet 1983 with its crisp finish, the ♼♼1983 auxerrois, and the ♼♼1983 johannisberg riesling, another British Columbia wine; the Ontario johannisberg 1982 gets ♼.

ALSO ❢ aurore 1982, ❢ seyve villard 1983, ❢ seyval blanc
RECOMMENDED 1982 and the ❢ chelois 1983, all produced in On-
tario; Domaine d'Or White, Franciscan Canadian
Chablis, Hochtaler, House Wine, Kurhauser Troc-
ken Sekt, Richelieu Canadian Champagne,
❢❢Golden Cream Sherry, Similkameen Superior
Red and Similkameen Superior White, both from
B.C., and Wintergarten.

Joseph Peller once described his father, Andy, as a "great bull of an
entrepreneur." This aptly characterizes the restless man who in 1961,
at age fifty-eight, moved halfway across Canada to establish Andrés
Wines. The youngest of Canada's large wineries, it has become the
most substantial of them all, operating six establishments across the
country with a combined storage capacity of 11.2 million gallons and
annual sales in excess of $55 million. Andrés has at least two things
its competitors lack: Baby Duck, the concord-based sparkler that was
for some years Canada's biggest-selling wine, and Joseph Peller, the
medical specialist who turned businessman to save the company from
collapse and who has surrounded himself with similarly tough-
minded employees.

The elder Peller was born in 1903 to German parents whose
livelihood included a small vineyard on the Hungarian Danube. He
apprenticed as a machinist and, when he emigrated to Canada in
1927, took a mechanic's job with a Kitchener brewery that was
resuming operations with the repeal of prohibition. A few years later
he moved to Toronto, where he worked in another brewery, Cosgrave's. When U.S. Prohibition ended in 1933, both Cosgrave
brewmasters moved to American breweries. Peller, then superintendent of the bottling line, was rushed through a six-month course in
Chicago and came back as Cosgrave's new brewmaster. When the
Second World War broke out, Peller's German background caused
friction with some fellow employees: he left to open a machine shop
in Hamilton, where he proved his patriotism by making, among other
products, rangefinders for the Canadian navy. Towards the end of the
war, he organized the Peller Brewing Company, secured a licence,
and began making beer in 1946. The Hamilton brewery's equipment
had been scavenged from five American breweries, all of which had

sprung up and then failed after Prohibition; he was to equip his first winery the same way.

Peller's brewery was a considerable success, both because of a postwar beer shortage and later, when competition intensified, because the irrepressible Peller found ways around Ontario's ban on the advertising of booze. Remembering that ice boxes still outnumbered

refrigerators, he formed an ice company that was free to advertise, using billboards and radio, where Gordon Sinclair read the commercials with puckish relish. The stress was always on the Peller name and not the ice, since the idea was to make people think of cold Peller's. Sinclair recalled: "Will Gent, an advertising man, dreamed up the idea of advertising the ice with a pause by the broadcaster. I was to talk about Peller's ... ice. The pause was important. Sometimes in taping the commercials, I'd make a fluff as we all do and sometimes Gent deliberately let them go as if to indicate I was a bit loaded. On ice!" Ontario's Premier Leslie Frost called Peller personally to complain. Peller shrugged off complaints, but he learned that bureaucrats have long memories when, a decade later, he applied for an Ontario winery licence.

In 1953 the brewing magnate E. P. Taylor, who had purchased Cosgrave's before the war, added Peller's to his empire with a rich offer. Andrew Peller found himself with a million dollars at the age of fifty. Ever restless, he bought the ailing *Hamilton News,* a paper started by newspaper unions in a strike against the reigning *Spectator*. Eight months later, when continuing losses forced him to close, he sold the building back to the unions and peddled the name to publisher Roy Thomson, who wanted the tax losses to offset profits elsewhere in his communications empire. The wine business had always intrigued Peller: now he began pestering the Ontario liquor board for a licence. The board first rebuffed him and then made the impractical suggestion that he produce only "Rhine wine," a style with which he would be crippled in a market then dominated by fortified wines. He had no doubt that he was being punished for the mischievous ice commercials, and headed for British Columbia.

In his autobiography, Peller recalled how surprised he was to see only 250 acres of vineyard in the entire Okanagan, a natural locale for vines. He found a 40-acre farm on the banks of the Similkameen River, which flows into the southern Okanagan, and turned for viticultural advice to a new acquaintance, Tony Biollo, a local grape grower and home winemaker. Biollo believed passionately in the Okanagan's potential: he had already encouraged Chateau-Gai to establish a winery there, and was later in the syndicate that established Casabello. Naturally, he encouraged Peller, and when the farm was acquired, operated it for several years.

While Peller was looking for a winery site, it was suggested to him that he might buy Calona, then unofficially on the market. Jordan's Noah Torno looked at it about the same time and decided that it was "a tin-pot affair." Peller reached the same conclusion: "Capozzi's winery reminded me of the old French wineries where the grapes were crushed in ancient wooden vats which had been used for generations." With Pasquale Capozzi asking the equivalent of $700,000, Peller thought it would take another million to put the winery in shape – "and I would still have an old facility." Instead, he built a winery at Port Moody, a Vancouver suburb where land was cheap. With good transportation available, Peller preferred to have the winery close to its market rather than the vineyards. After weighing mundane names such as British Columbia Winery, he decided to call it Andrés: it was his baptismal name, and besides, it had a French ring.

Like the equipment at Port Moody, the first winemaker, Wallace Pohle, came from California. A handsome, cigar-smoking figure, he was a good plant manager but a self-trained vintner. Some of the first table wines Andrés shipped were unstable, refermenting in their bottles and popping corks in the liquor board warehouse. When Peller started opening wineries across Canada, Pohle decided to go back to California. Julius Fessler, a San Francisco wine chemist, was retained for two years as a consultant before Guy Baldwin, a chemist from Christian Brothers, became winemaker, returning later to California and Paul Masson Vineyards. Andrés thus acquired a California style that distinguished it from other British Columbia wineries of the day—Growers, then the largest, was selling more loganberry wine than grape.

Because the grapes of the Okanagan were already committed to other wineries, and Peller's Similkameen vineyard was years away from production, Andrés purchased its initial requirement from California. When the winery applied for its first listings in early 1962, Peller was informed that his use of imported materials meant that his wines would cost fifteen cents a bottle more than his competitors'. It was a stroke of luck: "That horrid, additional fifteen cents acted like a magic wand ... if it was more expensive, it must be better." The liquor board's second order was double the first.

Intoxicated by his initial success at Port Moody, Peller welcomed proposals for wineries in Calgary and Truro, Nova Scotia. He expanded long before the undercapitalized Port Moody establishment had repaid its debts, and by 1964 he faced serious financial problems at three wineries. These difficulties and the endless travelling left him in a condition which his doctor son has described as "frazzled." It had not occurred to Joseph Peller, though he was nominally a director, to do anything but medicine until he became concerned about his father's business problems. His chosen career had already taken him far as an endocrinologist; at thirty-eight, he was chief of medicine at Hamilton Civic Hospital. Talking with the elder Peller, he concluded that he had no option but to take three months' leave and go to his father's aid: "We were a closely-knit European family." Andrew later described his son as ''the best thing that ever happened to the company.''

Joseph Peller underrated the problems, and by the end of his three-month leave he knew that the Andrés wineries were in deeper trouble than he had imagined. At the same time, he became intrigued with the business: he sold his medical equipment, resigned his vari-

ous appointments, sublet his home in the Hamilton suburb of Ancaster, and moved to British Columbia. By the end of the year, with some management changes, the Calgary and Port Moody wineries were functioning smoothly. And for Nova Scotia, Peller eventually found so competent a manager in Ralph Logan that Andrés captured 60 per cent of the provincial market. Nor has Logan's competitive business style dimmed over the years. When the struggling Chipman winery of Kentville, which had been losing money for nearly two decades, finally ceased operating in 1983, he swiftly bought the rights to Chipman's labels, including Golden Glow, a strong apple cider. His lightning move gave Andrés added space on liquor store shelves and prevented rivals from improving access to Nova Scotia.

Since Andrés wineries could not pay Joseph Peller a significant salary, he reopened his medical practice from 1967 to 1969, ''running the wineries on weekends.'' He felt that a winery was required in Ontario, if only to anchor the company geographically, but his initial submissions to the LCBO were no more successful than his father's had been until the LCBO chairman observed that the new Beau Chatel winery at Winona, owned by Imperial Tobacco of Montreal, might be for sale. The 1964 U.S. Surgeon-General's report on smoking had sent cigarette firms the world over into headlong diversification: Imperial had chosen wine, but after five years, in most of which Imperial lost money on wine, the firm was in retreat. Joseph bought the winery in late 1969, making ''a super deal.'' In Andrew Peller's view the deal was not as sweet as his son thought: ''I could have built the whole thing for half the money,'' said the one-time machinist who

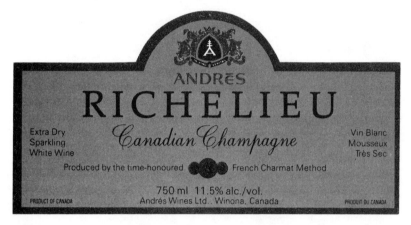

had scavenged bankrupt wineries and breweries. But it did give Andrés a running start in the big Ontario market, and two years later the Winona winery was operating at a profit.

Meanwhile, Joseph Peller completed the reorganization of Andrés's tangled structure. Each of the first three wineries had started as a separate corporation – Andrés in British Columbia, Anjo Wines in Calgary and Abbey Wines in Truro – to be grouped in 1965 under Gourmet Wines, a holding company. By 1969 the three were operating under the Andrés name with one board of directors. The Beau Chatel acquisition was followed by the 1974 purchase for $2.2 million of a winery in St-Hyacinthe, Quebec, which Calona had built and operated unsuccessfully. In 1975 Andrés bought the Valley Rouge Winery at Morris, Manitoba, which had been opened by the K-Tel organization, famous even then for hard-sell television promotion of popular recordings. No other Canadian winery has so many individual operations.

From the outset, Andrew Peller had grasped the advantages of having regional wineries in Canada, whether or not there is a local grape supply. In fact, a local supply can be a liability, since wineries can buy grapes and concentrates more cheaply from California or

Europe than they can from vineyards in Canada. But in Peller's words, "All the provinces are in the alcohol business," and express preference for local producers. Only companies with wineries in Quebec are allowed to market through grocery stores in that province, while firms with no wineries in Quebec rarely get listings even in provincial liquor stores. The six large wineries in British Columbia

are traditionally assigned an automatic sixty-six listings in liquor stores: Canadian wineries with no British Columbia base are on the same footing as foreign ones. Discrimination is also reflected in mark-up policies. Ontario, for example, marks up Ontario-made table wines by 45 per cent, other Canadian table wines by 85 per cent, and imported table wines by 110 per cent. British Columbia applies a 57 per cent mark-up to provincially made table wines, but 117 per cent to other Canadian and imported table wines. Of the six provinces in which Andrés produces wine, only one, Manitoba, so far lacks a preferential mark-up for local wineries. Andrew Peller's shrewdness in grasping the opportunity inherent in provincial chauvinism is one reason why Andrés is the country's largest producer. The chief reason for Andrés's dominance, however, is that remarkable and highly profitable product, Baby Duck.

The winery's first big success in the British Columbia table wine market had been a crackling rosé called Chanté, produced by Guy Baldwin and aimed at the market niche held in the sixties by the Portuguese rosés. Chanté was pressurized to two atmospheres with carbon dioxide; it came in red, white and rosé, and, best of all, its 7 per cent alcohol got it a federal tax break. At the time Joseph Peller spotted this, the tax on 7 per cent wines was twenty-five cents a gallon compared with $2.50 on sparkling wines such as champagne, and this gave Chanté a decided price advantage over higher-alcohol competitors. At the same time, a product called Cold Duck had become widely popular in the United States – an unpretentious, 12 per cent sparkling wine, typically sweet, made by blending reds and whites.

Wine critics have never taken Cold Duck seriously, and Peller himself was dubious as Andrés launched a similar product in Canada. It sold so well, however, that Andrés tried to register the name as its own brand, and very nearly succeeded.

Since Cold Duck had to pay the same excise tax as champagne, Andrés decided to develop a low-alcohol version. Named logically as Baby Duck, it waddled onto the market in 1971, a somewhat sweet blend of juice from labrusca grapes and water, sparkled with pressurized carbon dioxide. Labrusca are the lowest-priced grapes available since they are undesirable for dry table wines. Sweetened and with their acidity balanced, however, they gave Baby Duck a unique character that proved popular from the start. Despite a host of imitations, it held its position as Canada's single largest-selling domestic wine until sales reached a plateau in 1981 and Baby Duck was overtaken by Calona's Schloss Laderheim and other still, white table wines.

Heady success in Canada led Andrés to believe that Baby Duck could blast its way into export markets as well. One executive who held that view was Peter Green, a Briton recruited in 1976 from the cidermaker H. P. Bulmer, where as president he had tried to convince

Bulmer's board to distribute Baby Duck. Under Green's direction, Andrés backed a British launching with a $2.5-million advertising campaign in November 1979 and even dreamed of selling in France. One Andrés spokesman told a reporter, "They've never tasted concord grapes in France." They didn't want to, and the British didn't, either. Baby Duck was unable to penetrate either market to any significant degree, and by 1982, with Peter Green gone, Andrés withdrew almost completely from its European adventure.

The profitability of Baby Duck has given winemakers at Andrés wide latitude to innovate, to take a fresh approach to markets. As in other big Canadian wineries, they are required to deal with as many as forty different grape varieties, some vinifera, some hybrids and some labrusca. The challenge is immense. As Winona manager David Hojnoski says, "It literally staggers winemakers who come from other parts of the world." Andrés winemakers have become adept in the art of blending. Wines from the various grapes, vinified separately each fall, are clarified and stabilized as rapidly as possible after fermentation so that they reach the stainless steel tanks clean and sound. The blends for the various branded wines are prepared roughly once every four months, a cycle which enables the winery to bring fresh wines continually to market. It also gives the winery flexibility to alter blends as taste trends change. Blending cycles are also staggered so that fresh lots of wine are being bottled almost every week.

Andrés has also applied technology to the problem of preventing bottles from refermenting. Great pains are taken to remove microorganisms with fine filtering and to bottle under sterile conditions. The winery has refined the technique of removing tartrate crystals: wines are chilled rapidly below freezing for a brief period to speed formation of the crystals. "We do in ninety minutes what it takes Mother Nature six to nine months to do," Hojnoski says. Wine so treated is likely to reach the market sooner and in a fresher state.

This effort is all aimed at supporting the variety of brand-name wines with which Andrés attacks segments of the market. Its contender against German-style white wines is Hochtaler, a blend of johannisberg riesling, seyval blanc, aurore and two California viniferas, chenin blanc and colombard. Released in 1980, it has become Andrés's top-selling white. A fruitier and sweeter brand for the same market is Wintergarten, a blend of California vinifera and chiefly elvira, a labrusca variety. The Domaine D'Or brands, both red and white, are blends of French hybrid grape varieties. And to help reduce the surplus of reds, the company has released a grapy product with a brown kraft label, inexpensively priced and simply called Red Wine.

With aggressive blending and marketing, Andrés has captured a quarter of the entire market for Canadian wines. At the same time,

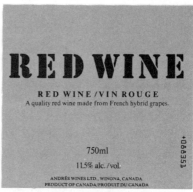

however, the firm's winemakers in British Columbia and Ontario are making smaller lots of noteworthy varietals. Ron Taylor, the veteran winemaker at Port Moody, first released a delicate verdelet in 1978 but not another one until 1982. He and Walter Gehringer, his German-trained assistant, made vintage whites from ehrenfelser and scheurebe, two excellent German vinifera hybrids starting to produce in quantity in that province. (Gehringer left in 1984 to start an Okanagan estate winery with his brother; his successor, Californian Mark Chandler, is proving as able.) At the Winona winery, Barry Poag evaluated nine different varieties made from the excellent 1982 vintage there, finally releasing varietals made from johannisberg riesling, seyval blanc, aurore and chelois. Using the Charmat process, he also made a 6000-gallon lot of blanc de blancs, a champagne-style wine blended from chardonnay and seyval blanc. A previous lot, about forty-five cases, was produced as a trial in 1979 and has been reserved as private winery stock for special occasions.

In other vintages, the Winona winery has even released a white varietal made from the red-skinned de chaunac grape, with the juice charcoal-filtered to remove colour. Andrés and other wineries now make white wine regularly from this grape, mainly for use in blends. In British Columbia, the de chaunac grape has long been the base of

Similkameen Superior red, a domestic table wine with which Andrés has won awards consistently since 1971 in eastern European competitions.

It was some time in 1977 that sales of imported table wines overtook those of their domestic counterparts. And while both segments of the industry have shown subsequent growth, domestics

continue to lag behind imports. Joseph Peller decided in 1980 to have a foot in both camps, and the company set up a California branch to buy and bottle bulk wines for the Canadian market. Andrés became Canadian agent for two small but prestigious California wineries, Heitz and Jekel. In 1982 the company acquired major interests in two Toronto-based importing agencies, one specializing in Italian wines and the other in German and French. "There is another half to the wine business in Canada," explained James Berry, an Andrés vice-president at Winona: "I'd rather compete against myself than have someone else compete against me." Thus has Andrés set its course to remain the largest and most profitable winery in Canada.

BRIGHT'S

ESTABLISHED 1874

COOPERAGE 11.4 million gallons

TOURS & TASTINGS are available at the Niagara Falls winery during business hours, Monday through Saturday; evening group tours by appointment. Tel. (416) 357-2400. The winery stands near the intersection of Dorchester and Thorold Stone Road.

In Oliver, British Columbia, tours and tastings are available Monday through Friday in summer, and in winter on Friday afternoons or by special arrangement. Tel. (604) 498-4981. The winery is 5.6 km (3.5 mi.) north of Oliver on the east side of Highway 97.

TASTER'S CHOICE includes the Ontario-made 🍷🍷🍷 1983 Aligoté, the Ontario-made 🍷🍷 1982 baco noir, a dry, full-bodied red and the best baco noir in Canada; the steely 🍷 1982 Chardonnay; two limited quantity British Columbia–made whites, 🍷🍷 matsvani 1983 and 🍷🍷 weiss burgunder, and the 🍷 Vaseaux Cellars Premium White from the British Columbia winery.

ALSO RECOMMENDED Bright's House Wine, 🍷 Bright's President Extra Dry champagne, the 🍷🍷 1982 chenin blanc from B.C., Club Spritz, L'Entre Cote red and white, the gewurztraminer, johannisberg rieslings, Quebec's Maximum Mousseux cider and Mon Village white wine, and B.C.'s Vaseaux Cellars Premium Red.

Adhémar de Chaunac, the French-born microbiologist hired by the T.G. Bright company in 1933, promised good table wines if his employer gave him $600,000 and twenty years in which to spend it on research and development. The request was entirely typical of the man. "If there ever was an individualist or a prima donna, it was Adhémar de Chaunac," recalled Meredith Jones, a retired Bright's president.

De Chaunac, who retired in 1961 and died eleven years later, was for three decades the outstanding winemaker in Canada. This was the consequence both of his ability and of his good fortune in being employed by the Hatch family which has run Bright's with paternal idealism since 1933. Then the country's largest winery, it was struggling against the general slide into economic depression when

Harry Hatch bought it in June of that year. Lacking adequate technical staff, Bright's had accumulated a substantial quantity of wine so bad that Hatch could only have it distilled to salvage the alcohol. A wealthy distiller and former partner in the Jordan firm, he could take the long view of the winery and the business in general, and over the next generation the Hatch family and Bright's had a profound impact on the Canadian wine industry. "They were the pioneers in changing Ontario viticulture," Toronto wine merchant Peter Chubb has observed, referring to the grape varieties which, at de Chaunac's urging, were imported from France after the Second World War: "Everybody sells the varietal hybrids today but Bright's did all the work."

The second-oldest continuously operating winery in Canada was established in 1874 on Toronto's Front Street by the lumber merchants Thomas Bright and F. A. Shirriff. To be closer to vineyards, it moved in 1890 to its current Dorchester Road location in Niagara Falls. Shirriff left the partnership to go into the jam business and W. M. Bright, the son of the founder, took over in 1910 to run the winery during the Prohibition years from 1916 to 1927, when Ontario wineries were producing the only legal alcoholic beverage. Many wineries failed quickly after Prohibition ended: all of them, burdened with surplus wines, were in difficulty. William Bright probably considered himself fortunate when he was invited aboard Harry Hatch's yacht, the *Anna Mildred,* and presented with an offer. Hatch controlled Hiram Walker, which also represented such distinguished European wine shippers as Nathaniel Johnstone et Fils of Bordeaux, Lanson of Champagne and the sherry house of Gonzales Byass.

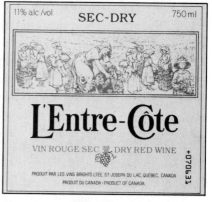

Harry Hatch began hiring professionals for Bright's as soon as he acquired the winery. One of the first was a winemaker, Dr. John Ravenscroft Eoff, a courtly Virginian gentleman who had been a food chemist with the Food and Drug Administration in the United States. He died in 1940, his contribution to Bright's overshadowed by that of Adhémar de Chaunac, who had been his assistant. A junior member of a noble French family, de Chaunac emigrated to Canada in 1907. He was a chemist with a Quebec dairy when Hatch bought a disused brewery in Lachine and converted it to a wine cellar. De Chaunac was put in charge of that conversion, his background in dairy sanitation well suited to the requirements of a good winery, and then moved to Niagara Falls to oversee the laboratory and, ultimately, all research and development.

In 1934 Bright's bought fourteen hundred acres of Niagara vineyard land and began planting such varieties as dutchess and delaware, readily available North American hybrids better suited than labrusca for table wines. By 1941 there were enough mature vines for de Chaunac to blend 5000 gallons of the winery's first major new table wine brand since Prohibition, Manor St. Davids sauterne. Later the brand became Canada's leading domestic table wine: Bright's continues to sell both red and white blends, with almost no promotion, to a loyal clientele.

De Chaunac argued that better wines yet could be made if the winery planted both vinifera varieties and the hybrids developed in France to overcome problems of weather and disease. The French would begin to limit hybrid plantings in the fifties, when it seemed that the prolific varieties would displace many traditional vinifera varieties to the detriment of their wines: in the mid-thirties, however, the hybrids were the wonders of viticulture. Early in the century, New York State's Geneva experimental station had begun planting vines produced by the pioneer French breeder Albert Seibel. In a scientific career which ran from 1874, when he was thirty, until his death in 1936, Seibel made tens of thousands of plant crosses. His work and that of such fellow hybridizers as François Baco, Eugene Kuhlmann, J.-L. Vidal and Bertille Seyve-Villard was known to de Chaunac and J.R. Van Haarlem, the grape specialist at the experimental station in Vineland, Ontario. Soon after de Chaunac joined Bright's, the winery, at his suggestion, planted Seibel 1000, one of the first French hybrids grown in Ontario. From this variety, later named rosette, he was able to make light, dry reds. Because the wines lacked character, however, the variety was never widely grown.

Both Bright's and Vineland were preparing to order vines from France when war broke out in 1939. The order was finally placed in 1945, with de Chaunac and Van Haarlem co-operating on the selection of varieties. The trial shipments included thirty-five French hybrids, among them all those that have since become commercially important, and four hardy vinifera: chardonnay, johannisberg riesling, pinot noir and perle of csaba. The decision to put in a major planting was made in 1947, and Bright's planted about forty thousand vines, encompassing all the hybrids, the next year. Some hybrids had been named, but many still bore only the breeder's number, Seibel 9549 being an example. As the varieties flourished, the wine trade realized that varietal wines would never be marketed effectively if the labels identified grapes by number, and in 1970 the Finger Lakes

Wine Growers' Association in New York began assigning names. Seibel 9110 became verdelet, Seibel 10878 became chelois, Seyve-Villard 5276 seyval blanc, and so on. Seibel 9549 was identified as cameo until the Canadian Wine Institute objected, since a member winery had registered this name as a trademark. Finally, a joint committee of Niagara and New York winegrowers decided in 1972 to name the grape for de Chaunac: the tribute was a fitting one, since this red-wine variety is the most widely planted in Canada and is planted extensively in the eastern United States, and all of these vines can be traced back to mother blocks at Bright's and Vineland.

De Chaunac was deeply touched by having the grape named for him at a ceremonial dinner in the Niagara Falls Club, but the irony is that, as a winemaker, he preferred the chelois, a more difficult grape to grow. Throughout his career, de Chaunac, as temperamental as an artist, was forever making difficult demands. ''De Chaunac was always critical of the board of directors, until we made him one,'' Harry Hatch's son Douglas has said. Nor was he ever afraid to argue with any of his colleagues. Meredith Jones has recalled a running disagreement which culminated when the winemaker marched into his office – ''He never walked, he stalked'' – and, finger wagging in accusation, snapped: ''Jones, you are a fool!'' This lack of diplomacy could be carried over into his private life as well. Edwin Haynes, then at Chateau-Gai, once invited the Bright's winemaker to supper and was stunned when the Frenchman, on arriving, announced that he would toss the salad. It was a perfectionist fetish that de Chaunac always repeated when dining with Haynes and his wife.

De Chaunac was responsible for making a bottle-fermented sparkling wine – the classic method for champagne – which was released in 1949 under the name President and has long been the largest-selling domestic champagne. The cuvée for this crisp, smoky-flavoured bubbly includes catawba, dutchess, delaware, rosette and seyval blanc. At first, the winery had bottles exploding from internal pressure until de Chaunac corrected this problem. They were then stacked to mature. "We did it without any idea of how to do it," Douglas Hatch remembered. "The first time a train went by, over went the pile. So we decided we'd better learn something about how to pile champagne. A group of us went down to New York State and learned the proper way, and then you couldn't push it over with a truck."

Of the four vinifera grapes in the postwar trial, Bright's decided in 1951 to concentrate on a six-acre planting primarily of chardonnay that has been described by Bright's research director, George Hostetter, as "the first successful planting of commercial vinifera east of the Mississippi in North America." These vines enabled Bright's to release what was called a pinot champagne in 1955 and a pinot chardonnay table wine in 1956; these are claimed to have been the first vinifera varietals marketed by a Canadian winery.

As quickly as the new hybrid grape vines began producing, de Chaunac began making new, non-labrusca table wines. A claret blended of chelois and rosette was added to the Manor St. Davids line in 1949, and a totally new Canadian burgundy was made from the maréchal foch grape. Meredith Jones, who travelled Canada extensively to market the company's wines, has recalled that de Chaunac's dry (or at least drier) table wines were a surprising success. At times, the packaging helped as well. After the Second World War, the Bright's agent in New Brunswick, an Italian-born soft-drink bottler by the name of Tony Buraglia, suggested that Manor St. Davids claret be put in a chianti-style bottle, round and stubby but without the straw basket, as a signal that the wine was dry and robust. For a long time, the claret in this bottle was one of the company's best-selling table wines.

Bright's shared its research information with the industry. It also began selling bulk wines to competitors, for it was the first winery with significant quantities available from the hybrid plantings. The purpose was both commercial and altruistic: "We felt that if Bright's was making something superior but others were not, we'd never convince the public that Ontario wines were other than garbage," Hostetter has explained. One such sale, involving several hundred thousand gallons of Manor St. Davids claret blend, was later released by three competitors under three different labels. The practice could have ironic results. "One day," Jones recalled, "my wife gave a party and she had some Manor St. Davids sauterne, nicely chilled. I got home just about the time the party was breaking up." One of the guests complimented Jones on the wine, but added, "Would you mind if I told you that London has a superior one?" Jones could scarcely contain himself, since the London wine was Manor St. Davids under another label. Bright's continued to sell table wines in bulk into the seventies, and even today supplies two other Ontario wineries with champagne.

Since 1946 the winery has spent more than $3 million on research and development and evaluated more than six hundred grape varieties; it currently has sixty under test on a plot near Harrow in southwestern Ontario. "If we had not done the work over the years," insists Hostetter, who succeeded de Chaunac as research director, "there would not be a viable Ontario wine industry." Research has also looked at winemaking techniques, the most recent being computer-controlled fermentation. When the firm opened its British Columbia winery, the nearby Inkameep vineyard had been growing a variety of exotic vines in test plots since the mid-seventies without any serious commercial evaluation of the grapes. Since the 1982 vintage, winemakers John Bremmer and Lynn Stark have made small lots of as few as a hundred bottles from nearly two dozen of these test varieties, enabling growers and wineries to taste the results and make the appropriate planting decisions.

Research is no substitute for aggressive marketing, however. Bright's sat out the pop-wine boom of the sixties that saw Andrés replace it as the country's biggest winery. Yet Bright's had had a low-alcohol beverage on the market long before Andrés was even formed. About 1950, the Ontario liquor board suggested, no doubt in the cause of temperance, that a low-alcohol wine be produced. The request was put to de Chaunac, who confirmed that 7 per cent alcohol wines were possible but technically tricky, since the alcohol would not be high enough to render the wine stable in the bottle. Bright's pushed ahead, however, proposing a shared-risk project to the family-owned Fred Marsh Winery in Niagara Falls. Marsh received the idea noncommittally, and then, "To our astonishment," Jones

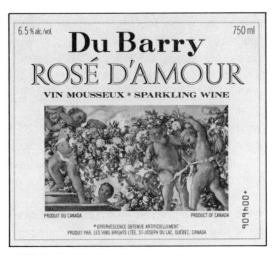

said, "one day we find Fred Marsh announcing a new low-alcohol wine called Winette." Because Marsh did not have as competent a winemaker as de Chaunac, the sparkling Winette soon began refermenting on liquor store shelves and had to be withdrawn. The disaster spelled the end of the winery, which Bright's bought in 1953, inheriting Winette, which is still being made, at the same time as it was introducing its own low-alcohol DuBarry Sparkling Rosé.

Bright's had been consistently profitable since 1934 when, in 1972, its profit peaked at $1 million on sales of $11 million. Five years later, the winery had slipped to an embarrassing $123,000 loss on $13.8 million in sales. Bright's was not alone: the major shift in Canadian wine consumption had begun. New strategies were clearly needed, and the recovery in Bright's fortunes was related to a shrewd hunch on the part of Meredith Jones, who had retired as president in 1963 but was still an active director. One of the bright young Andrés executives he admired was Edward Arnold, the son of a Steveston, B.C., fisherman, successful with the competitor firm but recently passed over for promotion. Jones concluded that Arnold might be ripe for a job offer, and broached the idea over lunch. The British Columbian, then only thirty-nine, joined Bright's as a vice-president in 1976 and within two years had become the winery's chief executive.

Arnold came from a winery which had made little fortified wine to one with extensive wood cooperage holding thousands of gallons of ports and sherries. Bright's Lachine winery, for example, had dominated the domestic wine market in Quebec until the early seventies with a sherry, a port and a sauterne. After 1972, however, new wineries sprang up that were dedicated to table wine production, and Bright's slipped to fifth place. The winery overhauled its Quebec product line and built or acquired the facilities to make table wines for the new and fast-growing market offered by food-store wine sales. By the end of the decade, it was in first place again. The Quebec strategy of replacing inexpensive and slow-selling fortified wines with new and better table varieties was Arnold's marketing thrust for the entire company.

The most successful of the new table wines, introduced in 1977, was Bright's House Wine. The white, with 9 per cent alcohol, was blended to compete with such medium-dry imports as Black Tower. The red, with 10 per cent, was soft, easy to drink, and as uncomplicated as the low-priced French and Italian reds. Drier versions were later introduced, and the brand has gone on to sell more than a million gallons a year in Canada. The name is simplicity itself, inspired by a question to Arnold from his wife: "Why doesn't someone put out a house wine?" It is to Bright's credit, in fact, that the winery has released fewer wines bearing so-called import alternative names than have many of its competitors. A number of Bright's brand names have drawn on company tradition. Manor St. Davids wines were first made from grapes grown in Bright's vineyards near the Niagara village of St. Davids. The Warnerhof label for German-style whites comes from a former Bright's vineyard settled originally in 1784 by a Swiss named Christian Warner. Vaseaux Cellars, a new Bright's label in British Columbia, takes its name from Vaseaux Lake near the Oliver winery and replaces the Entre Montagnes label, which had no local meaning.

In the eighties, Bright's is no longer to be found on the conservative sidelines when such new consumer tastes or fads emerge as the California-born popularity of low-calorie wines. There is no secret to stripping calories from wines: it is mainly a question of reducing alcohol content. Bright's entered the low-calorie market in 1982 with a cleverly crafted sparkling white called Club Spritz, containing only 5 per cent alcohol. The effervescence comes from mineral water, blended with wines made from such full-flavoured grape varieties as muscat and diamond. Unlike Winette, the wine was not left to sell itself: Club Spritz was launched with a $400,000 Ontario advertising campaign which made it even more successful than the winery had hoped. With new products aggressively marketed, Bright's restored its profits and more than doubled its sales to $40 million in the five years after 1978, when Arnold became president. It has yet to overtake Andrés as the sales leader in Canada, but by one yardstick, its storage capacity, or cooperage, it is slightly larger. While the Andrés winery at Winona holds wines almost entirely in stainless steel, Bright's has an astonishing amount of wooden cooperage, 6.5 million gallons, in its old Niagara Falls winery. Some of the wooden tanks, not suited for modern white wine production, have been dismantled and the staves used to panel the winery's large tasting room. However, the company's newest winery at Oliver, B. C., which opened in 1982, has 800 000 gallons of storage, nearly all of it stainless steel.

The Oliver winery satisfied a long-standing Bright's desire to be in British Columbia. The company has had wines on sale in that province since at least 1935. In the postwar years it looked twice at Calona, though on both occasions the asking price was too high, and in the mid-seventies Bright's made a serious bid for Mission Hill. The Oliver establishment occupies a $1.9-million building, erected by the Osoyoos Indian band to Bright's specifications and leased by the winery, which has invested another $3.5 million in equipment. Bright's has also contracted an additional two hundred acres of grapes from new plantings in the Okanagan.

A company with Bright's history was bound to transfer its taste for experiment to the new location. It has asked its British Columbia growers to plant two of the hybrids that have succeeded in Ontario, vidal and baco noir. In 1955 George Hostetter chose from an Ontario plot of baco noir one plant, or clone, with fruit that was less acidic and more full-flavoured than that of the other plants. It is this mutation – Hostetter's colleagues call it the George clone – that Bright's multiplied in its own vineyards and has now seen planted in the West. The wines from this clone have won more gold medals in international competition than any other Bright's red.

CALONA

ESTABLISHED 1932

COOPERAGE 4.8 million gallons

TOURS & TASTINGS are available daily at the winery on Richter Street, just at the edge of downtown Kelowna. For seasonal hours and group arrangements, telephone (604) 762-9144.

TASTER'S CHOICE includes the ♟♟♟ 1982 and 1981 chancellors, the former with an especially elegant balance of wood and dark fruit flavours, and the ♟♟ 1981 rougeon, also wood-aged, spicy with an aroma of orange peel. The winery offers an excellent selection of other varietals: a ♟♟ 1981 foch and ♟♟ chenin blanc, a ♟♟ 1982 johannisberg riesling, and a ♟ gewurztraminer of 1981. The best-selling Schloss Laderheim also gets a ♟.

ALSO RECOMMENDED Cuvée Blanc, Haut Villages red and white, ♟ Sommet Blanc and ♟ Sommet Red, and Tiffany White. Its Royal Red, a sweet red wine, for years was the largest selling domestic red.

It is told of Pasquale ("Cap") Capozzi, credited with organizing Calona Wines, that he once snapped back at a Vancouver panhandler looking for a quarter to buy wine, "How do I know you won't spend it on coffee?" The company's persistent image as a maker of panhandler wines has been a source of embarrassment to the winery, though the reputation has been salvaged in recent years by the success of Schloss Laderheim, Canada's most popular white wine by the time Calona celebrated its fiftieth anniversary in 1982.

The original proposal for the Okanagan Valley's first winery came from a restless entrepreneur and winemaker by the name of Guiseppe Ghezzi. Emigrating after the First World War, Ghezzi ran a Winnipeg winery that used Italian concentrates. The venture was not a great success, and in 1932 he moved to the Okanagan, where he recognized the commercial potential in processing surplus apples into wine and other products. He began enlisting support among the small

Italian community in Kelowna, whose leading member was Capozzi, a grocer who dabbled in real estate. Finally convinced, Capozzi began raising capital while Ghezzi ordered the necessary machinery from Italy.

The first crisis occurred with the machinery's arrival: there was not enough money to pay for it. Capozzi called a rally of Kelowna

business luminaries in the back of his store. The one agreeing to be president of the new company, called Domestic Wines and By-Products, was W. A. C. Bennett, a hardware merchant and community activist who was later British Columbia's premier for twenty years. A teetotaler, though not a temperance activist, Bennett was interested in seeing the company develop new Kelowna jobs and new apple markets. He drew no pay during his eight years as president. "If it hadn't been for Premier Bennett and the courage of that man, the winery would not be there today," Capozzi later said. Also unsalaried as vice-president, he joined the future premier in peddling shares across the British Columbia interior. A number of the new shareholders, investing fifty or a hundred dollars apiece, were Italians working at the big smelter in Trail: unlike others in those depression years, they had steady jobs and could afford to invest.

One of the winery's original employees, a twenty-nine-year-old electrician named Alex Ciancone, became foreman and had a hand in making the first apple wines. He operated largely from instinct, and his early products had a habit of refermenting on liquor store shelves, sometimes exploding the bottles. Even Capozzi described those wines as being among the worst in Canada. By 1933 Ghezzi, who moved on to start a champagne firm in Yakima, Washington, had installed his son Carlo as winemaker and general manager. A former Italian military pilot, the younger Ghezzi was a conscientious vintner

and a conservative manager who ran the winery until his retirement in 1961.

The winery barely survived those years: employees had to accept shares in part payment for wages. Yet money was somehow raised for the equipment, accompanied briefly by an Italian consultant, to make apple champagne by the Charmat, or bulk-fermentation, process, and

in 1935 the directors decided to branch out into grape wines. They also held a province-wide contest to find a new name, and a Fraser Valley woman won a modest cash prize for "Calona." Calona's Okay apple wines were joined by grape wines under the Royal brand, still in use today. Indeed, Canada's largest-selling domestic red table wine, at nearly 400 000 gallons a year, is Royal Red, with a sweetness code of four. Monsignor W. B. McKenzie of Kelowna helped, though more in image terms than in actual gallonage, by getting his bishop to sanction Calona's sacramental wine, to replace wine that the church was then importing from Spain.

When Bennett was elected to the provincial legislature in 1940, he sold his shares and resigned the presidency. Unlike Herbert Anscomb, who continued to run competing Growers Wines even while he was finance minister, Bennett did not believe an active politician should be associated with a company that depended heavily on government for marketing. Although Carlo Ghezzi was the logical successor, wartime sensitivities ruled out Italian names, and the job went to Jack Ladd, a Kelowna alderman and later mayor, and local

Studebaker agent as well as a founding shareholder. Ladd behaved like the cliché tightwad Scot, once reprimanding Ciancone and cellarmaster Enrico Guidi for the unauthorized extravagance of walling in the winery's fermentation room, even though most of the lumber was scrap. However, Ladd's parsimony and Ghezzi's winemaking kept Calona profitable until, in 1950 when annual sales had risen to $90,000, the decision was made to build the first stage of the current winery.

The original Calona establishment had been in what a company brochure has called "a decrepit old packing house." Bottling was done by hand in a basement with six-foot ceilings and eye-level beams. As president, Bennett tried to interest Bright's in the winery, and the Niagara Falls company sent out its accountant, who concluded that Calona was "a tinpot affair." The new Richter Street winery opened in 1951 with stainless steel tanks and automatic bottling machines. And in 1952, when W.A.C. Bennett became premier, the wine business began to look significantly more promising. Until then, Calona's market share had lagged behind Growers' because Anscomb, finance minister and Growers president, made sure that the deck was stacked in his winery's favour. The new premier now told the liquor board that there would be no more favouritism: British Columbia's two wineries were to fight it out in the marketplace.

As Calona's sales increased, Cap Capozzi began acquiring blocks of shares, stepped in as president after Ladd's 1957 death, and, to replace the ailing Ghezzi, installed his son Tom as executive vice-president and general manager in 1961. Capozzi management brought with it an aggressive style modelled on the Gallo brothers' operation in California, studied during a 1960 visit by Tom and his older brother, Joe. The Capozzis developed new labels, and in 1963, when they decided on distinctive bottles, they brought back some Gallo samples for copying by the Dominion Glass plant near Vernon.

Finally, in 1969, when the Gallo winery was the largest in the United States, the Capozzi brothers had the nerve to broach the subject of partnership. Calona wanted to sell shares to the Canadian public, and Tom Capozzi realized that a close relationship with the American company would make them far more attractive. "We've been imitating you for years," he told Ernest Gallo, but the poker-faced president said he would be interested only if his company got 51 per cent of Calona at no cost. "Mr. Gallo," Tom Capozzi retorted in anger, "if I'd wanted a job as a salesman with Gallo Wines, I'd have filled out an application." Gallo shrugged the remark off and took the Capozzi party to lunch, where he punctured their pride again by ordering for the entire table without consulting his guests. Capozzi, having decided that a deal was unlikely, waited until the waiter had reached the far side of the room and then called him back. "Waiter," he said, "I'll have the same thing Mr. Gallo ordered." Gallo never batted an eye.

An aggressive style was the Capozzi style even before they met Ernest and Julio Gallo. When the Princeton brewery went bankrupt in 1960, Tom, who was running his father's grocery store, put in a successful bid and then took a personal bank loan to pay for the stainless steel tanks and other production equipment of a quality superior to that already in the winery. With production capacity significantly increased, Capozzi then tackled the problem of markets by naming as Calona's national sales agent McGuinness Distillers, which secured listings across Canada. Some Calona products were already known in the east: there were stories of airline stewardesses returning to Toronto from Vancouver with gallon jugs of Calona's cheap and popular Red Dry.

"We had two or three lucky breaks," Capozzi has said. One of them was a drawn-out 1964 brewery strike that prompted British Columbia's beer drinkers to look for alternatives among domestic wines. "The amazing thing about a brewery strike is that your sales climb and they never drop back," Capozzi discovered. Another break was a federal program of grants and low-cost loans for job-creating investments in areas of high unemployment. Calona used it in 1965 to build a still for grape and fruit brandies to use in fortifying wines. And noting Gallo's success with Triplejack, an apple wine fortified to 20 per cent alcohol, the Capozzi family decided to launch a similar product in Canada. Unable to register the name Applejack, already in the dictionary as a generic term for apple brandy, Tom settled for DoubleJack. It was soon joined by GrapeJack, BerryJack, BlackJack and CherryJack. Sweeter than port and as alcoholic, the Jack wines enjoyed an immediate success among novice drinkers, some of whom even formed Jack wine clubs. The berry and cherry versions are still in Calona's list, though volumes have dropped since the sixties.

Occasionally, copying Gallo strategies did not lead to success. In 1957 the California company introduced its Thunderbird line of flavoured wines, and, when these flourished, the Capozzi brothers launched their juniper-flavoured Silver wine and citric-flavoured Golden. Both failed. Such problems aside, however, Calona's annual sales climbed rapidly from $373,000 in 1959, as Capozzi manage-

ment was moving in, to $3.5 million in 1971, when the winery was sold to Standard Brands of Montreal.

An American conglomerate, Standard Brands already owned a distillery in the United States and had just purchased McGuinness in Canada. Peter Mielzynski, who then ran McGuinness, advised his new employers that the real growth potential in the beverage business lay in wines, not spirits, and he told them to approach Calona. Tom Capozzi was not particularly interested in selling: he had just begun to build a second winery at St-Hyacinthe, near Montreal, and asked Standard Brands for $15 million, or $12.50 a share. "I couldn't believe they'd pay us twelve-fifty," he has since admitted. Nor, apparently, could Standard Brands, which countered with a six-dollar offer. Just as negotiations began to cool, arch-rival General Foods showed interest. Capozzi now told Standard Brands that the presence of another suitor was confirmation of his view that the winery was worth at least $10 million. The argument was persuasive, and they settled on $9.6 million. The brothers continued to run the winery for several years, until the new owners had assembled their own executive team. Tom Capozzi has stayed on as chairman of the board.

The Capozzis were fortunate in selling when they did, for the winery soon faced some serious new problems. The first was the million-gallon winery in Quebec, which began losing heavily as soon as it started operation in 1973. The St-Hyacinthe establishment had been built on the assumption that wine would be joining cider and beer on grocery store shelves, a boon that did not materialize for another five years: within a year, Standard had sold the winery to Andrés. A second problem was shared with the entire Canadian industry, as the explosive sixties growth in domestic wine sales flattened out. In the twelve months to 31 March 1973, Canadian liquor boards sold 15.9 million gallons of Canadian wine and 9.1 million gallons of imports. While import volumes doubled over the next five years, however, sales of Canadian wine would remain about the same.

During that period, Calona Wines desperately overhauled its product line to compete with imports. The burden of blending fell largely on Robert Claremont, who now runs his own estate winery in the Okanagan. A microbiologist, he was born in Toronto in 1943, and had worked for a Michigan winery, St. Julian, before joining Calona early in 1972. He and the Standard Brands marketing executives correctly diagnosed Calona's difficulties: in a flat market for Canadian wine, they had the wrong product in the wrong packages. Such distinctive containers as the flasks embossed with grape clusters that had worked in the sixties were no longer effective as consumers turned to imports in classic bottles. Those were changed, along with Calona's wines. Sommet Rouge, a dry red made from British Columbia and California grapes, was released in 1974 in a green Bordeaux bottle with a cork. It was joined the following year by Sommet Blanc, a dry white, a bottle of which was widely publicized as Calona's hundred millionth. The Sommet lines were followed by such brands as Palazzo Reale and San Pietro, reds blended to compete with popular, inexpensive Italians, and the Haut Village team, a red and a white in burgundy bottles.

These new offerings were all solidly successful: a decade later, the Sommets remain among the twenty most popular domestic table wines. And with Schloss Laderheim, first released in 1977, Calona scored spectacularly. "Schloss," the German word for castle, is a familiar one on that country's labels. One evening, over a bottle of the winery's port, Calona's executives decided to invent their own castle

as the vehicle for a new white that Claremont and his assistant Harold
Bates were blending from Okanagan riesling, verdelet and aurore.
With its Germanic label and brown rhine bottle, Schloss Laderheim
became the biggest seller in Canada by 1981, edging out Andrés's
Baby Duck 589 000 cases to 571 000 and accounting for a quarter of
Calona's total sales. Yet this very success precipitated a new prob-

lem. Even though Calona buys about half the grapes in the Okanagan,
it could not support Schloss sales with domestic grapes alone, and had
to alter its blend to accommodate grapes and bulk wines from
California. This gave Ontario wineries the leverage to argue that
Schloss, because of its California content, should be subject to a
higher liquor board mark-up than Ontario wine. The LCBO bought the
argument, changing its retail mark-up structure in 1981 to 45 per cent
for Ontario wines and 85 per cent for wines from elsewhere in
Canada. As if this were not enough, the Ontario board also introduced
a 25 cent handling charge on bottles of table wine from outside the
province. The result was precisely what Calona's local competitors
desired: the British Columbia winery's share of the Ontario market
fell from 9 per cent in 1981 to 4.5 per cent in 1982, stabilizing only
when Calona rolled back its prices to offset some of the mark-up.

  With success at the national level, Calona has faced the problems
of provincial chauvinism, and it has also been, as marketing and sales
director Bruce Walker puts it, "wrestling with its heritage." The

mid-seventies strategy was to distance the products from the old Calona name. A secondary label, Okanagan Cellars, came into use, and on such wines as Schloss Laderheim the Calona name was merely a fine-print reference. Walker, a former Andrés sales executive, has disagreed with that, and set Calona on the path of releasing distinguished varietal table wines which will enhance the winery's name. The decision is very much in the Capozzi style, since it echoes the image-building strategy of Ernest and Julio Gallo.

The varietal program, interrupted when Robert Claremont left Calona in 1979, was resumed after a new winemaker joined Calona in early 1981. Elias Phiniotis, who was born in Cyprus in 1943 and came to Canada in 1976 armed with a Hungarian doctorate in viticulture and enology and three years' experience at a Cypriot winery, had spent two years as technical director of Wine-Art, the Vancouver-based retail chain serving home winemakers, before moving to the Okanagan. Employment at the Uncle Ben and then the Casabello winery, where several new estate wineries had their first vintages made under contract, gave him experience with two of the newer red hybrid varieties in the Okanagan, rougeon and chancellor. In 1981 he persuaded Calona to contract tonnages of these varieties, and two years later they were in a new line of British Columbia–grown Calona varietals. From the 1982 vintage, a superb one in British Columbia, Phiniotis produced Calona's first johannisberg riesling, and the winery is contracting growers to plant vidal and seyval blanc, white hybrids proven in Ontario but not yet widely grown in British Columbia. With wines such as these, Calona will finally lay the lingering Jack-wine ghost to rest, much as the Gallo brothers have erased the memory of Thunderbird and Ripple with their oak-matured chardonnays.

CASABELLO

ESTABLISHED 1966

COOPERAGE 2.5 million gallons

TOURS & TASTINGS take place year-round on weekdays from 10 A.M. to 4 P.M.; for group arrangements telephone (604) 492-0621. The retail store at the winery on Main Street and Skaha Lake Road in Penticton is open Monday through Saturday from 10 A.M. to 6 P.M.

TASTER'S CHOICE includes the 🍷 1983 chardonnay, pale, lemony in colour, and bone-dry, the subdued 1983 gewurztraminer, the flowery 1983 johannisberg riesling and the appley 🍷 1982 chenin blanc. Among the reds, the 1983 chancellor is light, fresh and dry, and the foch-based Canadian Burgundy is dark in colour but light-bodied.

ALSO RECOMMENDED Burgon Rouge, Fleur de Blanc and pinot noir.

Antonio Biollo would have savoured the irony of John Labatt's 1972 offer to buy Casabello Wines of Penticton. Labatt was then taking over Chateau-Gai of Niagara Falls, a company Biollo, before becoming one of Casabello's founders, had tried to interest in establishing a British Columbia winery, only to be told that the quality of the grapes was too poor.

No doubt the rejection stung. A bulldozer operator in his Penticton youth, Biollo was a capable, self-trained grape grower. He certainly impressed Andrew Peller in 1961, when the founder of Andrés was looking for a site in the southern Okanagan. Biollo was hired to plant the new vineyard, and he ran it for several years until the two men parted over a now forgotten difference of opinion. He then developed an experimental vineyard near West Bench near Penticton, while seeking backers for a new winery.

In 1966 Biollo's enthusiasm finally infected Evans Lougheed, a Penticton businessman, and a group of his friends. Lougheed, born in 1914 and a university commerce graduate, had already done well in Penticton as a retailer and hotelier; he had sold his hotel and was looking for a new business idea when Biollo came along. The investor group they put together, including Vancouver forestry executive Chester Johnson and Cawston agriculturist James Dawson, raised the capital for what started as a $500,000 winery with $100,000 in federal grant money. Col. Donald McGugan, head of the provincial liquor board, insisted that the winery contract about 60 per cent of its

grapes before he granted it a licence. Biollo lined up growers and later, when the winery was operating, doubled as a salesman in the Okanagan until his 1970 death.

Lougheed and his directors had a choice between two Penticton sites for their winery: a four-acre plot in an industrial park and one of similar size on Main Street at four times the price. Lougheed, who wanted the latter site, asked the advice of a friend, Vancouver publicist Bill Clancey. The answer came, "You're in an industry where you can't advertise. Why not put it where a million cars go by?" The board of directors accepted this logic, and a decade later, when the winery was allowed to open a tasting room and retail store, it emerged as a major tourist attraction.

Casabello's first crush of October 1966 yielded about seventy thousand gallons of wine, including an Okanagan riesling, a grenache rosé (from imported grapes), a crackling rosé, a port and three generics still in the company's portfolio: Vino Rosso, Vino Bianco and Burgundy. Some of the varietals were released in fashionable kraft labels, now discontinued, and sold at a slight premium. Casabello was determined to position itself as a producer of quality table wines. Market penetration was difficult, given that advertising was not allowed and there were still very few self-serve liquor stores where new products, smartly labelled though they might be, were actually on view. Lougheed and his staff resorted to the tough slog of personal promotion, giving wine and cheese parties the length and breadth of the province.

Casabello managed to get through that first crush with consulting winemaker Wallace Pohle, formerly of Andrés. In the spring of 1967,

however, German-born Thomas Hoenisch, who had been a chemist at Andrés and then a winemaker in California, returned to British Columbia. Wooed by Casabello and Mission Hill, which had built a winery in 1966 as well, he chose Casabello, where he remained as winemaker until 1979. Demanding and abrasive, he viewed wine-making as 60 per cent art and 40 per cent science, yet once described the winery prosaically as a food-processing plant. Hoenisch called for vinifera plantings at a time when Okanagan growers were putting in hybrids, which he regarded as "fill-in or blending material." Vinifera were already grown successfully two hundred miles to the south in Washington State, and, he argued, they should grow in the Okanagan.

Biollo had planted various vinifera in his Penticton test plot with indifferent success. In 1967 he planted several hundred vinifera vines behind the winery in Penticton and was encouraged when they sur-vived a severe winter. When the company needed to expand its facilities, the vines were transplanted to the Osoyoos area, with the exception of some Thompson seedless vines which still flourish decoratively in front of the building. Many went into a vineyard acquired by Lougheed's son-in-law, Walter Davidson, with invest-ment from Lougheed and his brother Alleyn, who arranged to import vinifera including chenin blanc and semillon from the California winemaker and grower Karl Wente. These vines were sufficiently mature by 1978 for Casabello to make the first chenin blanc entirely from grapes grown in British Columbia. When the winter of 1978–79 devastated them, Davidson chose to replant with seyval blanc, a French hybrid from Ontario.

In the 1967 vintage, Hoenisch turned to Washington vineyards for vinifera, importing, among other varieties, a small tonnage of pinot noir. The strategy was to release named varietals using Washington grapes, to develop a following by the time similar varieties were producing in British Columbia. Though several vintages of pinot noir have been released in this way, doubt remains as to whether this particular vinifera, when grown in British Columbia, can produce a red of appropriate body. The 1967 strategy is working, however, with such white varieties as chardonnay, chenin blanc and gewurztraminer.

Casabello's consistent use of Washington grapes is due in part to the influence of Dr. Walter Clore, the long-time viticulturist on the state experimental farm at Prosser in the Yakima Valley. Clore's work led to the extensive vinifera plantings in growing conditions that are roughly comparable to those of the southern Okanagan. Casabello invited Clore to the Okanagan to advise its growers, since horticulturists at the local Summerland research station were dubious about vinifera grapes, and he told Lougheed and Hoenisch what they wanted to hear: the European varieties would grow in British Columbia. Test plots on Davidson's Osoyoos vineyard included gamay, pinot noir, cabernet sauvignon, chenin blanc, chardonnay, gewurztraminer and johannisberg riesling. The vines grew well until the winter of 1978–79.

After that winter's extensive frost damage, however, it was decided to replant with hardier white varieties and Casabello's viticulturist, Lloyd Schmidt, had to go far afield, to the Niagara nursery of Paul Bosc. Bosc is a meticulous grower of disease-free vines, and Casabello believed that the certificate from Vineland needed to accompany the shipment of five thousand seyval blanc vines would be issued routinely. With the Vineland grape specialist in hospital, they proceeded on a verbal assurance from his assistant. The vines were in the Okanagan ground when, in Lougheed's phrase, "the whole bureaucracy roof fell in on us." Casabello and the federal department of agriculture, concerned with preventing the spread of plant diseases, engaged in legal battles for three years until Ottawa was satisfied that the plants were healthy. Davidson had by then propagated a sound fourteen acres of seyval blanc.

Despite his vinifera preference, Hoenisch did produce sound wines from locally available hybrids. The best was Fleur de Blanc, a blend of 80–85 per cent Okanagan riesling and palomino, a neutral Califor-

nia white grape. First released in the early seventies, it has been one of the driest whites available and, perhaps for that reason, slow to develop a following. Roberta Jordan, who succeeded Hoenisch in 1979, refined the blend to give it a more vinifera-like character. Hoenisch also once made a barrel-aged maréchal foch, but market resistance to this varietal resulted in its being blended into Casabello's successful Canadian Burgundy.

The extensive use of oak cooperage for aging red wines was an early Casabello trademark. In fact, the pinot noir released from the 1967 vintage was inadvertently left in oak too long, with the result that the wine matured only after the mid-seventies. The subsequent pinot noir vintages of 1972, 1975 and 1978 spent much less time in oak. Over time, the winery disposed of its small barrels, retaining eight hundred-gallon French oak casks exclusively for aging pinot noir.

Casabello's move towards more winemaking in large stainless steel tanks has been triggered by its commercial success with proprietary blends. The Gala Keg bag-in-a-box line became a big seller, with Gala Keg dry white the winery's top brand. A light white wine called Capistro, based on a low-alcohol concept developed at Labatt's Bear Mountain winery in California, was introduced in

British Columbia early in 1982 and soon challenged Gala Keg for volume leadership. And the new sister company of Chateau-Gai contributed the name and blending concept for Alpenweiss, one of the top-selling domestic brands in Canada. These blended wines came so to dominate Casabello's list that by the early eighties the winery had begun to lose the enviable consumer reputation earned with its premium varietals. More recently, there has been a conscious effort to recapture some of that identity using the same varieties – chenin blanc, johannisberg riesling, gewurztraminer, chardonnay and pinot noir – with which Hoenisch began in the early seventies. Roberta Jordan's chardonnay wines continued to be dry and delicate, echoing Hoenisch's Alsatian style, but she preferred to round out the gewurztraminer and the rieslings with a touch of sweetness, and stressed the underlying fruity character of the chenin blanc. The style is being continued by Tom Seaver, who succeeded her when she retired in 1984.

Its early reputation as a producer of premium table wines set Casabello apart from British Columbia competitors. By 1972 the winery had been able to expand its storage capacity to 500 000 gallons, about five times the original size. And no sooner had it become profitable than an emissary from Labatt arrived with an offer to buy. Evans Lougheed and his fellow directors refused to sell a winery on the verge of success: Labatt countered with the idea of an option to buy the winery in five years at about eleven times whatever pre-tax profits then would be. This gave Casabello real incentive to increase its profits, as well as a bank guarantee which Lougheed saw as "almost unlimited availability of capital."

Labatt-backed capital enabled the winery to spend on product development. In 1974 it introduced generic wines packaged not in conventional bottles but in attractive carafes, a style pioneered by Paul Masson vineyards in California. They were an instant success, doubling the winery's sales and helping it get its first Alberta listings. The following year, Casabello became one of the first Canadian wineries to pick up the Australian packaging idea of four-litre polyethylene pouches, equipped with spigots and packed in cardboard boxes; a sixteen-litre size was later introduced for the restaurant trade, and again sales soared. In 1976 Casabello tripled its storage capacity to 1.5 million gallons, and since the Labatt purchase in 1978 it has gone to 2.5 million.

CHATEAU-GAI

ESTABLISHED 1928

COOPERAGE 3.5 million gallons

TOURS & TASTINGS are not available in Niagara Falls, but the retail store is open.

At the Alberta winery, group tours are available Monday through Friday by appointment. Tel. (403) 286-8511. The retail store is open.

TASTER'S CHOICE includes the ♈♈♈ Hallmark Dry Sherry, nutty and golden; the fruity ♈♈ johannisberg riesling, the ♈♈ 1982 chancellor, a dark and youthful wine to be cellared beyond 1986; the dry 1980 gamay rosé and the rosé-like 1980 merlot, also dry. The best sellers include Alpenweiss, Canadian Sauternes, Capistro, Cavallo Rosso, Edelwein, and the red and white Princières.

ALSO RECOMMENDED are the winery's other Hallmark sherries and its Charmat-process Imperials, brut and dry.

John Labatt of London, Ontario, which has been brewing beer in Canada since 1828, got into the wine business in 1965 when it bought the thirty-eight-year-old Parkdale company of Toronto. Parkdale turned out to be the first of five wineries in Canada and one in California purchased by Labatt. The Canadian group, operating under the Chateau-Gai umbrella in eastern Canada and Casabello in the West, now commands 12 per cent of the market for Canadian wines. Gradually, a corporate personality has blanketed enterprises with traditions ranging from, in Chateau-Gai's case, the production of sacramental wines for the Roman Catholic Church to, in that of a small Calgary winery, the making of fruit wines with suggestive names. By the eighties, the Labatt group's winemakers had come up with the Alpenweiss blend that is now among the largest-selling domestic white wines.

Chateau-Gai had emerged from one of the many winery mergers that followed the end of Prohibition in 1927, when, with the return to legal sale of beer and spirits, the majority of upstart wineries were no

longer viable. Early in 1928, A. W. Marsh's Stamford Park Wine Co.
of Niagara Falls, then Ontario's fourth largest, joined forces with four
smaller firms: Dominion Wine Growers of Oakville, founded in
1920, Thorold Winery, started in 1924, and Lincoln Wines of St.
Catharines and Peerless Wine Manufacturers of Toronto, both dating
from 1925. The new Canadian Wineries had a storage capacity of 1.1

million gallons and was for some years, until Bright's began expanding, the biggest winery in the country.

Stamford Park had also boasted of employing "an expert Chemist
... thus ensuring the technical application of recognized principles of
winemaking as practised throughout the world." But Sir Henry
Drayton, the commissioner of the new liquor board, was so unhappy
with the quality of some Canadian Wineries products that he sent an
English wine chemist, Dr. A. O. Blackhurst, to go through the
wineries with A. R. Bonham, the chemist for the Ontario Department
of Public Health. Some 130 000 gallons of wine were declared unfit
and dumped, and Marsh resigned. Blackhurst became Canadian
Wineries' new production manager, and he helped the company
acquire the exclusive twenty-five-year rights in 1928 to the Charmat
process for making sparkling wines. With this method, developed in
France in 1902 by Eugène Charmat, the secondary fermentation of a
sparkling wine, which traditionally occurs in the bottle, can take
place instead, and much more economically, in a large pressure tank.

Blackhurst seems to have resolved the company's quality problems, for in 1929 it was acquiring the 140 000-gallon National Fruit &
Wine Co. of Toronto. Four years later, when it became apparent that

American Prohibition was about to be repealed, Canadian Wineries built an establishment in Lewiston, New York, just across the Niagara River. When this winery opened for the 1934 crush, many in the industry greeted it as one of the world's most modern, chiefly because its tanks were made with a new alloy – stainless steel – developed by International Nickel. Because the company had the North American rights to the Charmat process, the winery was designed to specialize in sparkling wines. Not a success, it was sold to an American in 1937.

Things were going badly in the home market as well at this time, with company sales down to barely 200 000 gallons in 1936 from more than three times that amount at the end of the twenties. It was a poor performance that called to the scene one of the great characters of the Canadian wine industry. Alexander Sampson, born at L'Ardoise on Cape Breton in 1900, had risen to become national advertising manager of the *Halifax Chronicle,* where his performance had commended him to F.B. McCurdy, the Nova Scotia banker who owned the paper. McCurdy and the Toronto businessman W.D. Ross, later Ontario's lieutenant-governor, had picked up shares in Canadian Wineries' $1.6-million issue of 1928. When the company's fortunes began to slide, McCurdy sent Sampson to take over its management in 1936.

He got results: by 1940 the winery's annual sales had doubled to 400 000 gallons. Dictatorial and demanding, Sampson was feared and often disliked by his employees and industry colleagues. On his periodic visits to the Niagara Falls winery from Toronto head office, he would take his managers to a gruelling lunch. "One of us would get hell in front of the others," winemaker Edwin Haynes recalled. "By bawling somebody out and embarrassing him, he thought he would get more work out of him." A paternal employer as well as a browbeater, Sampson once asked Haynes why, after five years of marriage, he still had no children. Was there a financial problem? Haynes alertly agreed that there was, and won his first grudging salary increase from his bachelor boss. Haynes ultimately worked sixteen years for this man, whom he later remembered as "an S.O.B."

Sampson even looked like a tough egg: short, stocky, with flashing black eyes, a sharp prow of a nose and a large mouth, all set in a strong, square face. In Toronto he lunched at the fashionable Arcadian Court in Simpson's department store, where, as he strode to his regular table, he would ask loudly whether his bottle of Chateau-Gai was on ice. Yet he was not immune to sentiment, as shown in his relations with Thomas and William Comery.

For some years, until he bought a country home outside the city, Sampson lived at the Granite Club. One of the Comery boys was delivering a parcel to the club one day early in the war. Engaging him in conversation, Sampson discovered that the father had died and the

brothers were living in poverty with their sick mother. His heart stirred, Sampson took the boys in his care, became their official guardian, and saw to it that both received university educations. Tom Comery succeeded him as the winery's president. The greatest compliment the Comerys paid the man they called ''uncle'' was their adoption of his intensely held Roman Catholic faith.

That Chateau-Gai emerged from the war years a healthy company was due in no small part to Alexander Sampson. On Ross's death in 1948, Noah Torno of Jordan Wines quickly struck a deal with the other partner, F. B. McCurdy, to buy the company. A few days later, however, an embarrassed McCurdy learned that Ross had given Sampson an option to buy when the winery came up for sale, and Torno agreed to give him seven days to raise the money. ''Sampson was absolutely livid,'' Torno has recalled: the two were adversaries, and what's more, personal enemies. Sampson, who gained control of the winery through his personal company, Wine Securities, remained bitter, contending for years that Torno's bid had forced him to pay a premium.

Sampson managed to return a profit in each of the twenty-eight years he ran Chateau-Gai, though the company seldom emerged as an innovator. Edwin Haynes was restricted by his grapes: "In those days we had concord, niagara, catawba and, if you were lucky, delaware. And you had to make ports, sherries, varietals, vermouths, champagnes, the whole ball of wax out of those." One novelty that went unnoticed at the time was a 1949 sparkling rosé, believed by California wine writer Leon Adams to have been the first such rosé made in North America.

Under Sampson, however, the winery was commercially aggressive. It was the first Canadian winery to sell in Newfoundland after that province entered Confederation in 1949. In the fifties Sampson hired Col. Garfield H. Stevens, a retired Cameron Highlander, as his sales manager – a shrewd move, since the liquor boards of several provinces were headed by former officers. And though Sampson was frequently at odds with his colleagues, he also gave leadership to the industry as president of the Wine Products Association and then as the first president of its successor body, the Canadian Wine Institute, formed in 1948.

A talented promoter, Sampson wrung every ounce of publicity he could from his travels – advertising, after all, was not permitted. His annual trips to Europe were followed by press interviews in which he castigated national drinking habits. "The great weakness of Canadians in relation to wines and spirits is that too many of us have never learned to consume them while eating," he told one paper after a 1950 trip. Chateau-Gai pursued promotionally useful export sales and placed wines in European competitions, where entry fees usually procured an award of some description. Jordan's Noah Torno dismissed such awards as "phony," but Chateau-Gai boasted of them in its annual reports, particularly when, in 1954, the company won medals at a Paris show for a vermouth, a sherry and its Charmat-process champagne. The publicity Sampson generated from this latter product rebounded ten years later in the now famous "champagne" lawsuit over the use of appellations protected by French law.

Sampson was also interested in making his winery national. Frustrated by the failure to get good listings in British Columbia, he toured the Okanagan in 1959, where grape grower Tony Biollo, later a Casabello founder, gave encouragement and even took some local grapes to Niagara Falls. Sampson finally concluded that the quality of

British Columbia grapes was poor, however, and soon also dropped the idea of a winery in Nova Scotia. This goal was achieved after Labatt bought Chateau-Gai and put under its wing Normandie Wines, which had been started in Moncton in 1966 to produce blueberry wines.

A key development in the company's history was Paul Bosc's

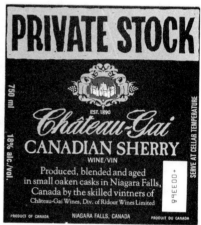

hiring as winemaker in 1964, the year of Sampson's death. The talented, Algerian-born Frenchman set out immediately to convert the company's list to table wines from the old reliance on sherries and sparkling wines. At Bosc's prodding, Chateau-Gai began planting vinifera and urging French hybrids on its growers, who responded better than they had in 1931, when company president K. H. Smith had labelled concord and niagara "objectionable" wine grapes. By the early seventies, Bosc was overhauling Chateau-Gai wines dramatically, his most notable success being a varietal maréchal foch that in 1974 replaced the company's burgundy – the first varietal foch in Canada and one of the earliest varietals to be promoted on television. Perhaps Bosc's most important wine for Chateau-Gai, however, was the later Alpenweiss, a German-style blended white released in 1978, which by 1981 had become the largest-selling Canadian white, and launched Chateau-Gai into a family of European-style proprietary wines, among them Edelwein and Cavallo Rosso.

One of Bosc's speculative wines turned into a commercial success. About 1970, a friend in an American winery told him about a new sparkling blend of red and white wines called Cold Duck, which was enjoying great popularity in the United States. On his own, he developed a sparkling blend of concord and white elvira. Cold Duck's success had also been noted by Andrés, which introduced it to Canada and tried to register the name. When Comery heard about this move, he asked Bosc how long it would take to make a comparable product. "Five minutes," Bosc said – the time required to fetch a

sample from his private bin. With this, Chateau-Gai blocked Andrés and in late 1971 began selling its own Cold Duck in Canada.

By the late seventies Labatt was firmly in control of the Chateau-Gai group. Its 1965 purchase of Parkdale, later renamed Chateau Cartier, had been successful, encouraging a major expansion into wine, and in 1972 Labatt took a five-year option to buy Casabello Wines of Penticton, British Columbia. Also in 1972, at the suggestion of Maritimer Norman Stanbury, who had helped Sampson raise the money to take over Chateau-Gai in 1948, Labatt made an offer to shareholders of the Niagara winery. When the Comery brothers resisted, Labatt enriched its offer until in the end it paid $15 million, about three times the Chateau-Gai sales figure for that year.

The purchase came at a time when the wine industry was entering a difficult period. That fall's unusually small grape harvest forced Bosc to buy concentrates in Spain, a move that skirted the ban on imports of grapes or juice maintained by the Ontario government since the twenties. Within five years, Ontario wineries would all be allowed to import 15 per cent of their requirements to give their wines a more "European" polish. While looking for raw material sources in

California, Labatt came across a near-bankrupt, farmer-owned co-operative for sale at Bakersfield. Taking it over in 1978 by assuming its debts, Labatt now was in the wine business in a major way, for Bear Mountain has ten times the capacity of Chateau-Gai and Casabello combined.

The brewery was also consolidating its eastern holdings. Parkdale

operations were shifted to the Chateau-Gai Niagara Falls plant on the site of the original Stamford Park winery, and the Normandie line in Moncton, where blueberry wine had been a commercial dud, was changed completely to emphasize table wines. In 1980 the brewing company decided to rescue yet another failing producer, Stoneycroft Cellars of Calgary. Under a young winemaker who had worked in California, Ignacious Chang, Stoneycroft was vainly attempting to attract attention with such products as Passion Frost, a sparkler made from Brazilian passion fruit and grape juice, Honey Rosé, a sweet crackling wine from British Columbia raspberries and Alberta honey, and a line of carbonated fruit wines under the brand Fanny Hill, recalling the heroine of a once banned, and therefore popular, novel, whose exploits inspired double entendre labels such as Bramble Bush. These dubious products were soon replaced by Alpenweiss and other less risqué, but more profitable, Chateau-Gai wines.

JORDAN & STE-MICHELLE

ESTABLISHED 1920s

COOPERAGE 6.5 million gallons

TOURS & TASTINGS at the Ontario winery in St. Catharines take place Monday through Friday at 10 A.M., 1 P.M. and 3 P.M.; weekends and evenings by arrangement. Tel. (416) 688-2140. The retail store hours are 9 P.M. to 6 P.M., Monday through Friday. Exit from the Queen Elizabeth Way on Martindale Road South and follow it until it turns into Louth Street South.

The British Columbia winery has tours and tastings Monday through Saturday at 11 A.M., 1 P.M. and 3 P.M.; group and evening tours by arrangement. Tel. (604) 576-6741. Retail store hours are 10 A.M. to 6 P.M., Monday through Saturday. Exit from the Trans-Canada Highway just over the Port Mann Bridge, and proceed south on 152nd Street to 54-A Avenue in Surrey.

TASTER'S CHOICE begins with some excellent ▼▼▼ johannisberg rieslings, the 60th Anniversary Special Reserve from the B.C. winery, a full-bodied wine from the 1983 vintage, and the Ontario winery's 1983 Special Reserve, another silky, elegant offering in the late-harvest German style. Ontario's ripe pinot chardonnay 1982 and 1983 vidal get ▼▼, though the winery's 1982 and 1983 Selected rieslings will be more widely available.

ALSO RECOMMENDED Canadian Rhine Castle (B.C.), Ontario's chelois and dutchess, Falkenberg, Ontario's foch, Interlude, Ontario's seyval blanc, the Ste-Michelle red and white Grande Cuvées, Spumante Bambino and the perennial best sellers Maria Christina and Toscano.

Once, during the seventies, Jordan hired a California-trained vintner from the more than one hundred responding worldwide to the company's advertisement. For all his sound theoretical qualifications, the new expert lasted only weeks at the St. Catharines winery, his career there cut short by a confrontation about the making of a blueberry-flavoured beverage known as Lonesome Charlie. The winery quickly hired another of the practical Germans who have given Jordan & Ste-Michelle a distinctive winemaking style over the past decade. They have never flinched at making Lonesome Charlie, for the profits from this and other pop beverages have made possible the commercial-scale production of elegant johannisberg rieslings that has set the Jordan & Ste-Michelle group apart from Canada's other national wineries. The company has a further peculiarity: the most complex corporate ancestry of any large Canadian winery, with roots in both Ontario and British Columbia.

Jordan's in Ontario traces its beginnings to a firm called Canadian Grape Products, incorporated in 1920 by Archibald Haines, later a member of the Ontario legislature. The winery was installed in the village of Jordan, west of St. Catharines, in a fieldstone building that had been put up in 1870 for drying apples. Still standing, it was in use up to 1980 as a sherry-maturing cellar. In 1926 W. B. Cleland, a Scottish-trained distiller, bought control of Haines's firm and reorganized it as the Jordan Wine Co. The new owner had gained special insight into the wine business as general manager from 1919 to 1921 of Ontario Government Dispensaries, the Prohibition-era forerunner of the liquor board. He also became a director of Distillers Corp.-Seagram, the international giant that Samuel Bronfman put together in the twenties. When Cleland decided to buy out his partners in Jordan, he did so with a loan from Seagram's that guaranteed the distiller first option on the winery whenever he decided to sell.

Cleland ran the winery until his death in 1946. The Imperial Bank, which was handling his estate, was evidently unaware of the Seagram's deal, for it approached Toronto's Torno family to propose merging Jordan with their Danforth Wines. The Tornos were in the wine business purely by chance. Fred Torno, who died in 1982 at the age of ninety-six, had been a lumber dealer and sometime investor in commercial real estate in Toronto when he acquired an empty store on the corner of Danforth and Hampton, across the street from a church. The first potential tenant to come forward wanted to convert the place into an urban winery. Torno was wary of the church's reaction, but he was anxious to rent and agreed, only to see his tenant-to-be fail to get a winery licence. Torno's friend Peter Quigley, a former banker and salesman, then suggested to a struggling Fort William winery that it relocate in the Toronto store. When the enterprise was offered for sale instead, the two Torontonians bought and relocated it in 1930 as the Danforth Wine Co. The pastor of the church across the street, far from exhibiting outrage, welcomed a neighbourhood business from which he could cadge sugar for needy parishioners and a few bottles

for the church parlour. Even luckier for Torno was the friendship between this clergyman, Rev. F.E. Powell, and Sir Henry Drayton, the crusty pioneer commissioner of the Liquor Control Board of Ontario. Other winery owners had to cower in Drayton's outer office; Fred Torno received the commissioner at the winery.

Fred's eldest son, Noah, impatient to enter business, resisted family pressure to study law and instead convinced his father to stake him for a year with five thousand dollars, roughly the cost of a law degree. He used the money in 1932 as a down payment on a bankrupt winery in New Toronto. His winery had no wine – he arranged to buy some from his father – but it did have a substantial building, and Noah brought up the obvious: a merger with Danforth Wines. When Peter Quigley, who had been managing the winery, sold his interest and bought a hotel, Noah took over, later bringing in his younger brothers Philip and Chum. By 1946 the Torno brothers had acquired several other wineries and built Danforth into a thriving firm. The New Toronto plant was used to bottle all Jordan and Danforth wines until it closed in 1968.

The Tornos learned about Seagram's option just as they were about to close the deal for Jordan, and Noah journeyed to Montreal to meet Bronfman. What the distiller wanted to know was, "If it's good enough for you, young man, why is it not also good enough for me?" The outcome was a partnership and close friendship with Bronfman that lasted until Bronfman's death in 1971. When Jordan lost money in 1948 – its only loss under Torno leadership – Bronfman would reassure his partner: "In business you need a long pocket and a stout heart." The distilling company took a 72.5 per cent interest in the winery and the Torno brothers, who were to run it, had the remainder. Danforth Wines operated under its own name until 1964, when it was merged with Jordan. By that time, Noah was immersed in other Seagram business interests, including real estate development, and Philip was running the winery. Chum had been sent to British Columbia in 1959 to build a subsidiary in New Westminster that operated under a variety of names – Pacific Western Wines, Westcoast Wines and, finally, Villa Wines – before it was absorbed into the reorganized Jordan & Ste-Michelle group in 1973.

On Bronfman's death, the Torno brothers exercised their option to buy Seagram's out. The distilling company, frustrated by Ontario's refusal to allow wine-grape imports, was more than willing to sell. To help finance their $20-million purchase, the Tornos found a new partner in Canadian Breweries, which carries on business today as Carling O'Keefe, a Canadian subsidiary of Rothmans International Ltd. of Britain. The brewing company secured an option to buy control of the winery and in 1972 exercised it. Buying Growers Wines of Victoria the next year, it then set about building a national

business around the talents of a series of German-trained vintners.

The first of these was Dieter Guttler. Born in Germany in 1945 and raised in South Africa, he apprenticed in winemaking before studying for three years at the Geisenheim research institute in his native Germany. Returning to Africa, he plied his trade for Rothmans there until he was dispatched to the newly acquired British Columbia winery. Growers had been the province's first, but by the early seventies its half-century-old plant and product line were both in dire need of overhaul. ''Our big sellers were still fortified wines and sweeter reds,'' Guttler discovered: in short order, he added the first varietals – ruby cabernet, chenin blanc, cabernet sauvignon and

grenache rosé, all made from California grapes. His intention, however, was to have good vinifera available in British Columbia, and
one sight of the Okanagan convinced him that it was excellent
johannisberg riesling country. Telling this to every grower who
would listen, Guttler also steered his winery into co-operating on
some trial vinifera plantings in the valley.

Guttler was transferred in 1978 to Jordan's Ontario winery, helping the company's veteran chief enologist make the transition to such
national table wine brands as Toscano and Maria Christina. William
Anderson had joined Jordan in 1950 and, because the market wanted
fortified wines, developed a sure hand with ports and sherries. But he
also made other new wines: in 1958, on orders from the Torno
brothers, Jordan released Canada's first brut champagne, a winemaking success but a sales flop. More successful was Jordan Valley Extra
Dry White Table Wine, also released that year and made entirely
from French hybrid grapes. One of Anderson's greatest commercial
scores, however, was a gin-flavoured, wine-based beverage with 20
per cent alcohol called Zing. The winery introduced it in August
1962, expecting to do a business of 14 000 gallons. To everyone's
surprise, 120 000 gallons were sold that year and 350 000 the following year. In just four months after its release, Zing had become the
largest-selling wine in Ontario. Its wild popularity attracted im-
itators, and Zing, having shared the action in the sixties, slid into
oblivion in the seventies; it was finally dropped in 1978, the year
Guttler arrived.

In Ontario, Guttler began making the johannisberg riesling that
Jordan first released in limited quantities and then, as plantings
increased, as a general listing in the province. When Guttler launched
his own Vineland Estates winery, its first offering in 1984 was also a
johannisberg riesling. He was succeeded in British Columbia by
Joseph Zimmerman, recruited through the Geisenheim old-boys'
network. Born in 1949 in Guldental, Germany, to a family that has
been making wine in Germany's Nahe Valley for generations, Zimmerman decided after graduating from Geisenheim to vacation in
British Columbia, in part to explore a job offer from Guttler. He
accepted the offer in time to help with the 1976 vintage, the last to be
done in the old Growers Victoria winery before production was
moved in 1977 to Surrey in the Fraser Valley. There, he continued the
conversion to white vinifera and German-style wines. In 1978 he was

the first to produce a commercial auxerrois from grapes grown by
George Heiss, who was to use the same fruit for a superb varietal
under his own Gray Monk label: a variation of the pinot blanc, the
auxerrois was destined, in Zimmerman's view, to be ''the chardonnay of the Okanagan.'' Another Zimmerman innovation was Falkenberg, a Germanic blend that includes verdelet, chenin blanc and
Okanagan riesling. He never produced a varietal from the Okanagan
riesling, however, for he disliked the wine the grape produced and
was offended at the name riesling being given to a grape that is not
even a vinifera.

When Zimmerman replaced Guttler at the St. Catharines winery in
,1980, he was succeeded in Surrey by Klaus Scherner, a 1977
Geisenheim graduate whose family had made wine in the Rhineland
since the seventeenth century. The johannisberg riesling Scherner
made in the sun-drenched British Columbia vintage of 1981 was from
grapes the grower had left on the vine until late fall. The result was a
rich, auslese-style wine of which Scherner was so proud that he took
five cases with him when he went back to Germany to help run the
family business. Scherner, who continues to consult for a group
planning a Vancouver Island winery, was replaced at Surrey by Jeron
Van Dijk, a graduate of the Weinsberg wine school that rivals
Geisenheim. But Geisenheimer Ivan Lessner became winemaker at
the Calgary winery, while Zimmerman, another Geisenheimer, remains in overall charge.

Jordan & Ste-Michelle has made strenuous efforts to propagate
better winemaking grapes and talk growers into replanting. By the
early eighties the company was employing seven viticulturists and
had seventy-four acres in Ontario committed chiefly to vinifera which
one Jordan executive called ''show-me vineyards.'' The winery also
runs a St. Catharines nursery that supplies vines for two small mother
blocks in Ontario and two in British Columbia, and has financed
contract growers to convert plantings to johannisberg riesling and
other premium varieties.

The emphasis on riesling grapes is the obvious result of recruiting
winemakers trained in Germany. ''What we are trying to do is what
we are most familiar with,'' Zimmerman said. Within a decade of the
Geisenheimers' arrival, Jordan & Ste-Michelle was producing
enough riesling of good basic quality, acceptable by German *tafel-
wein* standards, to support listings in liquor stores across Canada. A

fact of life, however, even for the Geisenheimers, has been the necessity of dealing with the labrusca grapes, such as concord and niagara, that are still grown in abundance. The company spent $1 million on a three-year program to develop a concentrator now being used to process labrusca juice. The juice is briefly exposed, in a vacuum, to heat which drives off the volatile substance, methyl anthrilate, that is chiefly responsible for the labrusca's so-called foxy aroma and flavour. The vacuum allows this substance to be evaporated at lower temperatures than in more conventional concentrators, thus avoiding the danger of leaving the juice with a slightly burnt or caramelized flavour. Jordan uses the results in its Toscano white and Interlude, a soft and fruity white featuring the normally pungent elvira grape.

Dieter Guttler, when he became Jordan's British Columbia winemaker in 1973, was astonished to find the product list dominated by fortified and sweet red wines. Such wines had been successful during the winery's previous forty-two years, since they were in tune with the popular tastes of the day. The success of Growers also owed a great deal to the colourful Herbert Anscomb, the barrel-chested, stentorian, British-born accountant who controlled the winery from 1927 to 1955.

The farmers who established the Growers winery immediately after Prohibition to process their surplus loganberries – a raspberry and wild blackberry hybrid – recognized the winery's need of an experienced general manager. In 1927 they installed Anscomb, who had already run the Victoria Pheonix Brewing Co. and who, as reeve of Oak Bay and later mayor of Victoria, was a rising public figure. Earlier, Growers had bought another loganberry winery, Richmond Wine Co., and, with Anscomb's 1936 purchase of Slinger's of Victoria – started by Steven Slinger, who bootlegged his loganberry wine from a pool hall during British Columbia Prohibition – the entire loganberry wine business was consolidated under one company.

The rich red loganberry wines, which typically were sweet and slightly fortified, have almost entirely disappeared from the market, but until the sixties were sold as far east as Quebec and were durable favourites at prairie weddings. The fortifying spirit was produced in Growers' own pot still, purchased in 1936, which also enabled production of a line of once popular wine cocktails: 45 Per, Bon Santé and Slinger's Gin Cocktail.

In 1936 Anscomb was elected to the British Columbia legislature as a Conservative of a stripe characterized by political rival and later premier W. A. C. Bennett, himself no pink liberal, as "extreme." In that same year, Bennett had taken over presidency of struggling Calona Wines, then the only commercial winery not under Anscomb's thumb. When teetotaler Bennett was elected to the legis-

lature in 1940, also as a Conservative, he severed all connections with the winery. He was sharply critical of Anscomb for not doing the same when in 1946 and again in 1950, he fought unsuccessfully to wrest the leadership of the provincial Conservatives from Anscomb. Bennett's failure as a Conservative resulted in him taking over the Social Credit party and winning power in 1952.

Bennett had reason to criticize. Anscomb had become finance minister in 1945 and, during his next seven years in the post, brazenly used his power to ensure that British Columbia liquor store listings guaranteed the substantial Growers market share. "It was unbelievable," recalled Meredith Jones, a former president of Bright's. Jones once squirmed with embarrassment during lunch at a Vancouver hotel as Anscomb, in a characteristically loud voice audible throughout the room, revealed that Chateau-Gai of Ontario had asked the improbable – a listing in British Columbia. Bright's itself, along with Jordan when it was still making wine only in Ontario, had only token listings; Noah Torno of Jordan believed that they were given as bait to

soften up one of the Ontario wineries as potential buyers for the day
when Anscomb would want to sell Growers. After the 1952 election,
in which Anscomb was defeated, the winery did come on the market
and Torno did look at it. He turned it down, partly because he did not
trust Anscomb's bookkeeping, but chiefly because "I couldn't see
that with Anscomb out of power, the winery would keep its share of

market.'' The conclusion turned out to be wrong: even though Bennett's liquor board played no favourites, Growers retained a solid
share of the local market and, under new owners, secured listings
across Canada by 1961. When Jordan did buy Growers in 1970 from
Imperial Tobacco for $10 million, it paid considerably more than the
$1 million which Anscomb had accepted in 1955.

Jordan's Villa Wines in New Westminster, B.C., selling 400 000
gallons by 1970, had outgrown its winery. With the Growers purchase, the mainland facility could be closed down. Operations were
consolidated temporarily in Growers' old Victoria winery, and the
search began for a new mainland location that would place the winery
closer to both its source of grapes and its major markets. In 1974,
when the search was beginning, Growers was renamed Ste-Michelle
so that Dieter Guttler's new table wines could develop a positive
image for a growing number of consumers who disdained the old-
time Growers and Slinger's wines. A decade after the name change,
the only product still bearing the Slinger name was Slinger's Grape,
the sweetest domestic red available in British Columbia.

The new Jordan & Ste-Michelle winery was opened in 1977, on a sixteen-acre site in Surrey, with an initial storage capacity of four million gallons and an optimistic design which would permit the winery to be tripled in size. Equipment brought from the Victoria winery included the now-retired pot still and sixty-five French-made, oval oak casks believed to be more than a century old. Ranging in size from nine hundred to sixteen hundred gallons, they are the survivors of eighty bought by Anscomb during American Prohibition from the Christian Brothers winery in California. After being cleaned and rebuilt, the casks are once more maturing wines in the classic manner.

PART II/2

THE SMALL COMMERCIAL WINERIES

BARNES

ESTABLISHED 1873

COOPERAGE 1.2 million gallons

TOURS & TASTINGS are offered Monday through Saturday from June to October at 10 A.M., 1 P.M. and 3 P.M.; November to May tours are on Saturday only, 1 P.M. to 3 P.M. Groups of fifteen or more may book day or evening tours year-round. Tel. (416) 682-6631. Take Seventh Street exit from the Queen Elizabeth Way just north of St. Catharines, and turn left on South Service Road to the winery.

TASTER'S CHOICE includes the ♈♈♈ 1983 johannisberg riesling, a full-bodied white with a touch of sweetness and an attractive, floral aroma; the ♈♈♈ Heritage Ruby Canadian Port, a rich and lingering wine, and the soft, fruity ♈♈ 1983 De Chaunac Limited Edition. The best of the Heritage Estates label is the ♈ Canadian Claret, a pleasing, honest blend of 70 per cent foch and 30 per cent California petite sirah. The Heritage Chablis and the German-style Weinfest are the company's best sellers.

ALSO RECOMMENDED the ♈♈ seyval blanc 1983; the pinot chardonnay 1983; the ♈♈ Heritage Cream Sherry, and the Heritage Canadian Burgundy.

Golden Diana's retirement in 1982 marked the end of an era at Canada's oldest continuously operating winery. The Canadian wine trade had still regarded it as a port and sherry factory when, on its hundredth birthday in 1973, it was sold to a British group by heirs of the founding Barnes family. The winery's list has since been transformed so dramatically that four of every five bottles now produced are table wines, among the most soundly made and reasonably priced such wines available in the country.

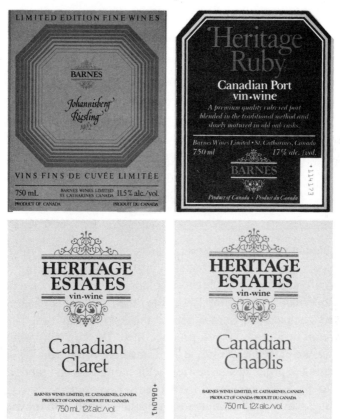

The Ontario Grape and Wine Manufacturing Co., as it was once known, changed its name in 1934, long after the brothers George and Thomas Barnes emerged as the controlling shareholders. Golden Diana – a sweet, sherry-style wine, possibly named for the diana grape – was one of its earliest brands and, until it was discontinued, one of the oldest in Canadian wine. One private Ontario cellar still contains a bottle of 1889 Diana, complete with its original cork and lead seal.

Legend has it that the lake boats plying the old Welland Canal frequently moored below the winery on its banks to be provisioned with barrels of wine after personal sampling by their officers. At the turn of the century, Barnes was one of the largest wineries in Ontario, reported as producing 75 000 gallons a year with a storage capacity of 250 000 gallons in 1894. One of the commercially sound and techni-

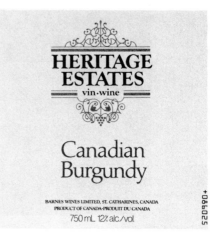

cally capable wineries to emerge from the gloom of Prohibition, Barnes opened a Toronto retail store in 1934, purchasing in 1936 the Fort William Wine Co., which had a store in North Bay, and in 1939 the Sunnybank Winery of Belleville, then Ontario's easternmost. Like its competitors, Barnes bought these struggling little firms for their retail licences, not their product lines. The company slumbered through the postwar evolution of Canadian wine-drinking habits, continuing to produce the sherries, with enough cheap brands among them to erode its reputation by the early seventies.

Barnes was one of a number of Canadian wineries to move at this time from family or individual control into the pockets of international corporations that could bankroll the important investments needed to keep pace with rapidly changing markets. (Toronto-based Turner Wines, established in 1885, was one of the few family wineries to refuse takeover bids, with the result that, no longer wanted by any suitor, it ceased business entirely in 1977.) One of the worldwide companies was the British food conglomerate Reckitt & Colman, which had been investing in wineries in Australia and the United States. After acquiring Barnes in 1973, it spent more than a million dollars over several years, including $400,000 on equipment for table wine production. Some of this money was raised by the sale of most of Barnes's hundred-acre vineyard, leaving a fifteen-acre frontage that is more important for the character it lends the winery than for the grapes it grows. The new owners also began installing new managers, one of them a sales supervisor who later became president, Jeffrey Ward. With twelve years in the British and European trade, he held his senior diploma in wine, one step short of the British trade's prestigious Master of Wine degree. Yet when Ward and his wife came to Canada to start a new life in early 1973, he was not planning to do so in the wine business. He had not realized that a Canadian industry existed, and his first bottle of Ontario table wine – the brand has diplomatically been forgotten – came as a rude surprise.

By 1981 Reckitt & Colman, apparently tired of feeding an old winery's appetite for money, offered Barnes for sale. A firm offer came from Gilbey Canada, the local subsidiary of a British distilling giant, only to be refused by the Foreign Investment Review Agency. The winery was finally purchased by Keewhit Investments, a Toronto holding company that is a vehicle for entrepreneurs Patrick Keenan and Fred McCutcheon; their subsequent FIRA-approved sale of a 49 per cent interest to Gilbey has given Barnes valuable access to the distiller's national sales force. "What it means to us," Ward explains, "is that we don't have to put Gilbey Canada on a commission. They get 50 per cent of the bottom line."

The new owners have continued investing heavily in a winery which still looks its age. Barnes is one of the more romantic wineries for touring: its cellars have catacomb-like passages and large wooden maturing tanks, aromatic after nearly a century of use. In the long term, ten 50 000-gallon oak tanks will be replaced by stainless steel ones, more appropriate for table wine production and much easier to keep sterile. Gradually, the firm's history, including photographs and documents from its early years, has been assembled in a large hospitality room.

The list of table wines now being marketed by Barnes reflects major changes in style and sales strategy that began in 1980. In common with such larger competitors as Andrés, Barnes has developed its own generic brands, aiming at the kind of distinctive identity that is not always achieved with varietal names. In fact, the winery only makes limited bottlings of its red varietals, maréchal foch and de chaunac, after concluding that consumers lacked the confidence, either in the grapes or in the Barnes name, that would propel either to a major market share. The foch now makes up 75 per cent of the blend in Heritage Estates Claret, the remainder being petite sirah from California, while de chaunac makes up the Burgundy. The inexpensive Heritage Estates series, with a rhine wine and a chablis,

has been successful since its introduction early in 1982. Other Barnes proprietary table wines have included Weinfest, a German-style white launched in 1981 with an aggressive, quarter-million-dollar advertising campaign, a Springwood label for labrusca-based offerings, and Beauvoir for premium-priced generics.

The other new varietals offered by Barnes have been whites, a seyval blanc, a chardonnay and a johannisberg riesling – prestigious but modestly priced, and designed to burnish the new image. The cheaper fortified wines have been dropped and replaced by a medium-priced Heritage sherry and port line. The sherry market has now stabilized after its sharp decline in the seventies, and Barnes believes that its expertise and its stock of aged sherries will win it an important share.

Behind the new style is Nikolas Opdam, born in Holland in 1951 and a graduate in organic chemistry from Brock University, who spent six years at Andrés before coming to Barnes in 1979. With resources like these, Canada's oldest winery has again become the forceful competitor it was a century ago. Sales by 1982 were running at about $4 million a year, with the target a doubling of volume by mid-decade. The ranks of the big six Canadian wineries are some way off, but Barnes is now solidly established in the second six.

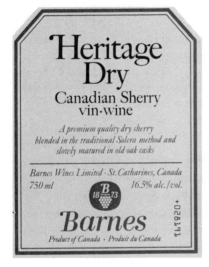
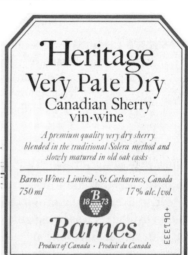

BEAUPRE

ESTABLISHED 1983

COOPERAGE 100 000 gallons

TOURS & TASTINGS are not yet offered at this new winery on the grounds of the Potter distillery in Langley, B.C.

TASTER'S CHOICE includes the Blanc de Blancs, a neutral-flavoured pale, dry white with a fruity aroma, and the light Canadian riesling. The Vin foch & Cabernet sauvignon is a medium-bodied light red with foch aroma; the cabernet is South American.

British Columbia's Terry family are competitive business people of the old school, uncomfortable with interventionist government. In the early seventies, the province in which they were operating their Potter Distilleries was being governed by social democrats who were not reluctant to intervene in business, supported by an aggressive union movement not reluctant to stand up to management. Potter's had been started in 1958 by businessman Ernest Potter and had been controlled since 1962 by Capt. Harold J.C. Terry and his son Frank. They were ready to expand into the wine business in 1974 when a rash of labour disputes swept British Columbia and changed their minds. They concluded that it would be prudent to reduce the risk of a single-province location by expanding elsewhere; they built a major distillery in Portland, Oregon, and a small one in St. Catharines, Ontario. The Beaupré winery, its name taken from a Potter-distributed French brandy, was finally built nine years later.

The delay seems likely to benefit the new winery. Far better grape varieties are under contract than was the case a decade ago, and the Oregon distillery has established an extensive sales network throughout the United States, including Hawaii. The American outlet may be useful: Beaupré has been awarded fewer listings than expected in British Columbia itself. Frank Terry has confirmed that ''we'll take a red and a white wine into the United States. All our distributors will buy from us. Despite the fact that there is a global surplus of wine, we can still participate in the export market.''

The $700,000 winery is a comparatively modest facility, given over mainly to stainless steel maturing tanks and served by the neighbouring distillery's high-speed bottling line. The grape-crushing facilities are located in the Okanagan, where the winery has contracted a total of ninety-five acres in four vineyards, the Terrys' argument being that crushing in the valley immediately after harvest

safeguards against deterioration in transit to the winery. The first Beaupré offerings – four whites and two reds, all generics – reached the market in October 1983 during the winery's first vintage, blended with bulk wines from competitors. The first wines made for Beaupré by Franz Helmer, formerly a winemaker with Jordan & Ste-Michelle, reached consumers in the summer of 1984.

Bulk wines for blending are also being purchased in the United States, a common practice among west-coast wineries. Generic blends form the base of Beaupré's production, but private reserve and varietal wines will be added. The varieties available to winemaker Helmer, in addition to chardonnay and johannisberg riesling, include Okanagan riesling, the valley's reliable standby, verdelet and inter-lake among the whites, and maréchal foch and baco noir among the reds. In fact, the extent to which Beaupré contracts new vineyard acreage in the Okanagan will help determine how rapidly it increases its listings in the home province. British Columbia authorities now insist that new wineries contract a significant supply of locally grown grapes rather than relying heavily on imported raw materials.

CULOTTA WINES

ESTABLISHED 1984

COOPERAGE Target is 100 000 gallons.

So powerfully are some people drawn to the romance of wine that the Liquor Control Board of Ontario entertains several inquiries and applications for winery licences each month. Jack Couillard, the board's assistant general manager, describes many such applicants as dreamers; most simply go away after a dose of his hard-headed realism. One dreamer who persisted was Peter Culotta, a Toronto businessman who braved two rejections before winning a licence in 1984. His winery's Columbus labels were among several new winery labels unveiled in Ontario that year, even though it was a difficult business year for domestic wines. The others include Seagram's Paul Masson, Vin Villa, Vineland Estates and Reif, all discussed elsewhere in this book.

Culotta was born in Toronto in 1920, the son and grandson of Sicilian pharmacists. His father, shortly after arriving in Toronto in 1910, had established the wholesale fruit and vegetable business which remains the cornerstone of the $25-million-a-year Culotta businesses. The operations, which included the import of wine grapes for Toronto's home vintners, were taken over by Peter in 1950. He subsequently began selling fresh grape juice as well to the winemakers. That whetted his desire to establish a winery, ultimately to be run by his food-technologist son, Christopher, born in 1961. The first Culotta application was filed in 1980; he succeeded, however, only after employing veteran Rudi Mueller as his consulting winemaker for the 1983 vintage.

Mueller, born in Dusseldorf in 1937, is the son of a Mosel wine-grower. He had worked and studied enology in both Germany and France, and left Europe for some North American experience in 1963. He intended to go directly to California, failed to get a work permit and came to Canada instead, planning to apply here for American papers. He certainly had not expected to pursue his craft in Canada, having been assured by a Canadian consular official in

Germany that there was no wine industry in the country. But three months after arriving, he found himself working in the cellars at Chateau-Gai. The following year, when Andrés started its Nova Scotia winery at Truro, Mueller was hired to supervise construction and the first vintage. He stayed there for twelve years, leaving in 1976 first to start his own Maritime winery. When that venture failed to come together, he joined Barnes in 1978, where he was one of two winemakers until he went to Culotta's aid.

Naturally, Mueller prefers making wines in the Mosel style with which he grew up. The first offerings from the winery include, therefore, one medium-dry white. However, the other two, a white and a red table wine, both are dry, for Mueller recognizes that Culotta's target clientele among southern Ontario's Italian community was itself raised with dry wines. The winery plans to make what Mueller called "ordinary consumer wines at reasonable prices."

During the 1983 vintage, Mueller produced five thousand gallons of wine in the Culotta grape juice warehouse at Oakville. Now, however, the juice business for home vintners, which is continuing, operates separately from the wine business. The Culotta winery was planned for a five-acre vineyard site just outside St. Catharines, located midway between the Barnes and Jordan wineries. The vineyard's labrusca grapes are to be replaced with premium hybrids and vinifera, though Culotta will buy most of its grapes from other growers. "We wouldn't even consider labrusca," Mueller said. About twenty thousand gallons of wine were planned for the 1984 vintage as Culotta gradually eases itself into the market, doing what Peter Culotta calls "getting the feel of it."

LONDON

ESTABLISHED 1925

COOPERAGE 2 million gallons

TOURS & TASTINGS are not offered at the winery on Wharncliffe Road, London.

TASTER'S CHOICE begins with a time-tested London product: the ♥♥ Dry Flor Sherry, pale and crisp for the sophisticated. Of the varietals, the ♥ 1983 maréchal foch is big, purple, fruity; and the ♥♥ 1983 baco noir is dark, with a cinnamon-like aroma; it is even better than London's prize-winning 1981 baco noir. ♥ Ancient Mead is the durable London exclusive – the only honey wine made in Canada. Best sellers are the winery's Chablis, Castini Bianco and the red, slightly foxy Bellavista de Chaunac.

In 1929 the Anglican bishop of Montreal, the Right Reverend J.C. Farthing, penned a remarkable testimonial for a wine produced by J.S. Hamilton & Co. of Brantford, Ontario: "For twenty years in parish work I used St. Augustine Communion Wine. . . . I know of no wine equal to it for sacramental purposes." Half a century later, Anglicans across Canada still use St. Augustine, a sweet red fermented to 16 per cent alcohol and made chiefly, as always, from concord and fredonia grapes. Its producer now is the tradition-conscious London Winery, one of the few in Canada to remain under the same family's control into the third generation.

St. Augustine stands for the quietly conservative approach to wine of the Knowles family that founded London in 1925. Another brand from that era, XXX Port, remains in the product line; the winery continues to produce substantial quantities of baked and dry flor sherries in the face of a trend away from fortified wines. It is the only Canadian producer – and perhaps one of three in North America – of mead, a honey wine of ancient origins. The winery's executives work in sober, dark-panelled offices, and technical staff, including the quiet-spoken Scots winemaker James Patience, are uniformed in neatly laundered laboratory smocks. Winery tours have been discouraged ever since a would-be visitor some years ago asked A.N. "Pete" Knowles, the man in charge, what the babysitting arrangements were. "I just don't like the public that close to me," he said later. "I do think it is difficult for people to do serious work with tourists milling throughout the sanitary food plant."

The Knowleses are descended from one of those Victorian British families that sent its young professionals out to the colonies. Several generations of the family lived and worked in the Bahamas, moving in a social set that included a plantation manager by the name of Neville Chamberlain, later the British prime minister who made the "peace in our time" Munich pact with Hitler. Chamberlain stood as godfather to Arthur Neville Knowles, Pete Knowles's father and London's founding president. Joseph Knowles, the founder's brother and the winery's general manager and vintner in its early years, was named after Neville Chamberlain's father. Pete Knowles, who bears his father's Christian names, has used the nickname for many years to avoid confusion: of his three sons in the winery, one is an A. Neville. This feeling for continuity applies equally to the business. Opportunities to sell have included at least one inquiry from the London-based Labatt brewing group, but, as Pete Knowles explains, "When you sell, all you have is money. To be in the wine business, you have to like it more than money."

The original Arthur Neville Knowles emigrated as a young electrical engineer and was soon running southwestern Ontario's largest electrical supply business. His brother Joseph had trained as a winemaker under a father-in-law who had a winery in Oakville, Ontario. The London winery the brothers established in 1925, with a modest 25 000 gallons of cooperage, was geared to selling ports and sherries in the London area. Until the new Liquor Control Board of Ontario began retailing wines in 1927, London's products were sold

through pharmacies on prescription. Their consumers were decidedly not table wine drinkers. In the words of Pete Knowles, "The original Americans and Canadians were hard-drinking and hard-living and hard-fighting." And the table wines London did attempt in the early days were unlikely to wean them from these ancient habits. Edwin Haynes, a veteran winemaker who worked at London in the forties, has recalled that one commercial failure was a bone-dry claret made entirely from concord grapes, a variety completely unsuited to be finished any way but sweet.

London's original licence was acquired from a would-be vintner by the name of Giovanni Paproni, who had planned to operate at Welland. With Ontario refusing to authorize new wineries, a situation that persisted for the next half-century, ambitious businessmen could expand only by buying existing licences, which included the right to operate retail stores. London made nine such acquisitions, five of them between 1935 and 1941. St. Augustine communion wine became a Knowles brand with their 1949 purchase of the J. S. Hamilton company, started in 1871 on Pelee Island at the southwestern end of Lake Erie. One of Hamilton's earliest brands, it has been sold in

Britain and the United States as well as in Canada, and continues to meet a small but steady volume of church demand. A white St. Augustine, developed some years ago in response to complaints about red wine staining church linen, has been discontinued because of poor sales.

In 1942, within months of each other, both A. N. Knowles and his

 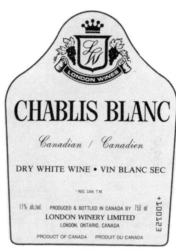

brother Joseph died of heart disease. A. N.'s wife, Evelyn, took over and recruited as general manager her brother-in-law, J. Laurie Kingsborough, who had been a salesman for a wholesaler of automobile parts. This team ran the winery for the next twenty years until Pete Knowles took over.

Knowles had wanted to study enology in California: prevented from doing so by wartime exchange controls on Canadian currency, however, he settled for a chemistry course in Canada before going to work for the winery in 1944. By then, Edwin Haynes, also a young chemist, was bringing to the vintner's job a professionalism that made London a rarity in an industry that emerged from Prohibition in so rustic a state that one of the LCBO's first acts was to organize winemaking courses. London's original winemakers also had some professional training: Haynes's immediate predecessor was Hugo Balderman, one of the first German enologists to work in Canada. When Haynes left in 1946, he was succeeded by Henry Schonfeld, a Polish-born enologist who left London in 1962 and in 1966 became the first winemaker at Mission Hill in British Columbia. His successor was Douglas Parker, a microbiologist previously employed in a tuberculosis sanitorium. Parker broke in James Patience, an Edinburgh-trained brewer who joined London in 1964 as a laboratory technician and took over in 1978.

Under Patience's direction, the winery finally made the commitment to table wines. In 1979 London released its chablis, a dry white

generic. The challenge from Italian generic wines has been met by such London brands as Castini Bianco, Castini Rosso and Londini, this last a red sold in a bottle that recalls a best-selling Italian red. All are comparatively dry table wines, a major change from an earlier time when London's Dinner Wine, in distinctive reclining-bottle containers, was medium-sweet to sweet. By 1982 the winery had also begun to release limited-edition varietals, including foch, de chaunac, and baco noir among the reds, and seyval blanc and johannisberg riesling among the whites.

The swing to table wines has required extensive upgrading of London's cooperage. Its two-million-gallon capacity, nearly all of it wood, ranged from the small oak barrels in the subterranean sherry cellars to 20 000-gallon fir and redwood maturation tanks. Much of this wood has been in use as long as London has made wine, and the housekeeping has been flawless. But white wine cannot be made in old port and sherry tanks. In 1982, for example, a maturing cellar with 80 000 gallons of wood cooperage was converted to stainless steel, with some tanks of only 7000 gallons to let Patience nurture table wines in small batches.

Conservative and traditional as London is, the winery's pitch has been enlivened by a certain inventiveness. Before 1960, when liquor and wine advertising was prohibited in Ontario, London gave away 50 000 pairs of salt and pepper shakers with the LCBO brand numbers of its leading products printed on them so that they would be fixed in the minds of consumers who, in that era before self-serve liquor stores, had to fill out order slips with these numbers. The winery had also been a pioneer in breaking away from the uniform bottle forced on producers by wartime constraints. As distillers began using distinctively individual containers for their products, Pete Knowles, then director of sales, quietly commissioned a decanter-style sherry bottle. He expected a storm of protest when the time came, at a wine industry meeting, to tell his peers about London's decision. To his immense relief, a Jordan executive disclosed a similar plan. "Jordan broke the code," Knowles remembers, "but we were the first ones on the market with a new bottle." Most of the curious shapes of that era have now disappeared, being too troublesome to handle on high-speed bottling lines.

London followed the Jordan lead of the early sixties with a gin-flavoured wine cocktail called Riki in the trend that produced such controversy in the wine business. "I can remember going to Nova Scotia and trying to get our brand listed," Knowles recalled. "They wouldn't have it. Zing had got there first and was outselling rum, gin and rye. Because of the lower price, the liquor commission's revenues were down and they were not in the least bit interested in taking on any new listings for this type of product." One winery after another dropped the product – except for London, never a company to make a rash move, and which still recommends its inexpensive Riki as a good base for punches.

London's mead was originally produced by a Sarnia beekeeper, Walter Strawa, who in 1960 received a special liquor board licence to make it. Strawa died shortly after starting his winery, and financially sound London took it over. Knowles found mead "a great door opener" for sales calls in the United States, where no similar domestic product was readily available. Sometimes described as the most ancient of man's fermented drinks, mead's popularity is declining with the consumer swing to drier wines, but it remains a personal favourite with Pete Knowles, who admits to a sweet tooth.

MISSION HILL

ESTABLISHED 1966

COOPERAGE 600 000 gallons

TOURS & TASTINGS take place hourly in peak season; group and evening tours by arrangment. Tel. (604) 768-5125. The sales room is open seven days a week from 10 A.M. to 6 P.M. Drive south on Highway 97 from Kelowna and watch for the winery sign about 3 km (1.9 mi.) past the floating bridge; turn onto Boucherie Road and follow the signs.

This winery's premium vintages from vinifera grapes are bottled under the Mission Hill label. Wines from hybrid grapes appear under the Pandosy Cellars label. The fruit brandies are sold as Great West Distillers.

TASTER'S CHOICE features the fine ♈♈♈1983 johannisberg riesling with its aroma of peaches and crisp, slightly tart finish, and, of the reds, the ♈♈♈1981 cabernet sauvignon, dark, intensely fruity, and still slightly tannic – leave this in the bottle to improve. The winery's unusually dark 1981 pinot noir also gets ♈♈♈. Other whites favoured include the golden ♈♈1981 gewurztraminer private reserve and the ♈♈1981 private reserve chenin blanc. The chardonnay and fumé blanc from 1983 also get ♈♈, and the former is well worth laying down. This winery offers ♈♈ port and sherry and excellent fruit brandies: ♈♈Bartlett Pear, clear, dramatic and delicate, is especially fine.

ALSO RECOMMENDED are the other gewurztraminers, chenin blancs, cabernet sauvignons, pinot noirs, and the winery's semillon, chasselas, seyval blanc, de chaunac, chelois and maréchal foch, its soundly made generics as well as its kirsch, apricot brandy and grappa.

Ben Ginter, the Canadian wine industry's most improbable owner, rarely spent to advertise his products: he could always count on free

publicity for being outrageous. In 1971, when Prime Minister
Trudeau mouthed an expletive in the House of Commons that was
later explained away as "Fuddle Duddle," Uncle Ben's Winery of
Westbank, B.C., moved quickly to register the phrase as the brand
name for a pink, sparkling pop beverage that it marketed against
Andrés's successful Baby Duck. Fuddle Duck was soon joined by

Yellow Bird and finally, Hot Goose, the latter a mulled red. None of
these wines is being made today now that Uncle Ben's, under new
owners, has become a sophisticated California-style winery, operating as Mission Hill Vineyards.

Mission Hill was the winery's original name when it was formed in
1966 by a group of Okanagan business people headed by R.P.
"Tiny" Walrod. A chemist, Walrod was already a major figure in the
Okanagan, having formed the company which developed the successful Sun-Rype apple juice brand. When that company was amal-
gamated in 1946 with B.C. Tree Fruits, Walrod became general

manager. "Tiny was a remarkable individual and he was a perfectionist," recalled Ian Greenwood, a later chief executive officer at B.C. Tree Fruits. "Not only did he have a beautiful voice, but he trained himself to paint, play the organ, fly airplanes ... and almost anything he tackled he did well." In 1964 Walrod left Tree Fruits to study the potential for a new winery, and in the Napa Valley of

California picked up the idea of having it look like a Spanish mission. He and his backers chose a dramatic hilltop near Westbank, with views of Okanagan Lake and the vineyards on its shores. The site presented certain practical problems when it came to water supply, but Walrod and his backers persisted, designing their winery with a bell tower and Spanish-style arches in the exterior frame. Mission Hill was also one of the best-equipped new wineries of the day. Before it was completed, Walrod died at age fifty-seven of a heart attack, and, without strong leadership, the winery slid into receivership, to be acquired in 1970 by Ben Ginter.

The bearded, barrel-shaped Ginter was a British Columbia folk hero by that time. Running away from his Manitoba home at age fourteen to work on construction, he started his own company in Prince George in 1948 and made a fortune in northern British Columbia over the next two decades. He found himself in the brewing business by chance when, in 1962, he bought the troubled Cariboo Brewing Co. in Prince George with the intention – or so he explained later – of storing his construction equipment in the building. But a little urging from the brewery employees encouraged him to see whether the native shrewdness that had made him a construction king would also work with beer. The new Tartan Brewing Company's labels were soon displaying Ginter's own smiling, crewcut portrait.

Uncle Ben's was the first canned beer in British Columbia, and Ginter began plans for breweries in Ontario, Manitoba, Alberta and the Vancouver area. The Alberta brewery was the only one open when his fledgling beer empire foundered in competition with national brands. Ginter later blamed most of his problems on alleged unfair tactics by John Labatt.

An entrepreneur used to bulldozing his way through problems, Ginter was the author of much of his own misfortune. The alcohol bureaucrats in government were outraged when he sold soft drinks in the familiar stubby brown bottles used for beer. They made him stop that, and they frustrated his efforts to cut prices, though Ginter fought one government-ordered price increase by taping a dime in every case of Uncle Ben's beer. Finally, a 1975 dispute with construction workers at the Richmond brewery site mushroomed to the point where the province's labour federation declared all Ginter products "hot." This meant that union members were expected neither to handle nor to consume them. The sanction was powerful enough to send the Ginter brewery and Westbank winery into receivership.

The winery had always been a poor cousin in the Ginter group, its product line dominated by Caravel Ruby Red, a sweet wine which was once the cheapest in British Columbia and a big seller on skid row. The winery's marketing lagged, despite such trendy inspirations as Fuddle Duck; in 1974 it was the last in the province to begin using corks instead of screw caps to seal its better offerings.

Joe Raffeiner, Ginter's long-suffering vintner, produced some good wines during this period. A 1974 maréchal foch was still winning approval from wine writers eight years later. When Mission Hill's current owners took over in 1981, they discovered barrel-aged dry sherry and ruby port of such quality that, bottled, it sold for ten dollars each, an almost unheard-of price for domestic fortified wines. Raffeiner had grown up and apprenticed in northern Italy, and he later acted as a consultant to several of the estate wineries. A Jehovah's Witness, he attracted some of his coreligionists to work under him, a common bond which may have helped the winery survive the several years when it was run by an accounting firm as receiver while Ginter and his bank joined battle.

Early in 1978, the receiver began selling off the various Ginter assets. A serious bid for the winery of nearly $800,000 came from Bright's, which had long been anxious to expand into British Columbia. Ginter successfully refinanced, topped the bid by a slim ten thousand dollars, and resumed control of what now became known as the Golden Valley Winery. Elias Phiniotis, who became winemaker while Raffeiner was consulting, began updating Ginter's thinking, convincing him, among other things, "that a winery with a 450 000-gallon capacity could not make a living selling only Ruby Red." The company plunged into the Germanic-style wine boom with a white called Schloss Weinberg and another called Harvest Pearl. Golden Valley recaptured enough of the British Columbia market so that Ginter was able to sell it in 1981, for about $4 million, to a group headed by the brash Vancouver wine merchant Anthony von Mandl, then only thirty-one. Ginter died a year later at fifty-nine, like Walrod, also of a heart attack.

Von Mandl is the antithesis of Ginter – a tall, slim, piano-playing bachelor, born in Vancouver to a family that came to Canada in 1947 after its textile plants were expropriated by the Czechoslovakian government. Just as aggressive as Ginter was, von Mandl is considerably more sophisticated in his dealings with bureaucrats. A 1972 commerce graduate from the University of British Columbia, he immediately set out to be a wine merchant, and in time was representing such top-selling European houses as Mommesin of France and Deinhard of Germany. For the Bordeaux shippers Yvon Mau et Fils, he blended to Canadian tastes in the widely popular St. Jovian brand of white and red wines.

To run the company, von Mandl hired a former adversary, Nick Clark, who had been in charge of Liquor Distribution Branch product listing from 1975 to 1980, during which time von Mandl had been struggling for listings of the European wines he represented. Born in Victoria in 1945, Clark is a McGill-trained industrial engineer. But nothing in his previous careers at Northern Electric, the post office and the LDB quite prepared him for what he and von Mandl found when they took over the winery in 1981. In Clark's words, it was "a shambles," having been run on such a shoestring that even lightbulbs needed replacing.

They moved swiftly to improve the winery technically and – with a $100,000 tasting room – aesthetically. For cash to service the debt load, they launched three pseudolabels: one German (Klosterberg Cellars), one French (Caves Chauvignon) and one Italian (Barbarossa), at the same time retiring the low-repute Golden Valley

brands. The pseudolabels have since been downplayed or dropped
altogether as the winery, through aggressive television advertising
and improved wines, established a following for its Mission Hill
labels and its second line, Pandosy Cellars. The Pandosy label, under
which Mission Hill's hybrid varietals and blends appear, refers to
Father Charles Pandosy, the pioneer Oblate missionary credited with

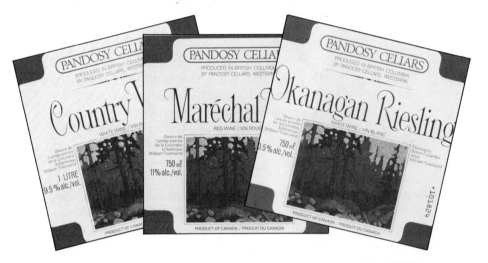

planting the Okanagan Valley's first vines in the 1860s. What has
emerged under these two labels is a wine and a commercial strategy
modelled as clearly on California as Walrod's original concept had
been.

There have been other innovations as well, among them the establishment of a sister distilling company, Great West, under whose
umbrella a small, copper pot still from Cognac, France, was installed
in 1983, enabling Mission Hill to make fruit brandies, or *eaux de vie*,
from locally grown pears, cherries, apricots and, of course, grapes.

Most of the distillery's volume, however, comes from the resale
under its own labels of bulk spirits purchased from distillers worldwide. A graphic example of Mission Hill's knack of seizing opportunity is provided by the winery's 1983 purchase of fifty-six Limousin
oak barrels in France. Von Mandl diverted the barrels first to Cognac
where they were filled with cognac that the distillery had purchased
and that was awaiting shipment to Canada. Profit on subsequent
cognac sales defrayed shipping costs for the barrels, which are now
maturing Mission Hill's premium wines.

OKANAGAN VINEYARDS

ESTABLISHED 1979 as Vinitera; reorganized under new owners in 1984.

COOPERAGE 55 000 gallons

TOURS & TASTINGS are available, and the retail store is open. Tel. (604) 498-4041. The winery is 4.8 km (3 mi.) south of Oliver, B.C., on No. 11 road just west of Highway 97.

The winery's initial products are all generics – a chablis, a burgundy, a premium dry red and a premium dry white – bread-and-butter wines, according to the winery. There are ambitious plans for varietals.

The picturesque Oliver winery, which reopened in 1984 under the new name of Okanagan Vineyards, had in its five years' existence added two footnotes to British Columbia wine lore: as Vinitera, it was the first cottage, or estate, winery to slip into bankruptcy, and as Okanagan Vineyards, it converted to a commercial licence, thus becoming the only commercial winery in B.C. with its own vineyard.

Vinitera was established by Joseph Poturica, who immigrated from Yugoslavia in 1954, and in 1967 converted a southern Okanagan orchard to a vineyard. A decade later, when the province began to license cottage wineries Poturica and his sons, Tony and Silvio, decided they could make a profit by producing their own wine, rather than selling the grapes. So they invested $500,000 in buildings and equipment; a distinctive feature of the winery is the storage tanks embedded horizontally into a hillside. The first wines, variations on Okanagan riesling, were released in 1979 from the previous year's vintage.

Sadly, those wines were somewhat rustic. Sales lagged and stocks accumulated until, in late 1982, Vinitera went into receivership. A number of potential buyers, among them Barnes Wines, looked at Vinitera during the next year and a half before a deal was struck. For most of them, the major hurdle was the requirement that they also buy an inventory of 53 500 gallons of bulk white wine that was becoming increasingly tired as it aged.

The group that finally revived the winery was headed by Alan Tyabji who was only thirty-nine years old in 1984. An earlier six-year executive career at Calona had ended abruptly when the winery, in one of those convulsive executive housecleanings not uncommon among conglomerates, fired him and four others on the same day. Tyabji immediately began planning a winery of his own. As it turned out, he got no further than registering a name – Oliver Cellars, now destined to be the second label at Okanagan Vineyards – before he got the chance in the spring of 1984 to be the operating head, and a modest investor, at Vinitera. The backers who put up most of the $500,000 to buy the winery were two Vancouver car dealers, brothers Bill and Don Docksteader. Bill, born in 1928, has become one of the West's largest Toyota dealers; Don represents Volvo; their father has been a service manager for a major Chrysler dealership. Neither claims to be particularly knowledgeable about wine, but Bill Docksteader has admitted: ''We're both smart enough to know we don't know anything about it and that we've had to hire the right people.''

Those people, besides Tyabji, included Randy Barichello, who had been controller at the Mission Hill winery, and William Finley, a veteran consulting winemaker who had been on staff at Calona in the early seventies and then ran the Labatt group's huge Lamont winery in California. It was his expertise that turned the tired white wine into money in the bank. Finley had previously refined a technique for wine revitalization that was last used on a major scale in postwar Europe to salvage unsold wartime vintages. Sugar and fresh yeast are added to the wine, starting a new fermentation which refreshes the wines. The resulting higher degree of alcohol is reduced to a normal table wine level by adding water. Finley thereby turned Vinitera's problem stock of bulk wine into a $100,000 asset for successor Okanagan Vineyards. With these wines, and mostly red blending stock from other wineries, Okanagan has re-entered the market with a group of generic table wines.

The decision to surrender the estate winery licence for a commercial licence was made by the Docksteaders. It was clear to them that, as investors, they could not make money within the estate winery limits. The estate licence prohibited a winery from producing more than 30 000 gallons a year, a volume barely sufficient for a profitable family operation and quite inadequate for a business with several salaried employees. By converting to a commercial winery, Okanagan Vineyards can produce as much wine as it can sell: the target is an annual 200 000 gallons. ''We want to stay small and premium,'' Tyabji says.

When the new owners took over, the 23-acre vineyard surrounding the winery was planted primarily with Okanagan riesling. They plan to replace nearly all those grapes with quality vinifera varieties chosen from those which have done well in recent research trials; another seventy acres of grapes have been contracted throughout the valley. These promise to produce distinctive wines towards the end of the eighties.

THE WINES OF QUEBEC

ANDRES

ESTABLISHED 1972

COOPERAGE 1 million gallons

TOURS & TASTINGS are held daily and evenings at the winery, at 3755 rue Picard, St-Hyacinthe; reservations are needed for groups. Tel. (514) 467-1562 (toll-free from Montreal) or 733-7468. From Montreal, take Highway 20 towards Quebec City and exit on 130 south into St-Hyacinthe.

The winery uses California and Ontario juice and grapes – no concentrates.

BEST SELLERS are Baby Duck and Hochtaler, a German-style medium dry white.

BRIGHT'S

ESTABLISHED 1933

COOPERAGE 1.6 million gallons in three wineries

TOURS & TASTINGS are available only at the St-Hyacinthe winery opened in 1971 as Vins LaSalle. Tel. (514) 731-1126. The original Lachine winery was acquired in 1933 and is used for maturing; the St-Joseph-du-Lac facility (La Cidrerie des Deux Montagnes) was bought in 1978.

The wineries use Ontario and California juice, and wine blends from Europe.

TASTER'S CHOICE includes the Mon Village white in the Bordeaux style and the sparkling, Charmat-process cider sold as Maximum.

CHANTECLER

ESTABLISHED 1972

COOPERAGE 1.25 million gallons

TOURS & TASTINGS daily at 2:30 P.M. beginning at the winery's attractive reception room, are available at modest cost to groups of thirty to sixty, food additional. Reservations are required a month in advance. Tel. (514) 469-3104 or 861-2404. On Highway 10 south from Montreal, Chantecler is on the left at the western edge of Rougemont.

Muted musts and fresh juice from California are used, as well as bulk blending wines.

BEST SELLERS include Table Ronde, a semi-dry red; the Chianti-packaged Rossini, and Rêve d'Eté, a medium-dry white. The company's Double Six cider claims 70 per cent of the Quebec market.

CORELLI

ESTABLISHED 1981

COOPERAGE 400 000 gallons

TOURS & TASTINGS feature wine and cheese parties by appointment.Tel. (514) 638-1333. From Montreal, cross the Mercier Bridge going southwest, then turn left for La Prairie on Highway 132; the winery will be visible on the right.

Corelli uses muted must and fresh grapes from Italy.

TASTER'S CHOICE is Castelnuovo, a Barolo look-alike from cabernet sauvignon and montepulciano musts, matured over oak chips to add bouquet and complexity.

ALSO RECOMMENDED are Entre Deux Pays and the sparkling Grand Mousseux.

GELOSO

ESTABLISHED 1965

COOPERAGE 2 million gallons

TOURS & TASTINGS are by appointment, with group facilities. Tel. (514) 661-0281 or 324-3100. Leman Blvd. in Laval's industrial park is reached from Highway 440.

Geloso works from muted Italian musts.

TASTER'S CHOICE includes the winery's Caberneaux, the fruity Réserve à Vincent, and the sangiovese-style Réserve du Patrimoine, all reds. For the best-selling Cuvées, Romaine Rouge and Orfée Blanc, see listings.

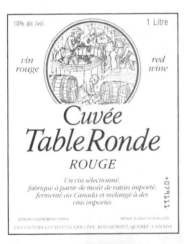

JULAC

ESTABLISHED 1972

COOPERAGE 200 000 gallons

TOURS & TASTINGS are scheduled during the blueberry harvest, August to mid-September. Tel. (418) 276-4120. The winery is on 7th Avenue, Dolbeau.

TASTER'S CHOICE is the winery's durable specialty, Dubleuet.

LUBEC

ESTABLISHED 1971

COOPERAGE 1 million gallons

TOURS & TASTINGS are readily available; groups need reservations. Tel. (514) 871-1197.

The winery at St-Antoine-Abbé uses muted musts and blending wines.

BEST SELLERS are La Nuit Volage and Tournefête, both red.

SECRESTAT

ESTABLISHED 1972

COOPERAGE 600 000 gallons

TOURS & TASTINGS are not available at this winery on the Trans-Canada Highway at Dorval.

California concentrates are used.

BEST SELLERS are Chambord, at 115 000 cases the second domestic red in 1983, and Servino.

VERDI

ESTABLISHED 1978

COOPERAGE 600 000 gallons

TOURS & TASTINGS feature a hospitality room for groups at 9355 Langelier in St-Léonard. Tel. (514) 328-2820. The winery uses California grapes.

BEST SELLERS are the reds Nuit d'Amour, Cuvée des Moines and the more complex Vieux Manoir, made of carignane, alicante, grenache and ruby cabernet.

VIGNOBLES DE QUEBEC

ESTABLISHED 1974

COOPERAGE 400 000 gallons

TOURS & TASTINGS are not available at the winery, which is in Hemmingford.

BEST SELLERS are Seigneur de Beaujeu and Petit Prince, both reds, and the Petit Prince Blanc.

THE WINES OF QUEBEC

Technology has triumphed over nature: Quebec, a province with no commercial-scale vineyards, has no fewer than eleven wineries. Technology allows these establishments, importing raw materials from several continents, to make palatable wines which are, at their best, a match for ordinary wines from anywhere in the world. The proof of this is the wineries' ability to survive in Quebec's extremely competitive market.

For Quebec's wine market is distinctively different. This is the only province in which red wines continue to outsell white, though the whites are catching up. It was also the first province to permit the sale of domestic wines and ciders in small food stores, creating a mass market that is certainly one reason why so many wineries operate there. At the same time, Quebec wineries are the only ones in Canada facing vigorous competition from the provincial liquor board, the Société des Alcools du Québec. The SAQ, North America's first state liquor monopoly when it was formed in 1921, bottles imported wines at its modern Montreal plant and markets them under it own labels. With a storage capacity of 3.5 million gallons, this plant is larger than any of the eleven wineries and, indeed, larger than most wineries in the country. The SAQ's listing policies severely limit the number of wines from other provinces available in its outlets. This measure of protection for Quebec wineries is less significant than it seems, however, when it is weighed against the market dominance of the SAQ's own imported brands. Its Cuvée des Patriotes, for example, was in early 1983 the second largest-selling red wine in Canada after Donini from Italy.

The long-sought permission granted at the end of that year for private wineries to bottle imports should improve their ability to compete with the SAQ and let them operate beyond the one-third-capacity level that has been the recent industry average. Wineries were also allowed by this move to increase to five from three the number of brands each can sell through food stores. It was a first step towards deregulation that will be extended to include an additional five brands per winery, and, after the middle of the decade, as many as grocers will handle. The SAQ's own food-store offerings were temporarily frozen at fifteen, then raised to twenty-five: store owners may handle as many or as few as they desire. Under this new policy, then, Quebec wineries can capitalize on a vast world surplus and offer Quebec consumers reasonably priced wines for years to come. That, after all, was the basic reason why the SAQ, many years ago, got into the bottling business.

Quebec's attitude towards alcohol has always been distinctive. The

11% alc./vol.　　　　　　　　　　750 ml

Cuvée des Patriotes

VIN ROUGE

IMPORTÉ DE FRANCE ET MIS EN BOUTEILLES PAR
SOCIÉTÉ DES ALCOOLS DU QUÉBEC
MONTRÉAL, QUÉBEC

narrow attitudes of Prohibition failed to take root there; in a national referendum of 1898, Quebec alone among the provinces voted against going dry, and by a resounding four to one. The province was rendered dry temporarily, along with the rest of Canada, during the First World War, when federal law required this sacrifice from the home front. The first to abandon wartime Prohibition, Quebec opted for a government marketing monopoly in the form of its liquor control board, first studied and then copied by the other provinces and by a number of American states. The original objective of curbing alcohol abuse was a genuine one: only since the Second World War have liquor boards been transformed into government revenue agencies. "Right from the start, there was a preoccupation with getting the population to consume less alcohol," recalled Daniel Werminlinger, a courteous engineer who retired in 1983 as the SAQ's president.

Quebec's comparative openness was an irritant to those provinces still under Prohibition. In 1924 Ontario's Board of Licence Commissioners, a forerunner of the liquor board, complained: "In recent years manufacturers of alleged medicated wines, especially in the province of Quebec, where their preparations were ruled as liquor . . . have been persistent in invading the Ontario market, and all over this province, and particularly in northern and eastern sections, these wines have been the cause of much intoxication.'' And in liberalization Quebec continued to lead the country. By 1932 it was the only province permitting the sale of wine with meals, a move which likely influenced T. G. Bright president Harry Hatch to buy a fifty-year-old brewery on the Lachine Canal in the Montreal suburb of Lasalle.

Using grape juice and wines from Ontario, the Bright winery – the original vintner was Adhémar de Chaunac – produced chiefly sherries, ports and a sauterne-style product; the wines were bottled under contract by the SAQ. In 1971, when expansion was in the air in the Quebec industry, Bright's bought a building in St-Hyacinthe, re-equipped it as a winery and bottling plant, and began producing nonfortified table wines. In 1978 the company purchased a defunct cider plant at St-Joseph-du-Lac near Montreal and, under the direction of the Bordeaux-trained winemaker Jean Berthelot, resumed cider-making and began producing table wines there as well. Since each winery is licensed separately, Bright's has been able to triple the number of listings it has in food stores, a circumstance that gives its wines the leading share of the Quebec market.

Soon after it was established, the Quebec liquor board began importing bulk wine and bottling it in the province. The quality-control laboratory set up to ensure that sound wines were being bottled remains one of the largest and best-equipped such facilities in the Canadian wine industry, making meticulous checks on all wines offered for sale in Quebec. The decision to import and bottle was made for two sound economic reasons: by buying in bulk, the board could reduce the cost of wine for its consumers, and the bottling plant created jobs in Quebec. The tradition of bulk bottling is venerable in the wine world. The British long bottled vast quantities of Portuguese port and Bordeaux claret. Quebec imported most of its table wines from France and most of its fortified wines from Ontario. Its consumers in the early years, like those elsewhere in the country, preferred port- and sherry-style wines to dry table varieties. The trend towards the latter began in the fifties with the arrival of immigrants from Europe, bringing with them a wine tradition and frequently also a winemaking tradition.

One such immigrant was Vincent Geloso, whose family had grown grapes near Naples. Geloso immigrated to Montreal in 1957 to escape a recession in Italy, and worked at a variety of jobs, from selling insurance to repairing sewing machines, until, in 1961, he began importing California wine grapes for fellow Italian immigrants in the city. "The men had to make their own wine," Tony Geloso, one of Vincent's three sons, has commented. "To the Italians, wine is as sacred as bread and pasta." Geloso's commercial success attracted competitors, including Giovanni Miucci, who had immigrated about

the same time and shared Geloso's attitude towards wine. Both men went on to establish commercial wineries.

Vincent Geloso was the first: in 1965, looking for a way to convert the six-week season for selling fresh grapes into a year-round liveli-hood, he received what is regarded as Quebec's first licence for a fully-functioning winery – Bright's Lachine winery was a blender and bottler of Ontario-fermented wines. "I don't think anybody took us seriously," Tony Geloso said of his father's first winery, which was unable to secure a listing in the province's liquor stores until

1971. "We just warehoused the wine." Total sales until that listing were 155 cases. In 1971 the winery sold six thousand, and volume growth since then has been "almost logarithmic," suggests Tony, a McGill business graduate who now runs the winery.

The early seventies saw the opening of several new wineries in Quebec. Their investors made some assumptions that turned out to be wrong, or, at least, premature. One was that permission was imminent for private companies to compete with the liquor board in bottling bulk imports. This undoubtedly motivated the French producer of Dubonnet to become one of the original investors in Chantecler, only to pull out as the winery slid towards commercial failure. Another assumption was that Quebec-based wineries fermenting imported raw materials would have ready access to markets in other provinces. This was Seagram's strategy in 1972 when it sold its interest in Jordan's Ontario winery and built Secrestat in Dorval, a suburb of Montreal. A third assumption was that food stores, where apple cider appeared on shelves beside the beer in 1971, would soon be dealing in wines as well.

However, neither Ontario nor British Columbia, the two major wine-consuming provinces outside Quebec, was prepared to give Quebec wines a significant number of listings, unwilling to see their grape growers compete with the world's vineyards via the fermentation tanks of Quebec. Maj.-Gen. George Kitching, head of the Liquor Control Board of Ontario in the early seventies, firmly resisted applications from the SAQ which wanted to sell its Quebec-bottled imports in Ontario. To impress on the Quebec board the reason for his refusal, he arranged for Canada's liquor board general managers to hold one of their regular meetings in the Ontario wine-growing area around Niagara-on-the-Lake. Indicating the passing miles of vineyards as they drove to the meeting, Kitching told the Quebec delegates: "That's why we can't list your stuff." In retaliation, the SAQ delisted many Ontario wines. Today, major Canadian wineries with no wineries in Quebec – notably Calona, Jordan, Barnes and London – have few wines on Quebec's list and rarely secure new listings. Typical was Jordan's 1983 experience when it submitted its Maria Christina red table wine, a big seller in Ontario. The SAQ quality-control laboratory rejected the samples on the somewhat dubious grounds that they were oxidized, a fault unlikely in products of a modern winery.

Quebec's new wineries struggled financially until, in 1978, they were allowed to market through small food stores. Calona suffered such disastrous losses at the St-Hyacinthe winery it opened in 1972 that the facility was sold to Andrés within a year. Chantecler went through several sets of owners, barely avoiding bankruptcy. The food stores – about ten thousand of them, excluding supermarkets – offered a seasoned network that had sold beer for about twenty years. The impact was significant. In 1977, the last year in which wines were sold through liquor stores alone, sales totalled 44.8 million litres. Six years later, total wine sales in Quebec had risen to 60.6 million litres, a third of which was sold through food stores. The eleven Quebec wineries shared among them a food-store sales volume of 12.2 million litres, with the SAQ accounting for the other 7.8 million. Listings have crept up from the initial two allowed each winery, while the SAQ's continued significant share contributed to its "dividend" to the provincial treasury that in the year ended 31 March 1983 amounted to $275 million on total sales of $787 million.

Its multiple roles, in fact, make the SAQ quite unlike other Canadian liquor boards. It operates on such a scale as a marketer that, five or six times a year, a 750 000-ton bulk tanker is chartered to deliver European wines to the port of Montreal. A tough and direct competitor of the domestic wineries, the SAQ also governs in one way or another nearly all the channels through which its products are marketed, and, on certain brands, even undersells them. Another sore point with the wineries has been the board's periodic tendency to turn wines down for reasons the private industry believes are technically indefensible. Secrestat once decided to lighten the colour of its rosé, a brand called Pica, and happened to submit a truckload which included cases of the darker old blend. The SAQ laboratory spotted the variation, rejected the wine and ordered eight thousand cases destroyed. Secrestat afterwards made its colour change much more gradually. Another new wine was turned down for the thoroughly subjective reason that it lacked flavour. Wineries resent the board's potential power to "assassinate" products competing with its own house brands. The most recent revision of the winery regulations makes provision for an interprofessional committee to which wineries can appeal if they believe the SAQ has been arbitrary.

The almost total absence of commercial grape growing in Quebec has sparked some intriguing solutions. In 1971 Vincent Geloso began

importing fresh grapes from Italy in refrigerated shipboard containers. After three years, he admitted this was impractical: during the
two-week ocean crossing, the grapes were vulnerable to mold and
dehydration, and handling costs were excessive. Geloso then brought
in so-called muted musts, freshly crushed grapes or grape juice
heavily sulfured to prevent involuntary fermentation. Now, he and

his enologist, Dr. Nicola Vellusi, choose their grapes in various
Italian vineyards at harvest time and supervise processing there
before consigning the must to the sea journey. The grapes, after being
pressed, are bathed in nitrogen – an inert gas which drives off oxygen
and preserves freshness – and between five hundred and a thousand
parts per million of sulfur are added, ten to twenty times the quantity
used as a sterilant and preservative in finished wines. It is removed at
the winery, usually by briefly heating the juice under a vacuum,
which vaporizes the sulfur. Fermentation then proceeds as normally
as it would in Italy. Most winemakers would prefer to work with fresh
grapes, but, if that choice is not available, certainly prefer muted
musts to grape concentrates. The concentrating process, which in-
volves more heat, imparts a slightly baked or caramelized flavour to
the finished wines, particularly unattractive in white varieties.

The original Geloso winery was in Vincent's home. In 1973 the
current plant was built in an industrial park in the north Montreal
suburb of Laval. Production expanded until Geloso's offerings
ranged from the first Charmat-process sparking wine made in Quebec
to herb-flavoured, vermouth-style aperitif wines. Its pioneering success encouraged competitors into the market, creating the current

overcapacity. "At eleven wineries we're way too much," Tony Geloso noted sadly.

Giovanni Miucci's Corelli winery, opened in 1981, is the eleventh and most recent of Quebec's wineries. Like Geloso, he began importing California grapes, but soon decided that his clients, primarily other Italian immigrants, wanted wines that tasted like those they had

known in Italy. He turned first to European concentrates and then, in 1964, began importing containers of muted must for his clientele. When he and his partner, Vincent Morena, opened Corelli in the village of Ste-Catherine, a half-hour drive south of Montreal, they continued using the muted must of grape varieties familiar to their Italian-trained winemaker, Carmine Saccareccia. They also import bulk wine for blending and even bring in small quantities of fresh Italian grapes.

The Corelli wines, not surprisingly, have a pleasantly Italian style. Castelnovo, the winery's dry red, is a blend of 30 per cent cabernet sauvignon, 35 per cent montepulciano, and various fresh grape varieties it aims, with reasonable success, at the style of a simple Barolo. A technological trick gives the wine oak complexity without barrel-aging: the blended wines are circulated gently between two 5000-gallon tanks, one of which contains a pad of oak chips. Corelli's white, called Entre deux Pays, is made from the must of verduzzo grapes from the Veneto viticultural district of northeastern Italy. The Charmat-produced sparkling Grand Mousseux is made from pinot blanc must, also from the Veneto.

The one Quebec winery using fresh grapes consistently is Verdi, which shares an Italian heritage with Geloso and Corelli. Verdi's founder, a food wholesaler named Vincent Cacciatore, began importing California wine grapes to Montreal in 1967, and in 1978 built a large, well-equipped winery in St.-Léonard, another Montreal suburb. Laurent Vivès, Verdi's French-trained winemaker, blends a broad range primarily from seven varieties, among them ruby caber-

net, grenache, alicante and carignane. Ugni blanc, a variety of Italian origin also grown in California, serves as the foundation for most of the Verdi whites, notably the crisply dry Tourbillon d'automne. Vivès's use of fresh grapes yields some of the best Quebec-made table wines. The vintner has also tried some daring technical experiments, among them making a dry white wine, never released commercially, from maple syrup.

Verdi is required to use fresh grapes for its kosher wines, of which it is the only Quebec producer. These originated at a Jewish New Year meal attended by Cacciatore: when he complained to his host that he found the traditionally sweet kosher wines difficult to consume with food, he was challenged to make dry ones. The challenge was passed on to Vivès, who since 1980 has been making four of them from fresh grapes with no additives, in sterile conditions, and under rabbinical supervision. Verdi offers two white kosher wines (one semi-dry) and two reds (one also semi-dry), marketed under the brand Kineret, the Hebrew name for the Sea of Galilee. They are sold across

Canada, except for British Columbia and Ontario, and are exported to the eastern United States.

Among the group of Quebec wineries founded in the early seventies was Julac at Dolbeau, in the Lac St-Jean region about a hundred miles north of Quebec City. Julac's blueberry aperitif, Dubleuet, fortified to 15.5 per cent alcohol, resulted from research done by the

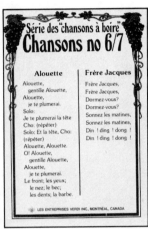

company in conjunction with Laval University and the provincial Ministry of Agriculture and Food. Various other Canadian wineries making wines with a blueberry base, Andrés Moody Blue in British Columbia being one example, have usually discovered that the fruit is technically challenging and not always accepted by consumers. Julac has persisted, however, and more recently began research on dry table wines from the berry.

Wild blueberries thrive in the wooded region around Lac St-Jean, particularly on land swept by forest fires. During the twenties, the Trappist monastery at Mistassini, near Dolbeau, operated a plant making blueberry conserves. Even before that, farmers in the region were harvesting the berries, not just for their own tables but also for commercial sale: by 1945, they were gathering an estimated 21 million pounds a year. This had declined to about 3 million pounds by 1961, one factor being better forest protection and thus fewer fires to create berry patches. Since then, the blueberry industry has been reorganized into producer co-operatives or commercial companies, of which Julac is one, and a degree of cultivation has taken place in the blueberry groves themselves. By 1976, when Julac first introduced Dubleuet, it was in charge of a 3500-acre grove; the productivity of that property has risen from 65 000 pounds to nearly 1.8 million in the harvest of 1983.

Only a portion of this production is required for the Dubleuet that

Julac makes every year. The berries chosen for winemaking are crushed and pulped and left in fermentation vats for four to five weeks, after which the juice is taken off, filtered, and allowed to age for a short time. Meanwhile, the herbs used in the Dubleuet are soaked in alcohol, and this flavoured alcohol is blended with the fermented blueberry juice. The wine is then pasteurized and bottled. The first offering in the harvest of 1976 went into only twenty-four SAQ stores, but once the product began selling, distribution was extended to all stores and then, in 1978, to food stores. Julac has responded by doubling the size of its winery in 1979 and increasing cooperage to 300 000 gallons. The company also markets Cuvée Val Jalbert, a dry white table wine blended from muted musts and bulk wines which has developed a reliable reputation.

One industry leader who in the early seventies believed that the Quebec government would quickly liberalize wine sales was Tom Capozzi, then president of Calona Wines of Kelowna, B. C. With the aid of a $200,000 federal industrial development grant and a $75,000 provincial subsidy, Calona opened a million-gallon winery in 1972 at

St-Hyacinthe, southeast of Montreal. Shortly after the winery was opened, Calona was acquired by Montreal-based Standard Brands, which quickly concluded that the losses there threatened Calona's existence. The winery was sold in 1974 to Andrés, which succeeded with its popular Baby Duck and other national brands.

Also in 1972, a group of Quebec City businessmen, in conjunction with France's La Compagnie Générale des Produits Dubonnet-Cinzano-Byrrh, built a 750 000-gallon winery at nearby St-Augustin and began marketing wine made primarily from concentrates. Chantecler's products were not well received and, as the winery's losses piled up, one of the creditors, Redpath Sugar, found itself owning most of the shares by default. Redpath, having no desire to stay in the wine business, arranged the sale of its shares and the Dubonnet interests in 1976 to a group headed by Jean-Denis Coté, the former manager of an apple co-operative who in 1971 had formed a cider company at Rougemont, about forty miles east of Montreal.

A dapper and sophisticated bookkeeper, Coté was considering a career in politics and planned to run the cider concern only until it was established. His interest in food and wine pushed public life aside, however, and in 1975 he obtained a winery licence. The purchase of Chantecler enabled Coté to obtain needed equipment at a reasonable price. Its inventory could be salvaged only by blending with bulk imports; when this was sold, the old labels were retired. The use of concentrates was discontinued in favour of muted must. With the new Chantecler products being released just as grocery-store distribution began, the winery has succeeded in making 80 per cent of its Quebec sales through the stores.

Apple ciders remain an important part of Chantecler's business. It is one of three commercial cider makers in Quebec, the others being Bright's, which has rejuvenated a cider-producing plant at Lac St-Joseph, near Montreal, to make a sparkling wine, and Lubec Inc. at St-Antoine Abbé, towards the American border. Lubec was established in 1971: its annual production of about sixty thousand cases consists primarily of wines made from European and South American musts. Despite its start as a cider company, its largest-selling product is a dry red wine, La Nuit Volage.

Both Lubec and Chantecler are located in prime Quebec apple-growing regions. At Rougemont, Chantecler ferments about a million litres of apple juice each fall, making still and sparkling ciders, apple brandy, and vermouth-like aperitifs. Coté claims that his Bellini brand was the world's first "vermouth with an apple base," though Bright's now offers a comparable product called Allegro. Despite the ingenuity Chantecler and Lubec have brought to making apple beverages, the Quebec cider market collapsed from 1 million gallons in 1974 to about 300 000 gallons ten years later. One explanation for this is that the ciders fell victim to competition from wines once both were being offered in food stores.

The newcomer to the Quebec wine scene with the most impressive credentials has been Distillers Corp.–Seagrams, the Montreal-based giant. By 1972, when it built Secrestat, Seagram's controlled the Paul Masson winery in California, Barton & Guestier, a 250-year-old Bordeaux wine shipper and G.H. Mumm & Co. of Champagne. International wine interests have since expanded to include investments in Portugal, Italy, Australia and New Zealand. In Canada, Seagram's controlled the Jordan winery from 1948 until 1972, when it sold the Ontario firm. "Our company was disenchanted with the whole Ontario scene," said Harold Abney, a veteran Seagram's executive and whisky blender, who was Jordan's marketing manager at the time. "There just weren't enough good-quality grapes in Ontario to make quality table wine there." It was fourteen years before the company changed its mind. In 1984 it converted an industrial building at Beamsville, Ontario, into a 200 000-gallon winery, operating under the name Paul Masson & Co.

La Maison Secrestat in Dorval, adjacent to the Trans-Canada Highway and not far from the airport, cost Seagram's $3 million. It is the only Quebec winery totally committed to vinifying grape concentrates, most of which come from California, where the winery is aided by Paul Masson. Secrestat has never used fresh grapes and has rarely used muted must, but winery manager Jean Martin, a former distillery chemist, manages to vinify concentrates with sufficient skill to put his dry Chambord among Canada's ten best-selling red wines. Lacking Ontario or British Columbia listings, however, the 600 000-gallon winery, like others in Quebec, has not been able to use its full capacity. Seventy per cent of Secrestat wines, backed effectively by television advertising, sells through food stores.

With its international connections, Secrestat recognized the demand from foreign wineries for Canadian bottling facilities, if only because great savings can be realized by shipping wine in bulk rather than in heavy bottles. In 1979 Riunite, the huge Italian wine con-glomerate, proposed that the Secrestat plant become its bottler for Canada and the eastern United States, with a potential volume of 500 000 cases a year. Harold Abney was receptive but unable to get approval from the Quebec government, which is believed to have wanted the Riunite business to go to the SAQ bottling plant. The Italian shipper finally dropped its idea and expanded its own bottling lines in Italy.

But the episode galvanized other Quebec wineries into action. Chantecler's Coté, taking the lead in developing a brief to the provincial government, surveyed ten of the largest foreign shippers of wine to Quebec. He learned that while all were prepared to have their bulk wines bottled in Quebec, only two were willing to give such contracts to the SAQ. The others all believed bottling contracts should remain independent of the state marketing monopoly, allowing wineries to adjust, move, or cancel such contracts without worrying about reprisals in the marketplace. Coté then assembled data on the industrial benefits that would flow to Quebec's bottle and carton manufacturers if wineries were permitted to bottle foreign wines for North American distribution. Both he and Abney argued that the American market would accept Quebec-bottled European wines as readily as European-bottled ones, given adequate quality controls. In 1983 Coté's campaign finally won the Quebec government's acquiescence to having its private wineries operate as contract bottlers.

The dream of vineyards in Quebec has flickered constantly since Jacques Cartier and Samuel de Champlain found native grapes flourishing in what they called New France. Count Justin de Courtenay, who later had a successful vineyard near Toronto, tried to grow grapes near Quebec City about 1860, giving up only when he failed to get a subsidy from the government. Georges Masson, a French-born biologist who taught at the agricultural school in Oka, west of Montreal, experimented with vines there as early as 1935. "The reason for importing grape vines to Oka was pure curiosity," Masson said. "Vineyards were then almost nonexistent in the province of Quebec. Since French hybrids had been doing very well in the cold region of Lorraine in France, I wondered whether they would survive in Canada. My father sent me about six cuttings – three baco and three de chaunac – which were planted on the south slope of a gully. Nearby was a building on the west side, and trees on the north and east sides. This was an ideal spot: snow accumulated early and remained until spring. The vines were not buried in earth. It should be kept in mind, however, that young vines are more resistant to cold than old ones.'' He left the school six years later, and nothing much came of this viticultural trial. "No one showed any interest," he lamented in his 1979 book, *Wine from Ontario Grapes*. By that time, he had retired to the Niagara Peninsula, where people did show an interest.

In 1970 Gérard Millette, a professor of soil science at Macdonald College in suburban Montreal, received a modest provincial research grant for a viticultural trial. Geloso helped him secure fourteen vinifera varieties from Italy, and he also planted fifteen French hybrid varieties. The trial was a failure: the vineyard was so deficient in heat units that Millette was reported to have considered either warming the vines with microwaves or laying heat-retaining asphalt between the rows. Subsequently, federal and provincial grants have aided experimental vineyards in the apple-growing districts at Rougemont and Rigaud, east of Montreal, and at St-Bernard-de-Lacolle, south of Montreal near the American border. Chantecler took part in the Rougemont trials, in which six acres were planted with a variety of vinifera and hybrid vines in 1977. While nearly all the varieties suitable for the Niagara also mature in Rougemont, the vines are 10 to 15 per cent less productive, and this, in Coté's view, spells the difference between commercial success and failure. At St-Bernard-de-Lacolle, French-born vineyardist Michel Croix, who was associated with the Chantecler project, has a small vineyard whose vines are leased to home winemakers. Meanwhile, scientists at Laval University in Quebec City are trying to develop cold-resistant grape rootstock.

At Dunham, a village near the American border, Christian Barthomeuf, a fruit farmer from Montpellier in France, has planted a ten-acre vineyard with vinifera and French hybrids. Barthomeuf believes that his slate-like vineyard – he even calls it Domaine des Côtes d'Ardoises – has a Bordeaux-like microclimate, and he is determined to be producing commercial wines from his grapes later in the eighties. ''People are tenacious, even against the greatest odds,'' former SAQ president Daniel Werminlinger said, skepticism blending with admiration in the tone of his voice. The dream lives on.

ESTATE WINERIES

REIF

ESTABLISHED 1983

COOPERAGE 20 000 gallons

TOURS & TASTINGS The attractive tasting room is open from 10 A.M. to 5 P.M. during winter months, and later in summer. Telephone (416) 468-7738. The winery is on the Niagara Parkway between Line 3 and Line 2 roads.

TASTER'S CHOICE includes the fruity ♥♥ 1983 johannisberg riesling, the fresh but elegant ♥♥ 1983 siegfried rebe and the silky ♥♥ 1983 vidal.

VINELAND ESTATES

ESTABLISHED 1984

COOPERAGE 20 000 gallons

TOURS & TASTINGS The sales room is open and visitors are courteously welcomed. Telephone (416) 562-7073. From the traffic light in Vineland, where Highway 8 passes through town, proceed south uphill to Moyer Road, then west to St. Urban Vineyards. Distance from the light is 3.6 km (2.2 mi.).

TASTER'S CHOICE is the ♥♥ St. Urban's Riesling Late Harvest 1983, a complex, full-bodied and intense johannisberg riesling. This impressive first release from the winery bodes well for planned 1984 vintage releases of bacchus, chardonnay, seyval blanc and vidal, as well as riesling.

THE GERMAN INFLUENCE

In 1970 a German textile salesman named Walter Hainle, who had grown up in the wine region of Württemberg, became gravely ill with an ulcer, and was advised by his doctor to simplify his style of life. He decided to move his family to Canada – a niece in British Columbia had been urging him to do so for some time – and the result has been beneficial for both Hainle and Canadian wine.

By the summer of 1973, he had begun planting a vineyard on the steeply pitched slopes above Peachland, B.C., as the first step in developing a winery to be operated by his young son, Tilman, a 1982 graduate of the enology school at Weinsberg, Germany. By that time, the cellar of the Hainle house, which overlooks the vineyard, contained no fewer than nine vintages of rare eiswein, one from each year but one since 1973. Eiswein (''ice wine,'' made from night-harvested frozen grapes) is a concentrated, sweet tour de force, a vintner's conceit produced in limited quantities in Germany. It is usually reserved for the maker's personal hospitality; if sold at all, it ranks among the most expensive commercial offerings. None had ever been released by a Canadian winery, though the elder Hainle, now bronzed and fit, could easily have been the first to do so. In the 1982 vintage, he made small quantities of eiswein from three different grape varieties: the johannisberg and Okanagan rieslings, and gewurztraminer.

Germans and their cultural cousins, the Austrians, have been having a profound impact on the wines of Canada in recent years, bringing with them skills and instincts accumulated for generations. In British Columbia, grape growers are in the last stages of a lengthy trial with German vinifera obtained from Dr. Helmut Becker, the world-renowned director of grape breeding at Germany's Geisenheim Institute. Becker, an advisor on cold-climate grape growing to New Zealand, the state of Washington and eastern American states as well, has persuaded an increasing number of Okanagan growers that grapes for outstanding wines can be raised successfully in the valley. He has pointed out repeatedly that the 50th parallel, which runs through the wine-growing district near Geisenheim, also runs through the north Okanagan. And his influence has spread indirectly through graduates of his institute now working in Canada. Walter Gehringer, for several years an assistant winemaker at Andrés in Port Moody, B.C., became the first Canadian-born Geisenheim graduate in 1979. His brother, Gordon, completed his five years there in 1983 and turned his attention to the family vineyard at Oliver, the base of a future Gehringer estate winery.

The Gehringer brothers are among a growing number in the Canadian wine industry who have been trained at Geisenheim or one of the other wine schools of Germany and Austria. The list includes consultant Rudi Mueller, formerly at Barnes; Ernst Fischer, general manager of Montravin Cellars and, before that, winemaker for Chateau-Gai; Thomas Hoenisch, now retired but winemaker at Casabello from 1967 to 1978; Helmut Dotti at Mission Hill; Jurgen Helbig and then Andreas Gstaltner at Hillebrand; Franz Helmer at Potter's Beaupré winery; Tilman Hainle, Walter's son, at Uniacke; Walter Strehn, owner of the Pelee Island winery; George Heiss, Jr., whose father established Gray Monk in the Okanagan, and Joseph Zimmerman, the latest in a considerable roster of Geisenheimers who have directed winemaking at Jordan & Ste-Michelle Cellars since 1973. Even those not trained in Germany, such as Inniskillin's Austrian-born Karl Kaiser, a chemist and microbiologist from Brock University in St. Catharines, have brought the traditions and standards of Europe to the art of making wine in Canada.

The vinifera most widely planted in Canada since the late seventies has been johannisberg riesling, the classic German cold-climate grape. Jordan & Ste-Michelle's winemakers, who had a traditional familiarity with the variety, began urging their growers to plant it in the middle of that decade. As a result, the winery now markets johannisberg riesling in significant commercial quantity in both Ontario and British Columbia. The majority of other wineries in these two provinces also offer rieslings in rising quantity as plantings mature. The fact that this riesling has been the most successful grape in the Becker trial plots of the Okanagan only reconfirms the variety's adaptability to Canadian conditions.

The Canadian wine industry has had the benefit, not only of German grapes and German training but of German investment as well. Scholl & Hillebrand, a major wine shipper based in Rüdesheim, acquired a 51 per cent interest in the Niagara's Newark winery in

1982, promptly renaming it Hillebrand Estates and proceeding to expand. The German company has also shown interest in having a British Columbia winery. A second example is a trio of Ontario vineyards, one owned by Dieter Guttler, who manages the others for German investors. The German-born Guttler was the first Geisenheim graduate at Jordan's before leaving to grow grapes and then develop his own winery, Vineland Estate Wines, which opened in 1984. Yet another instance is the shy bachelor farmer Ewald Reif, who has opened the petite Reif Winery Inc. near Niagara-on-the-Lake with the aid of investment capital from the family winery run by his brother in Germany. Taken together, the Guttler, Reif and Hainle stories sum up the differing but equally important impacts German traditions have had on Canadian wine.

Dieter Guttler was born in 1945, the grandson of a German winemaker and son of a manufacturer of winery equipment. After graduating from Geisenheim, he gained practical experience in the industry in South Africa, where his parents had emigrated in 1950, spending most of his time there with Distillers Corporation's Oudemeester winery. Distillers is part of the Rothmans International group that acquired control of Jordan & Ste-Michelle in 1972. When the new owners discovered the technical inadequacies of their wineries, they sent the intense and ambitious young Guttler to take charge at Ste-Michelle, then located in Victoria. He was startled to find it still committed largely to making and selling red wines, either sweet or fortified. The table wines then on the Canadian market from many domestic wineries were distressing: he recalled that the Ontario table wines he first encountered were "absolutely poor," while those of British Columbia were palatable, in his view, because of the presence in their blends of wines from California or Washington vinifera. He quickly tapped these same grape sources to make the first varietal table wines released by Ste-Michelle in its then thirty-year history: a chenin blanc, a ruby cabernet, a cabernet sauvignon and a grenache rosé, a zinfandel being added later on. All these varietals have been dropped from the Ste-Michelle line except for the chenin blanc, a sturdy and popular white.

Guttler was not impressed by the winemaking qualities of the red hybrid grapes and Okanagan riesling grown in British Columbia. "I maintained that the Okanagan was one of the most ideal places in which to grow johannisberg riesling," he said. "I tried to motivate the growers.'' That understatement hardly does justice to the aggressive, heated and sometimes arrogant exchanges that took place between the young Guttler and the older, conservative valley growers. Within a few years, Guttler was seriously planning a vineyard and winery for neighbouring Washington in partnership with Robert Holt, then general manager of Ste-Michelle and now a grower in the Similkameen Valley of southern British Columbia. Guttler had even secured an immigrant visa for the United States when, in 1978, his employer promoted him to the Jordan winery in Ontario. The ambition for independence remained, however, and he left the large winery two years afterwards to run his own vineyard. This, together with the two others managed for German investors, supplies grapes for the Vineland Estates Winery, whose first release predictably was a johannisberg riesling.

Significant amounts of German capital have been invested in Canadian agriculture since the seventies, so much, in fact, that some provinces have legislated restrictions on nonresident ownership of farmland. Vineyard land has not yet been made out of bounds to foreigners, fortunately, and several groups have funded plantings in Ontario. One investor in the Guttler group is Johny M. Vesque, an international salesman for the giant German wine co-operative Zentralkellerei Badischer Winzergenossenschaften (ZBW). Vesque, who invested privately and not on behalf of ZBW, has explained Canada's attraction as its stability and considerable distance from probable zones of war. A leading member of the syndicate participating with Guttler is Hermann Weiss, a German grape nurseryman wanting to sell virus-free vines who concluded that he could best break into the Canadian market with a vineyard investment. A similar strategy motivated the Germans and Austrians behind the Rhine-Danube Nursery at Leamington, Ontario, which was briefly associated with the Pelee Island winery and has a corporate link with Hillebrand Estates.

Vesque, Weiss and their associates realized that agriculture ventures could not be managed successfully from afar. Guttler purchased a forty-acre vineyard near Beamsville, Ontario, and the German syndicates purchased the nearby sites of fifty acres apiece now known as the St. Urban and St. Hilarius vineyards. The Germans transplanted not only names but also grape varieties, putting in primarily johannisberg riesling vines when many other Ontario growers were still playing it safe with the hybrids, seyval blanc and vidal. Guttler and his partners have also planted chardonnay and two German vinifera hybrids, optima and bacchus, and are likely to add gamay or pinot noir. Shrewd and practical, they have put in several white hybrid varieties, grapes which can be sold to the larger wineries or used in generic blends. In this planting program, they have taken a technique from the colder regions of Germany to safeguard their vines: plowing furrows of earth against the lower parts, shielding them against frost. The graft and lower buds are protected: even if the rest of the vine suffers severe damage, it should be able to regenerate from those buds, and, at worst, will miss only one season's production. Guttler feels ''a lot safer doing it that way.''

Guttler's first commercial crop, nearly all of it johannisberg riesling, was vinified in 1982 by Barnes. A delicately floral white, it is believed to have been the first vinifera varietal that winery had sold in its 109-year history. The grapes will not be available to Barnes indefinitely, however, since Guttler opened his own winery in 1984. The Guttler winery will offer not only rieslings but, when vintage conditions are favourable, late-harvest wines and perhaps even eisweins as well, for the eiswein challenge seems to run in the blood of many German-born winemakers.

Ewald Reif's forebears have made wine for generations at Neustadt in the Rheinpfalz, where he was born in 1937. His fascination with Canada began when he was still a teenager reading travel literature. He visited in 1968 and again in 1969, when he explored North America extensively by car and began thinking of returning to be a farmer. Finally, in the spring of 1977, he bought an eighty-three-acre vineyard by the Niagara Parkway first planted only nine years earlier and entirely with labrusca and less desirable hybrid varieties. He later bought a neighbouring forty-seven acres with a similar planting history. Reif's German experience was entirely with vinifera grapes, and, since he could see no reason why the same varieties could not succeed in the Niagara Peninsula, he immediately began a long-term replanting to chardonnay, kerner, gewurztraminer, gamay beaujolais and, of course, riesling. He also concluded an agreement to sell his grapes to nearby Inniskillin, whose winemaker, Karl Kaiser, shared with him the German language and traditions.

He made wines for his own consumption but had no idea of developing a commercial winery until his brother at the home winery encouraged him to do so. This encouragement has been tangible: cash arrived from Germany and essential winemaking equipment as well, including 4500 gallons of wooden cooperage. Reif prefers to have his white wines spend some time maturing in these German oak ovals, though he concedes that most of his cooperage will be stainless steel, which is easier to maintain. The winery is in the barn of a historic stagecoach station on the Reif farm. Its immensely thick stone walls mean that the aging cellars remain cool in summer and relatively even year-round. Reif's wines indicate a preference for making whites where acidity is balanced carefully with some residual sugar – the way most German whites have been made for centuries. He has contended that Niagara-grown johannisberg riesling grapes, if made into bone-dry wine, are not intense enough in flavour. A trace of sweetness, however, brings out the flavours very nicely.

Walter Hainle was born in 1915 in the south German town of Neckarweihingen. His father, a butcher, also operated a guest house, and as a youth, Hainle accompanied him on visits to the area's wine growers to purchase supplies. Their home was even located in an old vineyard, where he learned viticulture the practical way.

Coming to British Columbia, the Hainle family had spent more than a year searching for a vineyard site when they chanced upon one with a commanding view of Okanagan Lake that recalled their native Germany. It had the remains of a homestead, long abandoned, on a knoll with a dramatic, wind-blown southern slope. Hainle first planted Okanagan riesling and maréchal foch because no other varieties were readily available from local nurseries. Subsequent plantings have included johannisberg riesling, gewurztraminer, chasselas, pinot blanc and pinot noir. The foch vines have been replaced, and the Okanagan riesling vines, too, are giving way to other varieties. Not entirely, however: Walter Hainle is one of the few Europeans to admire this grape, which he crops very sparingly at only one and a half tons an acre (about a third of the valley average) to concentrate the flavours.

For nearly a decade, Hainle grew grapes and made wine chiefly as a hobby. There has never been a hobbyist so meticulous, and no more proof of this is needed than his glory, the eisweins. Grapes are deliberately left on the vine well beyond the end of vintage; while the vines have leaves, the fruit continues to build in sugar, but after the leaves have fallen, it begins to shrivel, concentrating the sugars and the flavours. To get the ultimate concentration, however, it is necessary to pick the grapes when they are frozen and press them in the frozen state. The sugary juice, which does not freeze as quickly as the water in the fruit, oozes from the press and is then fermented. The wine is costly, since many grapes are required for even a small quantity. But perhaps the most difficult aspect of eiswein production is the harvest itself. In the vintage of 1982, for example, Hainle and his family picked very early one morning late in November when the temperature had dropped quickly and suddenly to minus 17°Celsius. They worked with tractor headlights illuminating the vines, anxious to get the picking done before the sun rose and the grapes began to thaw. The juice was incredibly rich and sweet. ''I think we made a world record eiswein,'' Hainle has said, for the natural sugar content was about three times the normal sweetness of juice fermented into table wines.

ANDREW WOLF

ESTABLISHED 1976

COOPERAGE 30 000 gallons

TOURS & TASTINGS are not available at the Cochrane, Alberta,winery, but are planned for the proposed Stony Plain winery.

TASTER'S CHOICE is the winery's deep, full-bodied Canadian burgundy. Gramma Mary's Honey Wine, an interesting rosé made with grenache grapes and the lightest touch of honey wine, is sold only at the winery. Best sellers are the riesling and cabernet.

Alberta has four commercial wineries and the irrepressible Andrew Wolf had a hand in founding three of them, the latest being his Andrew Wolf Cellars in Cochrane. By the spring of 1984, Wolf, at age sixty-two, was planning a replacement for the cramped Cochrane winery, a grandly conceived $2-million, 400 000-gallon establishment to be housed at Stony Plain, west of Edmonton, in something that could pass for a French chateau. "It's my last one," Wolf has said. "It's the flagship of my career."

Wolf's life in wine has resulted from marriages which linked his family to that of Andrew Peller, the founder of Andrés. Peller and Wolf's father, also named Andrew, had married sisters in Hungary, and when the elder Wolf decided to immigrate to Canada in 1927, Peller travelled with him on the same ship. The fortunes of the two families remained linked: after the Peller brewery opened at Hamilton, young Andrew Wolf studied to become a brewmaster. Later, when Peller started Andrés in British Columbia, Wolf worked for his uncle again at a variety of tasks ranging from vineyard management to sales. When the Anjo winery, with Peller sponsorship, was started in Calgary in 1964, Wolf was on hand to negotiate the licence with nondrinking Alberta premier E. C. Manning. Wolf has recalled that the premier had the elementary shrewdness to ask where the new winery would get its grapes, since none were grown in Alberta (none are grown there still). Wolf replied, "How does Safeway get its

grapes?'' He knew the answer from his association with the Port
Moody winery, which had had to rely on California grapes initially
because the Okanagan vineyards were committed to other wineries.
Imported grapes have allowed the Alberta wineries to flourish for two
decades.

Shortly after Anjo opened, Wolf and his uncle clashed over policy.

The parting was abrupt, but Wolf did not miss a step: by 1966, he had
found partners and financing in Calgary to establish Chalet Wines as
the first in a planned coast-to-coast chain. Wolf had also planned to
produce low-priced table wines from imported vinifera grapes, but
the action in the Canadian wine industry during the sixties centred
around various pop wines, culminating in Andrés's Baby Duck.
Chalet's version was called Luv-A-Duck.

The grand plan for a national chain ended when Imperial Tobacco,
then collecting wineries, bought 49 per cent of the Calgary company.
Shortly thereafter, the tobacco company decided to get out of the
business, and its holdings in the West, including the Chalet interest,
came under Jordan & Ste-Michelle control in 1975. Wolf sold his
own interest in Chalet and was about to start an independent company
when another group of Calgary investors beat him by founding
Stoneycroft winery. Stoneycroft was soon in difficulty – it was
ultimately absorbed by Chateau-Gai – and Wolf incorporated Andrew Wolf Cellars in 1976. Since he had no winery building, he
installed forty used whisky barrels in his two-car garage in suburban
Calgary, and made wine that fall using imported grapes and a hand-

operated Italian crusher. Later, he hauled the barrels of wine to a modest cinder-block building in the industrial park at the foothills ranching town of Cochrane.

The head start gained in his garage, while not strictly legal, allowed Wolf to release his first four wines to the Alberta liquor board in 1978. All varietals from California grapes, they were zinfandel, cabernet sauvignon, chenin blanc and riesling. Then he hit on the idea of having his imported grapes frozen just after harvest, keeping them in cold storage and fermenting them in his limited facilities throughout the year. This enabled him to buy a greater variety of grapes, make more types of wines and gain the liquor store visibility which comes with a large number of listings. Subsequent Wolf releases, none vintage dated, have included pinot noir, chardonnay, chasselas, french colombard, golden muscat, grenache rosé and a variety of generic blends. And he has only begun to explore the potential of frozen grapes. In the proposed Stony Plain winery, with its larger volume, he would like to have as many as two hundred different wines for sale.

In the main, they will be designed as straightforward drinking wines, what Wolf calls "working man wines." The consumers he is after are just beginning to discover the taste of viniferas but are not yet prepared to pay a great deal for their wines. By not setting his aim immodestly high, Wolf has also conceded some of the limitations of frozen grapes as raw material: the wines in general are softer and not quite as well structured because, in freezing, the grapes lose some of their natural acidity. Wolf has tried to combat this, which can result in bland wines, by buying grapes whose acidity when fresh is higher than other winemakers prefer. He also continues to use fresh grapes, both for blending wines and for making "wine for my ego."

His wines have been sold entirely in Alberta. Like other small wineries, Wolf has sought private-label sales but, being Andrew Wolf, he has done so with a refreshing touch. Two of the winery's employees are skilled in calligraphy and, for a premium of fifty cents, will inscribe a name and brief message on otherwise preprinted labels. These personalized bottles have proved so popular as gifts that, before Christmas, the winery employs a third calligrapher as well. More conventional private-label sales are made as well to restaurants and consumers purchasing large lots.

CHARAL

ESTABLISHED 1975

COOPERAGE 60 000 gallons

TOURS & TASTINGS daily, except Sundays and holidays, at 11 A.M., 2 P.M. and 3 P.M. The shop on Highway 3 just west of Blenheim, Ontario, is open from 10 A.M. to 6 P.M. For group tours and information telephone (519) 676-8008.

TASTER'S CHOICE features the ♥♥baco noir, with a complex aroma that shows some wood and a flavour balancing acidic crispness with the fruit. Also meriting ♥♥ are the winery's full-bodied seyval blanc, its aroma recalling apples, and the 1982 vidal, very German in style. Charal offers a promising ♥ léon millot, a delicate ♥chardonnay and a ♥1982 johannisberg riesling.

ALSO RECOMMENDED are the Chandelle rosé, 1982 siegfried rebe, maréchal foch and Première rouge.

Alan Eastman, a lean, tousle-haired farmer, is jarringly unromantic about wines. A self-taught vintner, he won a gold medal at Pennsylvania's 1977 Wines Unlimited competition with the first commercial wine from his Charal Winery, a 1975 chardonnay. Personally, he is not a fan of chardonnays. Despite that, and despite the fact that the grape is difficult to grow, it remains in his vineyards mainly because wine consumers have accorded it special prestige. "I'm in it for the economics," Eastman snaps. He is the third generation of his family to operate Eastman Fruit Farms on fertile soil which slopes gently towards Lake Erie just west of the town of Blenheim. Because the lake moderates the winters in this sunny, southernmost region of Canada, grape growing flourished here at the turn of the century before being displaced by tobacco and tomatoes, more profitable crops and less subject to disease. By the late sixties, rising production costs were upsetting the economics of some of the Eastmans' crops. Alan, schooled in business administration, took a hard look at alternatives with his father, Ralph. "We were looking to increase the acreage of a fruit crop which could be mechanically harvested and treated in a mechanical means,'' Alan Eastman has said.

They chose grapes. For many years, they had successfully grown peaches, which are even more sensitive to weather. The Eastmans were reasonably certain that they would have little difficulty with hybrid grape varieties. They were reassured by their 1968 test plots –

plantings which marked the revival of viticulture in southwestern Ontario – and within four years, a tenth of the three-hundred-acre farm had been turned over to the new crop. The unusually late frost that snapped across southern Ontario on 10 June 1972 gave the province's grape growers their lowest harvest in a decade. Alan Eastman was lucky: the damage to his young vines was comparatively minor, and he planted a further thirty acres the following year. More plantings in succeeding years have put nearly two hundred acres into vines, making Charal basically self-sufficient. The independent-minded Eastman likes it that way. ''When we grow our own grapes, we don't have to depend on schedules. We don't have to harvest them today even if it is raining. We can wait for tomorrow. *We* decide what we do.''

He has planted more than thirty varieties, chiefly French hybrids: seyval blanc, aurore, dutchess and vidal among the whites, and foch, baco noir, villard noir, de chaunac and léon millot among the reds. The two major vinifera varieties in the Charal vineyards are chardonnay and johannisberg riesling. The chardonnay suffered enough bud damage in the winter of 1980–81 to prevent Charal from offering wine from that vintage, but both varieties produced the following year, as did the German vinifera hybrid, siegfried rebe, which several growers have now planted in Ontario.

Eastman has been less successful with red vinifera grapes. Gamay beaujolais proved to be disease-prone in southwestern Ontario's warmly humid spring climate, and pinot noir suffered winter damage. Mildew could be held at bay with fungicides: it had been a scourge of turn-of-the-century growers in the area, offsetting the advantage that an average one extra growing week gave their grapes over Niagara's. Eastman and other southwestern Ontario growers still have the problem of excessive soil fertility which promotes overly vigorous vine growth. The solution is aggressive pruning to channel the vine's energy into fruit production instead of overabundant leafing.

At first, Eastman sold his grapes to Niagara wineries. He decided to apply for a winery licence when Ontario lifted its fifty-year freeze, calculating that grape growing would be most profitable if he could add more value right on the farm. The Eastmans already were selling their own fruit and other products directly to the public from a large, modern fruit stand beside the highway. That stand was expanded to include a winery store and tasting room.

The Charal winery, its name derived from Eastman's own first name and that of his wife Charlotte, was established in 1975 with a thousand gallons of chardonnay and dutchess which were enough to convince the liquor board of his competence. The licence to sell was finally granted in 1977, but the winery store had to be delayed a year when the Eastmans discovered that their own Harwich Township was one of the few remaining dry areas in Ontario. A local plebiscite was quickly organized and 70 per cent of the voters approved the sale of alcohol.

The Eastmans have invested more than $1 million, installing new and modern winery equipment. The make-do, baling-wire artistry practised by some farmers is not for Alan Eastman. Wherever practical, vineyard and winery operations have been standardized and mechanized. Most wines are bottled in green burgundy bottles. In the fields, Eastman uses a crusher in parallel with a mechanical harvester: the unit deposits the must in the crusher's five-ton tank, metering in the minute quantity of sulphur needed to prevent oxidation. When the tank is full after perhaps half an hour, it is hauled to the nearby winery. Eastman believes that the speed with which the grapes move from vine to winery reduces processing problems and enhances the flavours and the freshness of the wines.

The Charal white wines all are cool-fermented at 55° to 60°

Fahrenheit and matured in stainless steel tanks, for Eastman believes white wines can be ruined by wood-aging. His rieslings and chardonnays are consequently dry and delicate in flavour, with flowery aromas. The winery's 1982 vidal, a first release for Charal, is soft and fleshy with a pronounced fruity aroma. The seyval blanc, perhaps because of the Blenheim soil, is distinctively different from other Ontario seyvals: intensely perfumed and full-bodied and nutty in flavour, recalling chenin blanc.

The fruit wines – Vinacopia white made from apples and pears and Vinacopia red made from strawberries and apples – are other examples of Eastman's passion for vertical integration. Apples, pears and strawberries are all grown on the farm, with the best grades sold directly to consumers and the rest vinified: it is more profitable to sell as wine than at distress prices as low-grade fruit. The same reasoning also led the Eastmans to install a bakery in the fruit store, which already had cheese and meat counters. The winery now supplies everything necessary for wine-country luncheons, including picnic benches on the property.

Alan Eastman's aversion to oak does not extend to red wines. He buys new American oak barrels in which to mature a portion of his red wines, some of which may then be blended with reds matured only in stainless steel. Used barrels later can be sold to home winemakers, who buy ten or fifteen tons of Eastman's grapes each fall.

With increasing winery production, Charal has sought distribution in western Canada as well as in Ontario. There have also been export sales to the United States. The winery has begun opening its own retail stores, the first being in London, two hours down the highway. The choice of London rather than more convenient Windsor was once again commercial: London's quarter-million citizens depend for their prosperity on such solid industries as finance and insurance, not the cyclical car business.

CHATEAU DES CHARMES

ESTABLISHED 1977

COOPERAGE 129 000 gallons

TOURS & TASTINGS are offered year-round, except on Sundays; groups larger than ten should reserve. Tel. (416) 262-4219. Look for the winery at the corner of Creek Road and Line 7, east of the hamlet of St. Davids near Niagara Falls.

TASTER'S CHOICE are the ♥♥♥ 1982 pinot noir, a dark, well-balanced red for laying down, and the ♥♥♥ black-label Estate chardonnay, crisp and dry in the Burgundy style, with complex aroma and flavours from oak maturing. The winery also releases gold- and white-label chardonnays: all are elegant and among the best coming out of Canada. Worthy of special mention are the flowering but crisp ♥♥♥ 1983 black-label johannisberg riesling, and the complex ♥♥ 1981 auxerrois. The gamay nouveau is a good example of the nouveau style. The winery's best-selling Sentinel red and white get one ♥ apiece.

ALSO RECOMMENDED are ♥ aligoté 1981, ♥ Cour blanc, gamay beaujolais of various vintages, Primeur rouge and ♥♥ seyval blanc.

Paul Bosc's first bottle of Canadian wine came as something of a shock. At Christmas 1963, he was a poor, new immigrant working as a cellarman for the Quebec liquor board, and happened to win a bottle of sparkling rosé in the office pool. This good fortune, he decided, would save him the cost of imported champagne for seasonal toasts. The wine's pronounced labrusca flavour so startled Bosc and his guests, however, that the entire bottle went down the sink. Since that Christmas, Bosc has done much to move the Canadian wine industry away from labrusca grapes and towards premium hybrids and vinifera, first during his influential fifteen years making wine for Chateau-Gai and then, since 1978, at his own Niagara winery, Chateau des Charmes.

He was born in 1935 in Algeria, where his family had a vineyard and were independent producers until Algerian winemaking was reorganized under co-operatives. Bosc, a graduate enologist from the University of Dijon in Burgundy, then worked as manager of one of the largest of these co-operatives until the Algerian revolution led to the expulsion of many of the French. He went back to France, but his

sense of being a stranger there prompted him to try Canada, where his technical background quickly got him a job in the cellars of the Quebec liquor board, long a major bottler of imported wines, including Algerian reds. His break came when he happened across a bottle of wine from Chateau-Gai in Ontario which contained commercially unacceptable sediment: "So I called them, thinking they would probably need somebody with some knowledge to prevent that kind of problem. And sure enough, they did. They asked me to come down to Toronto to talk to them and, two days after, I was hired." Thus began his career as Chateau-Gai's chief winemaker and director of research.

At the time, Ontario wines were still made chiefly from the labrusca grapes that had marred Bosc's first Canadian Christmas. The swing to hybrid varieties was just beginning. It could not happen quickly enough for Bosc, who wanted growers to move beyond the hybrids to vinifera right away. The Vineland authorities promptly told him that they never would flourish in Canada: if Niagara's humid summers failed to ruin the grapes with mildew, the cold winters would kill next year's buds.

Bosc's determination was ebbing until he saw the vinifera vineyards of Dr. Konstantin Frank in neighbouring New York State. Born

in the Ukraine in 1899, Frank had emigrated to the United States in
1951, and despite awesome technical qualifications, spent two years
as a vineyard worker before convincing a New York winery to hire
him for the cultivation of vinifera grapes. He started his own winery
in 1965, producing exceptional wines from vinifera grapes and con-
founding the strongly held official skepticism of the viticulturists at

the state's Geneva Experimental Station, even more conservative
then their colleagues at Ontario's Vineland station. Frank had no
trouble convincing Bosc, who came back believing that he was being
misguided by the experts: "They were saying the vines wouldn't
ripen. It wasn't true. We get here just as high a sugar, if not higher,
than they get in Burgundy." He persuaded Chateau-Gai and some of
its growers to begin planting such varieties as pinot noir, cabernet,
merlot and gamay beaujolais, and, by 1972, was impressing wine
writers as well as the trade with experimental lots of vinifera wines.
Leon D. Adams, in the second edition of *The Wines of America,*
described Bosc's 1972 wines as "three of the best Canadian reds I
have thus far tasted."

The commercially significant development at Chateau-Gai during
Bosc's time as winemaker was not the vinifera planting but the
conversion of the winery's raw material base from labrusca to French
hybrids. Of all the labrusca varieties, Bosc considers the niagara the
least palatable. The grape, basically a white version of the concord,
was used in Chateau-Gai champagne. For a year and a half, Bosc
badgered the company to change the blend, and finally, after
threatening to quit, he was allowed to experiment with a new blend,
using vinifera and hybrid grapes. His judgement was confirmed when

the wine was chosen for a social function during a royal visit. Meanwhile, the winery's claret, made from the ill-reputed concord, was selling poorly. In 1974 Bosc changed it to a blend of equal quantities of chelois and de chaunac. The resulting dry red table wine, renamed Seibel after the French hybridizer who developed the varieties, was an immediate success.

In 1974 as well, Chateau-Gai decided to replace its burgundy, selling a modest five thousand cases a year, with a named varietal, maréchal foch. It was the first varietal foch on the market and certainly the first to be advertised on television. The pitchman was the dark-complexioned, mustachioed Bosc himself, "the guy with the French accent and the Italian look." The wine sold several times better than its predecessor until the rest of the industry began releasing foch varietals as well. The commercials had done a better job promoting the grape than promoting the name of the winery. When some other foch releases turned out be be mediocre, everyone shared the poor image and most major wineries, Chateau-Gai included, discontinued it as a varietal. The thrust since then has been to develop and market proprietary wines so that successes do not create bandwagons for the competition.

But Bosc was bent on his vinifera dream. In 1977 he and Niagara Falls lawyer Rodger Gordon bought a sixty-acre farm on Four Mile Creek Road, east of the hamlet of St. Davids in the Niagara Peninsula. Correcting its poor drainage by increasing the number of tiles below the surface, they planted chardonnay, riesling, pinot noir, gamay beaujolais and aligoté. Another hundred acres purchased elsewhere in the Niagara region has since been planted with premium hybrids such as seyval blanc.

Putting the winery's entire home vineyard in vinifera grapes was an acknowledged risk Bosc believed he had to take. His vines came through the severe 1980–81 winter with little damage because earth had been hilled up to cover the grafts. Bosc leaves as many as four trunks growing, not just one, playing the odds that not all four will be damaged equally in a hard winter, and the healthiest survivor will be the base for the following season's growth. His vines are also trained close to the ground, to benefit from the extra heat reflected by the earth and, as an added precaution against frost, are grown at a density of thirteen hundred per acre, nearly double the conventional density in Niagara vineyards. This practice limits the productivity of each

healthy vine to perhaps six or seven pounds of fruit – another risk
Bosc felt he had to take. Many attempts to grow vinifera in Canada
have failed because growers tended to overcrop the vines: the competing hybrid varieties have generally proven capable of producing
two or even three times as much fruit as most vinifera, but overcrop-
ping the vinifera prevents them from maturing their wood early

enough in the fall to be safely dormant when freezing temperatures
take hold.

Bosc, whose nursery now supplies vinifera vines to many other
growers, has also turned Chateau des Charmes into a centre for
serious viticultural research. In 1982, with a $500,000 grant from the
National Research Council, the winery employed the scientist John
Paroschy, with a Geisenheim doctorate on winter injury to vines, to
identify the hardiest and most productive clones, or mutations, of its
vinifera.

Grapes from major clones are vinified separately to evaluate the
performance in the winery as well as in the vineyard. During the 1982
vintage, the winery acquired sixty-six French barrels of Allier oak,
preferred in Burgundy for maturing chardonnays. Special cuvées of
each of the selected clones were fermented and matured in those
barrels to be sold as special bottlings, thus yielding both research
results and a profit. Under a 1983 agreement, Ottawa will fund about
half the $260,000 cost of a trial for concentrating grape must by a
process of reverse osmosis. Bosc's aim is to remove a certain amount
of water from the must in order to intensify character and increase
sugar content. If the process is commercially feasible, it will help
improve the quality of wines in marginal vintages or those vintages

when rain at harvest has diluted the grapes. Such basic research is needed in Canada because French winemaking experience cannot be merely transplanted. "One problem they have in France," Bosc believes, "is that they are so bound to tradition that even if they find a better clone than the one in Meursault, for instance, they wouldn't touch it. We have to make our own tradition."

In its first full commercial year, ending in mid-1980, Chateau des Charmes sold fewer than seven thousand cases of wine. As additional vines have come into production, however, the winery has almost doubled its sales in each succeeding year. Bosc has begun to plan expansion which will take the winery to 100 000 and perhaps even 200 000 cases. Unlike most estate vintners, he has set no limit on maximum size: "You don't have to be small to be good."

Unquestionably, Bosc is good. It is a matter of opinion whether his best wines so far are his rieslings – as Inniskillin's Donald Ziraldo believes – or his chardonnays. Both grapes are processed in a variety of styles and released with different labels, giving consumers a good deal of choice. The white-label wines from Chateau des Charmes are generally those made with French hybrids or grapes purchased from various growers. Gold-label wines are made from grapes grown at Nokara, a gravelly vineyard owned by contract grower Dick Koop. On this soil, the grapes produce somewhat lighter wines than on the heavier clay loams which predominate around the winery itself. Wines from the home vineyard always have a black label and, in Bosc's view, are more full-bodied and aromatic. Other vinifera varietals from these two vineyards underline Paul Bosc's Burgundian preferences in wine. The 1981 vintage included an aligoté, widely grown in Burgundy, and an auxerrois, a grape from Auxerre near Chablis. While auxerrois is also grown in British Columbia, Bosc was the first in Canada to grow aligoté commercially. And the reds from his vineyard and the Nokara estate include Burgundy's two classics, the gamay beaujolais and pinot noir.

In 1982 Chateau des Charmes made a nouveau style from the gamay to compete with the new beaujolais wines. Its release revealed that Bosc has lost none of his television pitchman's instinct for promotion. It is an established French tradition for the winemakers of Beaujolais to release some of the vintage early in November, when the wines are perhaps forty-five days old. Gradually, this has become a madcap fad, with perhaps a third of all beaujolais now being rushed to every corner of the earth to be drunk while it is young and fresh. The technique used to produce drinkable wine within six weeks is called carbonic maceration, and Bosc, with a federally funded research project on this technique behind him, wrung the maximum publicity from his gamay nouveau. He invited volunteer pickers from some of his major customers, chiefly Toronto hotels and restaurants, to harvest and crush the gamay grapes at the winery. When the wine was ready, it was served with considerable fanfare to invited guests at a party in Toronto's posh Plaza II hotel that was timed to coincide with the Canadian arrival of the French beaujolais nouveaux. Another supply was air-freighted to a Paris restaurant for tasting that same day. And even more fanfare surrounded the release of his 1983 nouveau. That fall, Bosc secured the co-operation of Air Canada and the Holiday Inns to have samples shipped for simultaneous, television-linked tastings in eight cities, ranging from Paris to San Francisco.

CLAREMONT

ESTABLISHED 1978

COOPERAGE 65 000 gallons

TOURS & TASTINGS take place Monday through Saturday from 10 A.M. to 4 P.M., with groups by appointment. Tel. (604) 767-2992. From Highway 97 just north of Peachland, turn uphill 2 km (1.3 mi.) on Trepanier Bench Road.

TASTER'S CHOICE is the charmingly dry 1983 pinot gris, combining a delicate bouquet with good body and balance, and the full-bodied sauvignon blanc and gewurztraminer from the same year.

ALSO RECOMMENDED are this winery's Okanagan riesling, blended Vin Blanc, and Rougeon.

There were times when the problems of running a winery nearly broke the determination and the amiability of Robert Claremont. The worst years, he discovered, are the second and third, the years before a winery has found markets for all the wine made since opening. "That seems to be behind us now," he said with relief in 1983 – the fourth year he has run the Claremont estate at Peachland in the Okanagan. The establishment itself is a year older, having started under the ownership of Marion Jonn as the first of the estate wineries now dotting the valley.

Bob Claremont's ambition had once been to become a brewmaster. When he left the University of Guelph with a microbiology degree, however, none of the brewers was hiring. Instead, he became a laboratory technician at Jordan's St. Catharines winery in 1967, moving the next year to become an assistant winemaker for St. Julian, a million-gallon winery in Paw Paw, Michigan. Four years later, when he was ready to move back to Canada, he was recruited by Calona Wines, where he soon found himself senior vintner at a critical time in the Okanagan winery's history.

Calona's new owners asked for the redesign of a product line too heavily committed to fortified fruit wines and sweet wines at a time when consumer tastes were changing. And Claremont set out to meet the new demand for table wines in the European style. His outstanding success was Schloss Laderheim, a blend of Okanagan riesling, verdelet and aurore, later of California varieties as well, marketed in a brown Rhine bottle with a label oozing oom-pah-pah. Although Claremont winced at the presentation, Schloss became the country's largest-selling white wine within five years.

As Schloss Laderheim was taking off in 1977, the British Columbia government altered policy to begin licensing small, or cottage, wineries. Emboldened by his successes at Calona, Claremont decided in early 1979 to go it on his own. He had no financial backing, nor could he find a vineyard for sale with the essential ingredients of good grapes and easy public access for consumers. He was ready to give up when Marion Jonn offered a complete package. Claremont's only regret, as he admitted later, was that it was too big: "There was too much administration involved. I'd have preferred to start from scratch."

The Bulgarian-born Jonn, who claimed a lineage going back to the Roman legionaries, had been a computer analyst in Edmonton until, in 1972, he bought thirty-five acres at an elevation of sixteen hundred feet above Peachland, with a spectacular view of Okanagan Lake and an ideal southern slope, gravel soil giving good drainage, and a cleft in the mountains to the west ensuring a constant circulation of air – a safeguard against frost. By the mid-seventies Jonn had planted about twenty acres in grapes and began selling the fruit. It was so good that skilled amateurs who bought the grapes found themselves making prize-winning wines. Jonn became a keen home vintner himself, and when the government policy changed, he decided to start a small winery of his own. Its grandiloquent title of Chateau Jonn de Trepanier (the vineyard lies at the end of Trepanier Bench Road) typified his exuberant approach to everything.

Eager to be the first of the estate wineries, Jonn took a major gamble by making twelve thousand gallons from the 1977 vintage, five thousand of Okanagan riesling and seven of rougeon and maréchal foch. He had no winery licence, since the province had yet to write the regulations putting its new policy into effect. Indeed, he did not even have a winery: the grapes were crushed and the wine made in the Uncle Ben establishment at nearby Westbank. Meanwhile, with the government promising its regulations by April 1978, Jonn designed his winery to be built that spring. When the regulations had not been issued by mid-June, Jonn, facing a tight construction deadline for that fall's vintage, began building without the licence. Although the licence was later issued, the delays meant that some of the 1978 crop was still handled by Uncle Ben. Lacking a formal background in enology, Jonn may well have welcomed help from professional winemakers.

Jonn's surprising decision to sell out the following summer was never explained, not even to Claremont. "I think he was scared," Claremont believed. "There are a lot of people who love the romance of it, but there's also a hell of a lot of business involved." Backed by three silent partners, he paid slightly over $1 million and took over just two days before the 1979 vintage, to discover gratefully that Jonn had equipped the winery so well that no mechanical problems were encountered. Marion Jonn later moved to Ontario, and, after brief thoughts of developing a vineyard amid the sand dunes of Prince Edward County on the Lake Ontario shore, left the wine business altogether.

Although Jonn had regarded vinifera grapes such as pinot noir and chardonnay as "absolute winners," he committed the vineyard largely to proven if pedestrian varieties: six acres of Okanagan riesling and three acres each of the prolific red French hybrids, rougeon and maréchal foch. The two largest vinifera blocks were two acres each of gewurztraminer and New York muscat, a spicy blending variety. Claremont has since planted johannisberg riesling, and, with "the same red grape surplus as everyone else," will increase plantings of this white variety at the expense of the foch and rougeon. There are much smaller plantings of pinot noir, merlot, semillon and pinot blanc.

The practical Claremont had become used to making virtue of necessity. At St. Julian, he had had to craft a variety of wines chiefly from two labrusca varieties, concord and niagara. At Calona, there had been a conscious corporate decision to produce varietal wines exclusively from grape varieties proven in the Okanagan at a time when the other large British Columbia wineries were releasing such wines as zinfandel and cabernet sauvignon, made entirely from imported grapes. Claremont and Calona both believed that selling wines from grapes not adapted to the Okanagan merely developed the taste for imports. The stand became more apt when he purchased his own winery, for estate wineries are forbidden to import grapes or juice.

Claremont's style leans towards honest, full-flavoured, even rustic wines. His earlier white vintages were made by giving the grapes skin

contact – even two or three days in the case of gewurztraminer – to develop body and character. The reds also received plenty of skin contact and prolonged aging in the recoopered whisky barrels Marion Jonn had installed, an approach that yielded zesty, deep-coloured wines. And with the exception of an off-dry muscat riesling, the wines were usually dry. Gradually, however, Claremont has moved towards lighter reds and whites that are more delicate, less alcoholic, and even a shade off-dry. ''I like Vin Blanc,'' he has said of the winery's best-selling generic blend, ''because I like things bone-dry. But if I made all of my wines bone-dry, I'd go broke.''

The spectre of going broke haunted all the new estate wineries during the period of high interest rates in early 1982. Financial pressure eased in 1983 as interest rates dropped, and Claremont signed a distribution agreement with a new agent, Estate Wines of Kelowna, run by two former marketing colleagues from Calona. Earlier, Claremont and his wife, Lee, had tried to handle their own marketing, summed up in the boast that the annual advertising budget was only sixty dollars. Experiments with agency selling had been unhappy: one agent placed a shipment of Claremont wine in Seattle and another in Nova Scotia, but with no follow-up for repeat orders.

Estate Wines, which also represents Uniacke and Gray Monk, has a more practical strategy. Much of the wine is sold directly to British Columbia restaurants under special labels incorporating the establishments' names. Keg Restaurants take a private blend that Claremont makes exclusively for them. But some of Claremont's most sought-after wines, sold out quickly at the winery's tasting room, are

the limited editions that have included gewurztraminer, pinot blanc, pinot gris and sauvignon blanc, the latter a personal favourite of the maker. These wines are further distinguished by singularly attractive labels, conceived by Lee Claremont, which feature reproductions of watercolours by Les Weisbrich, a New Denver, B.C., artist. The artist's paintings have themselves been displayed and sold through the winery's retail store. The winery has also hosted local craft fairs as part of the Claremonts' commitment to art. There is, after all, much art in winemaking.

COLIO

ESTABLISHED 1981

COOPERAGE 200 000 gallons

TOURS & TASTINGS are by arrangement only. Tel. (519) 738-2241. In Harrow (Highway 18 south of Windsor), look for the sign on Queen Street.

TASTER'S CHOICE includes the "riservas," the ▼▼▼ Rosso and ▼▼ Bianco, both rich, ripe wines, the red dark and full-bodied, containing foch, chelois and cabernet sauvignon — winemaker Negri's favourite. The winery also produces a ▼▼ 1982 johannisberg riesling, delicate with a refreshing tartness, and a fruity ▼▼ 1983 riesling. Two well-crafted labruscas are the ▼ Fragolino and ▼ Perla.

ALSO RECOMMENDED are the best sellers ▼ Colio Bianco secco and the corresponding Rosso, the Rosata and a remarkable ▼▼ Seyval blanc.

The idea for Colio Wines was born in Italy during a 1977 ceremony twinning the cities of Windsor and Udine. Mentioning the revival of grape growing in Essex County, Ontario, Windsor's hinterland, one of the Canadian contingent made the casual suggestion that some of Udine's winegrowers consider an investment there. The result was a joint venture between the Italian wine group Il Castello and a group of Toronto businessmen of Italian descent headed by Enzo DeLuca, whose Siena Foods is a large Ontario distributor.

The winery that emerged is thoroughly Italian in style. Its vintner, Carlo Negri, arrived in time to handle the first crush in 1980. His experience includes fifteen years with Collavini, an important export-oriented winery based in the northeast Italian Friuli region, of which Udine is the capital. In a modest building screened by houses in the little agricultural town of Harrow, Negri uses gleaming, modern equipment, described by an envious colleague as "a winemaker's dream," to craft vintages that are strongly reminiscent of these origins.

Colio was built with an initial 200 000 gallons of cooperage, a volume most other small wineries regard as their ultimate size. And Negri's wines are priced aggressively in a range that takes on the other mass producers, not the cottage wineries. Yet the company's start in the Ontario market was comparatively slow. One former general manager, Charles Cologne, has suggested that Colio suffered

from an initial sales contract with distillery representatives, ''natural enemies'' of wine. However, aggressive selling allowed Colio to expand into western Canada and the United States.

There has been some controversy over whether the Colio name and labels qualify as Canadian. Through their ambassador to Canada, Italian authorities have lodged complaints and even lawsuits about various designations in the Canadian wine industry, and the Harrow winery has come in for special criticism since the Friuli region contains, just by the border of Yugoslavia, a wine-growing district of some reputation called Collio. The Canadian variant was indeed transplanted, as a matter of shareholder sentiment, though cautious legal advice led to an ''l'' being dropped. And to further compound any potential for confusion among consumers, Bright's has released a wine named Collina in a bottle similar to the ones used for many Italian imports and some Colio wines, including the best-selling Colio Bianco.

Negri has now proved through several vintages that he is every inch a craftsman. Initial offerings were all generics, since Colio, like some other wineries, preferred to develop consumer acceptance for brands, rather than varietals. The winery's Colio Riserva Bianco, a dry white with a ripe, fruity bouquet, is made primarily with seyval blanc grapes. The Riserva Rosso, a personal favourite with Negri, is chiefly maréchal foch. The nonreserve Colio Bianco brand is produced both semi-dry, with a slight sweetness recalling German-style whites, and

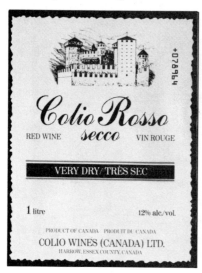
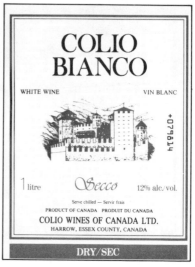

dry (labelled ''secco''), with a remarkably nutty or earthy finish reminiscent of some of the whites of Friuli.

In his first vintage, Negri also experimented with two of Ontario's classic labrusca grapes, the concord and the niagara. From the concord, he vinted a crackling red that the winery calls Fragolino. It delivers all the grape's intense aromas and fruit flavours and relies on a sweet finish to balance the foxy character. From the niagara, Negri fashioned Colio's Perla, not quite as sweet as the red, but full-bodied and very fruity. Both are remarkable achievements from a winemaker new to the varieties, and they appeal to Canadian palates of the old school.

The 1982 vintage provided Negri with the grapes for Colio's first varietals – a foch, a crisply dry seyval blanc and an elegant johannisberg riesling, the latter good enough for a silver medal at a major American competition. His 1983 varietals were even more promising. All are from young vineyards in Essex County, a thoroughly non-Italian designation which is prominently displayed on the labels.

DIVINO

ESTABLISHED 1983

COOPERAGE 22 000 gallons

TOURS & TASTINGS are now limited to the wine shop, open Tuesday through Saturday during business hours. Tel. (604) 498-2784. Three km (1.8 mi.) south of Oliver, B.C., on Highway 97, turn west onto No. 8 Road and follow it uphill to the end, taking the left fork.

TASTER'S CHOICE is the cabernet nouveau, a fresh rosé-style wine and a ♥ pinot bianco, a crisply dry white. Bacaro, a sturdy red for everyday use, is the winery's best seller.

Joseph Busnardo was raised on a farm north of Venice where his father, Luigi, grew a little bit of everything, including silkworms. The young Busnardo, who studied at the agricultural school in Cone-gliano, noted for its viticultural training, "never liked any plant but grapes." His rustic Divino winery now overlooks fifty acres of vines producing perhaps a hundred varieties of grapes, most of them vinifera, some unique to Divino in Canada. So stubbornly proud of his vines is Busnardo that he refuses to sell any grapes to the commercial wineries that once discouraged him from planting vinifera at all.

A compact man bursting with energy, Busnardo came to Canada in 1954 as a twenty-year-old bachelor and drifted west through a variety of jobs until he ended up as a construction worker in Vancouver. In 1967, however, he found a seventy-acre peach orchard on an east slope south of Oliver, protected from both the desiccating winter winds and the excessive afternoon sunlight of the south Okanagan's fiercely hot summers. He reasoned that if peaches grew there, so would his beloved vinifera. His intuition was also resonant with memories of vineyards in the mountains of northern Italy, where winters can be as cold as the Okanagan's.

Planting vinifera in 1967 meant going against all the best advice then available from the provincial government and the commercial wineries. With great difficulty, Busnardo wrung government approval to import twenty-six varieties of grapes from Italy – all of them had to be quarantined for a year on Vancouver Island before being released – and another fifty-six from the University of California at Davis, certified free of viruses and so not liable to quarantine. With these varieties on order or in the soil, Busnardo began canvassing wineries for contracts for his grapes. Greeted with skepticism and, at times, derision, he was advised to put half of his vineyard in the bath grape, a red labrusca that is completely out of favour today, and the other half in French hybrids. And he was not even offered a premium price for his vinifera, which typically produce only a quarter to half as much fruit per acre as the prolific but lower-quality hybrids. His battles for grape contracts discouraged him and so sapped his financial resources that in 1977 he gave up farming and went to work for the city of Penticton as a heavy-duty mechanic: "I closed the farm down, I didn't even prune the grapes."

What brought him back to his vines was the winter of 1978–79, remembered in the Okanagan as the worst of the decade, with frost and winds hitting before snow had fallen to protect the vines. The winter kill was extensive, especially among the French hybrid vines on the large acreages between Oliver and Osoyoos. Expecting the worst for his vineyard as well, Busnardo found that many of his vinifera had survived: he also found new heart to return to commercial grape growing that spring, convinced that the winter had supported his confidence in at least some of the classic European varieties. "Anything to do with pinot," he has advised. "To be on the safe side of the game, the pinot side is a possibility." Accordingly, pinot blanc is the single largest planting in his vineyards. Another eight or nine acres are planted to the Italian variety garganega, which is the principal grape in Soave, the best-known white wine of the Veneto area anchored on Venice. This grape also makes up about a quarter of the blend in Bacaro, and Busnardo believes it gives that red its lightness. The various hybrid varieties planted in the early years have disappeared almost entirely through either disease or neglect. Busnardo has only three vines left of Okanagan riesling, a grape he thinks is a hybrid from a seed – yet one more theory for the genealogy of the most widely planted white in the Okanagan. The rieslings in the Busnardo vineyard are either of the johannisberg riesling variety or the unrelated riesling Italico, both far better winemaking grapes.

Once he had gone back to serious grape growing, Busnardo decided to get a winery licence. Being Joe Busnardo, however, he wanted it issued to his requirements, not those of the bureaucracy. In the Italy where he grew up, people haul their demijohns to the local winery to fill up with everyday wines, a practice that does not inhibit wineries from selling their finer offerings by the bottle. Busnardo proposed that Divino work on the same principle, selling about two thirds of its wine in bulk, chiefly to the Italian community in Van-

couver. He could not understand why there should be any objection to this: he would not be competing with the restaurant wine trade or the commercial wineries, since his demijohn wine would go typically to people who had been buying fresh grapes to make their own. The bureaucrats reacted with horror, especially when they suspected that Busnardo was stubborn enough to bootleg if he did not get a licence. So he was licensed on the same restrictive terms that apply to other cottage wineries.

The winery is a haphazard affair, with evidence on every side that Busnardo has had to be very careful with his money. When he was unable to get sufficient stainless steel tanks to handle the 1982 vintage, he built the necessary forms and poured a dozen thousand-gallon tanks of glass fibre. Nor is Busnardo a professional winemaker: "I'm making a wine the primitive way, the way my father made wine. I just throw in the grapes and hope for the best." His commercial debut was marked by trial and error. A five-thousand-bottle shipment of pinot blanc had to be recalled for refiltering when the harmless but unsightly residue of a fining agent began settling out in each bottle.

Divino's first offerings included the Bacaro and pinot blanc, followed by a blended nonvintage cabernet and a rosé called Clavel – the Spanish word for pink carnation – made by blending pinot gris and traminer. A chardonnay has also been released. They are made by an admirably and courageously determined man: "I care about the grape, I was stubborn enough to prove that the vinifera grapes will grow. I never bow to anybody."

GRAND PRE

ESTABLISHED 1977

COOPERAGE 20 000 gallons

TOURS & TASTINGS are by arrangement. Tel. (902) 542-7511. Take Exit 10 off Nova Scotia Highway 101 for the village of Grand Pré, continue west and watch for the winery on a hill.

TASTER'S CHOICE includes the ♈♈♈ L'Acadie Blanc produced from a Vineland hybrid Ontario has lost interest in — dry and tart with hints of complexity and a good wine for food. The winery's use of Russian varieties has also been notable: Cuvée d'Amour and severnyi both get ♈♈♈ .

It is a mark of Roger Dial's persuasive enthusiasm that more than three dozen farmers in Nova Scotia's Annapolis Valley have contracted to grow grapes for his Grand Pré Winery. With people still telling him that wine grapes simply will not grow in the district, the windows of his study look out on a ten-acre hilltop vineyard, some of which has been producing since the early seventies. Dial believes Nova Scotia has the potential for two to three thousand acres of vineyard to produce for a growing regional wine market. "I don't know what the climate constraints are," he has said. "The major constraint is lack of confidence." His own confidence has been contagious. The Winegrowers Association of Nova Scotia formed in

1982 included, besides Dial, two German-born growers, Hans Jost
and Walter Wuhrer, who plan estate wineries of their own.

Grape growing in Nova Scotia has a long but modest history. The
Agriculture Canada research station at Kentville has been experi-
menting since 1913 with such limited success that a departmental
publication observed caustically in 1971 that nothing had been

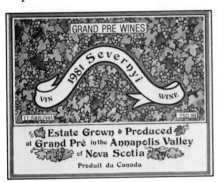

achieved but the identification of a few table varieties. The station
learned that the concord seldom matures in that short, cool growing
season, and another labrusca variety, van buren, which can be harvested in the Niagara Peninsula by late August, is barely mature by
October in Nova Scotia. Curiously, Dial has three rows of the latter
variety in a different microclimate and does manage to mature them.

The Dalhousie University economist Norman Morse planted some
table varieties in 1970 at Grand Pré, a crossroads hamlet better known
in Canadian history as the home of Acadians whom the British
expelled in the eighteenth century. Morse's planting also included
several wine grapes, and Dial, who had been teaching political
science at Dalhousie since 1969, began buying them to vinify at
home. Born in California in 1942, Dial had absorbed the basics of
enology while working his way through university in California, first
as a wine salesman and then as a partner in the Davis Bynum winery
in Berkley, which has a reputation for sound, if rustic, wines. He had
no intention of pursuing it as a career when he brought his doctorate in
Chinese politics to the Halifax faculty. After making wine with the
Grand Pré grapes, however, he prevailed on Morse to replant with
wine grapes and then formed the syndicate which now owns the
vineyard and the winery – at ten thousand cases a year, one of
Canada's smallest.

Advised that vinifera would not grow, Morse and Dial planted three acres in 1978 to a mixture that included two hardy amurensis varieties from Russia, so named because they are native to the far-eastern Amur River valley. Originally among a number of Russian varieties brought to British Columbia in the early seventies by plant breeders at the Summerland research station, these two were not planted on a commercial scale in either British Columbia or Ontario, but some cuttings were sent to Kentville, and they have grown so well for Dial that at least one Okanagan grower took cuttings in 1983 for commercial trial in the West. In 1979 Dial decided to challenge the sketchy Kentville trials by planting vinifera varieties as well, including chardonnay and gewurztraminer. He was risking his neck: "What I knew about grape growing when I left California was where you take the truck to pick them up."

The climate records he studied suggested that two bad growing years could be expected in each decade. As it happened, the first one came in 1980, when the vineyard was moving to commercial-scale production, and the weather was so bad that even Dial was shaken: "1980 was the worst year in more than a hundred and twenty years of climate reporting in Nova Scotia. This one was way off the graph." He was able to salvage the vintage only because warm weather at the close of the season matured grapes to the point where he could finish nature's work by chaptalizing, adding sugar, to the crush at fermentation. The high levels of fruit acids, characteristic of less than fully mature grapes, were reduced naturally through malolactic fermentation, in which the tart malic acid in the wines is converted to mellower lactic acid. Because of that unusually cool summer, Grand Pré's bottling of the 1980 foch was low in alcohol at 9.5 per cent, and lacked the depth of subsequent vintages. It was still well enough crafted, however, to give the winery its instant high reputation among the region's wine drinkers. And Dial relaxed, certain that if he could make adequate wines in such a difficult vintage, he would be able to handle future surprises from Nova Scotia's climate.

The high acidity of 1980 is also typical of some grape varieties, including the red French hybrids and the amurensis. While it presents a challenge to the winemaker, Dial insists that it is an advantage in his style of winemaking: he prefers to give most of his wines prolonged barrel-aging and recognizes that acidity lends them a natural stability that preserves their soundness. Dial is aiming for wines that will require long-term bottle-aging, an approach recalling the mammoth reds made in California in the decade after he left to teach in Nova Scotia.

Vintages since 1980 have been better, encouraging Dial and his partners to plant a second vineyard, this one twenty-two acres, at Lakeville, about fifteen miles from Grand Pré, with varieties that include two large blocks of the German vinifera hybrids, kerner and bacchus. In addition, the growers put under contract in 1983 planted thirty thousand vinifera and hybrid vines. Grand Pré's ambitious plan is to contract for 250 acres of Nova Scotia– grown grapes, the best 20 per cent to be vinified by Dial and the remainder sold to other vintners.

The Dial home at Grand Pré is a restored 1819 Georgian house. In the adjacent low-budget winery, Dial works with a simple basket press rather than a high-volume but expensive screw press. For fermentation tanks, he has purchased inexpensive unused versions of the square, glass fibre tanks in which Maritime fishermen store the catch before processing. As well, the bottling line is almost a hand operation. The money has been spent where it really counts – on French, American and Yugoslavian oak barrels.

The Grand Pré wines are truly originals among Canadian wines, given the unique varieties in its vineyards and Dial's own winemaking style. He first made a trial lot of the white that is now called L'Acadie Blanc in 1976 from V. 53261, a hybrid developed at Vineland in a 1953 cross, some cuttings of which were planted at Kentville in 1972 and at the Grand Pré winery about the same time. Although Vineland later discontinued Ontario trials of the variety, Dial, with two and a half acres planted, has produced a remarkable wine. By leaving the juice in contact with the crushed grape skins for as much as thirty-six hours, he has extracted layers of rich flavours for a golden-hued result that recalls a California sauvignon blanc. Dial has found that earlier vintages, with aging, develop a burgundian complexity. The 1982 vintage has become a relative rarity, since much of it was purchased for a 1983 banquet for Prince Charles and Lady Diana. Dial's success has rekindled Vineland's interest in the grape.

Equally remarkable are the results achieved with the winter-hardy, early-maturing Russian varieties. Grand Pré has now planted five and a half acres of miczurinoweic, more commonly rendered as michur-

nitz and, on the winery's baroque labels, Cuvée d'Amour. The red has
been made in commercial lots since 1980. His second amurensis
variety, with a mere half-acre planted, is severnyi, which produces a
dark, inky wine with a dramatic bouquet and spicy flavours; a
port-style wine has also been produced from the 1982 and 1983
vintages of these black-skinned grapes. A third variety still under test
is dalniewostoznd ramming – abbreviated, for obvious reasons, as
dalnie – of which Dial is establishing a one-acre planting.

   Even if his wines were not so interesting and well-crafted, Dial's
success in opening up a third Canadian grape-growing area would
make him a figure of some importance. He has convinced many
people that the wine grape has a future in Nova Scotia, among them
his son Adam, who plans to study enology at the University of
California at Davis. Sadly, still among the unconvinced is Nova
Scotia's liquor board, which failed, in a 1983 revision of liquor laws,
to permit cottage wineries to sell directly to consumers from the
winery.

GRAY MONK

ESTABLISHED 1982

COOPERAGE 30 000 gallons

TOURS & TASTINGS take place anywhere between 10 A.M. and 5 P.M.
Monday through Saturday, when the winery retail
store is open. Winter hours may be shorter. Groups
are advised to make appointments. Tel. (604)
766-3168. Take Okanagan Centre Road off Highway 97 just south of Winfield, then Camp Road.
The particularly attractive site overlooks the lake.

TASTER'S CHOICE features the ♟♟♟ pinot auxerrois and the ♟♟♟ pinot
gris, both best sellers: the greenish-gold auxerrois,
its bouquet recalling apples, is dry without being
austere, and the pinot gris — source of the Gray
Monk name — is soft and full-bodied. Outstanding

as well are the ❦❦ gewurztraminer and ❦❦ kerner, the latter combining dryness with a full-bodied, suave texture.

ALSO is bacchus.
RECOMMENDED

George and Trudy Heiss in 1975 were the first grape growers in the Okanagan to apply for an estate winery licence. By the time they opened their picture-postcard white-stucco winery establishment in 1982, however, five other estate wineries had opened, and one had already failed. The Heisses were late because they had changed their winemaking plans dramatically to replace their hybrid grapes with classical vinifera varieties. The result has been wines of such quality and unusual interest that Gray Monk has drawn praise even from the prestigious Guntrum winery in Germany, where son George Heiss, Jr., did a practical apprenticeship during his enology studies at Weinsberg. The Guntrums became such close friends, in fact, that they sent across the bottling line in a container along with Guntrum wines for sale in British Columbia liquor stores.

George Heiss, born in Austria in 1940, met Trudy, born in Germany in 1941, in Edmonton, where they were both hairdressers. Tiring of operating a hair salon, and, encouraged by Trudy's father, Hugo Peter, who had been growing wine grapes near Winfield, they decided to become farmers in the Okanagan. They bought a small orchard on a steeply pitched, westward slope which catches not only the long afternoon sun but the reflected heat from the lake's surface as well. Although it is at the north end of the Okanagan, its slope and proximity to the lake give it much the same heat units found a hundred miles farther south at Oliver.

Along with other new growers at the time, the Heisses planted hybrid varieties – foch and Seibel 1000, also called rosette and sometimes used for rosé wines. "We didn't know any better," Trudy has said. "There weren't really many varieties available and there was no guidance from the big wineries." Nor was there much guidance from the government agricultural authorities, aside from the advice to play it safe with cold-hardy hybrids already proven in Ontario. Information in German grape-growing periodicals to which Hugo Peter subscribed, however, convinced them to convert to vinifera. In the spring of 1976, after three years of badgering the federal government for the needed import licence, they got two thousand vines of auxerrois, fifty of pinot gris and a mere ten of gewurztraminer from France. These varieties set the future course of the vineyard and the winery. Later, Heiss imported other varieties, including kerner, bacchus and limburger, from Germany. Some of

the varieties in the vineyard have been propagated from tissue cultures taken at the experimental station in Saanich, a technique Heiss has found to yield occasional curious results with some German vinifera crosses. Kerner, for example, is a cross of johannisberg riesling and trollinger, the latter a spicy red grape: some of Heiss's tissue-culture kerners reverted to their genetic parents, with the result that he now has some random riesling vines and one random trollinger. Care is taken to propagate new vines only from the original, or "mother," plants rather than from second- and third-generation vines, to avoid chance mutations in the vineyard.

Heiss is a meticulous and cautious grower, grafting all his vinifera plants onto disease-resistant rootstock, an exacting and time-consuming exercise. He has used primarily SO4 (Selection Oppenheim number four), a root that resists such major vineyard afflictions as phylloxera and nematode and also enables vines to mature their fruit as much as ten days earlier. Such artful management attracted the admiration of Dr. Helmut Becker, head of the Geisenheim school, when he first toured the Okanagan in the mid-seventies. Also struck by the Rhineland-like microclimate of the Heiss vineyard, Becker offered to send for testing a selection of varieties nurtured at the world-renowned Geisenheim research plots. Heiss, who became chairman of the viticultural research committee of the grape growers' association, recognized this offer as a major opportunity, and the association raised funds from federal and provincial governments for a long-term trial of the Becker plants.

The two and a half acres of auxerrois began producing in 1978, before Heiss was ready to build his own winery, and that year and the two following he sold the grapes to Ste-Michelle, where the vintners produced a delicate, youthful white. Vintages produced since by Gray Monk show increasing depth of character as the vines mature. The vineyard also includes five acres of pinot gris, a white variety sometimes known also as Gray Monk, the source of the winery's name; the first vintage was released from the 1980 harvest.

George and Trudy Heiss believed their own winery could succeed only by converting from the hybrids generally available to major wineries to small acreages of distinctive varieties. An estate winery, with its higher costs, could not compete with the large commercial wineries if it produced similar wines. Trudy Heiss comments: "We just can't sell a bottle of wine for $3.50. We have $2.50 worth of grapes alone in a bottle of our wine." They believed that they must plant distinctive grape varieties and make wines which "would give the imports a run for their money." In doing so, they took a serious commercial risk with expensive varieties, unproven locally, that do not bear as prolifically as the hybrids.

Recognizing that their careful research into viticulture had not necessarily equipped them to be winemakers, the Heisses turned to two of the better professionals in the Okanagan, John Bremmer and Lynn Stark of Bright's, formerly both of Andrés. Until the $400,000 Gray Monk winery was completed in the summer of 1982, wines were also cellared and bottled at Bright's Oliver winery. Co-operation flowed in the other direction as well: George Heiss served as consulting viticulturist to the Bright winery when it was being established, and he has sold it some of his hybrids. The 1981 Gray Monk vintage totalled a mere 5200 gallons, and the 1982 vintage about 7500. Some varieties have been made in extremely limited quantities – only three hundred bottles of 1982 gewurztraminer, for example. The winery also produced very little bacchus, a white dessert wine, and rotberger, an interesting dry rosé. As the Heiss vineyard matures, production will rise slowly towards the thirty-thousand gallon limit imposed on estate wineries.

HILLEBRAND

ESTABLISHED 1979

COOPERAGE 100 000 gallons

TOURS & TASTINGS are available at the winery during business hours; groups by appointment. Tel. (416) 468-7123. Watch for the white, colonial-style building on Ontario Highway 55 just west of Virgil, near Niagara-on-the-Lake.

TASTER'S CHOICE are the novel ♙♙1983 Eiswein, the ♙♙ spicy, peppery gewurztraminer 1983, the ♙♙ gewurztraminer 1982, pale, gold, dry, and also spicy, and the best-selling ♙♙ Schloss Hillebrand in the German style, its charm coming from the morio-muskat grape in the blend.

ALSO RECOMMENDED are the Etienne Brûlé red and white blends, the chardonnay, Chevalier Rouge 1981 and the ♙ 1983 seyval blanc.

Joseph Pohorly, aged forty-seven in 1979, was the oldest Canadian to start a new winery since Andrew Peller did so in 1961 at age fifty-eight. It took Pohorly less than three years to realize that the debt incurred just might outlive him. The discovery coincided with the decision by a major German wine firm to invest in Canada. In 1983 Pohorly's Newark Wines became Hillebrand Estates Winery, controlled by the German investors but managed by the founder, who, relieved of debt, now has a fine technical staff behind him and the time to devote his amiable personality to selling wine.

Winemaking began as a hobby with Pohorly. Born in Vineland, Ontario, he pursued twin careers as a civil engineer and teacher, painting professional-quality landscapes to relax. In 1968 he bought a ten-acre peach orchard near the hamlet of Virgil, southwest of Niagara-on-the-Lake, and began replacing the trees with vines. Three years later, he bought a twenty-five-acre farm nearby and planted vines there as well. The hobby evolved into a business until, in 1979, he and his family risked $150,000 in life savings and a $500,000 bank loan to equip a winery.

Pohorly indulged a taste for romance and history in choosing the title: Newark was the original name for Niagara-on-the-Lake. One of his first generic reds, a blend of foch and le commandant, was grandly named Wellington. He called his de chaunac rosé after his wife, Elizabeth, and a slightly sweet white generic blend was known as Lady Anne after the second name shared by his wife and three

daughters. Yet other labels had a ring of nobility, among them Chevalier Rouge – 95 per cent foch, but sold as a proprietary blend since foch is hard to sell as a varietal – and the dry white blend Comtesse Blanche.

In the first commercial vintage of 1979, Pohorly produced only 5000 gallons of wine. This grew rapidly to 45 000 by the 1982 vintage, and the current target is about 200 000. The investors in 1982 who enabled this expansion are the prestigious Scholl & Hillebrand firm of Rüdesheim, Germany, controlled by the Unterberg family whose bitters is a popular tonic in that country. The company already held a controlling interest in the Toronto wine-import agency of Peter Mielzynski and was making an investment in the Rhine-Danube Nursery of Leamington, Ontario. It offered $2 million for 49 per cent of the winery, a figure Pohorly's competitors regarded as generous. A modest added investment made through Mielzynski Agencies effectively gives the Germans 51 per cent, with Pohorly and his family owning the remainder.

The impact has been far more profound than a mere name change. Pohorly, recognizing his technical limitations, previously had relied on Vineland's Horticultural Products Laboratory for analyzing his wines. Jurgen Helbig, a Geisenheim-trained winemaker from the Rheinpfalz, came over as enologist for the 1983 vintage and plugged this technical gap. Under Helbig's direction, the winery's generics have been reworked and a new product, Schloss Hillebrand, created for successful entry into the market for German-style white wines.

When he returned to Germany, he was replaced by Austrian-trained Andreas Gstaltner, who has confirmed the winery's new direction. The Wellington and Chevalier Rouge brands have been sidelined for a new blend, Baron Rouge, and its sibling, Baron Blanc. Two well-crafted new blends were released for the Ontario bicentennial under the historic name of the explorer Etienne Brûlé.

Three of the original Newark white vinifera wines – chardonnay, riesling and gewurztraminer – remain in the winery's product range, though the style has changed somewhat under the new winemakers. The flinty rieslings have become a bit fatter, while the gewurztraminer, perhaps Pohorly's best varietal, emphasizes its fruit and spice more than ever. The chardonnays, which Pohorly made without oak-maturing to emphasize the grape's delicate fruit, are destined for some oak treatment and should emerge with greater complexity. The winery's varietal seyval blanc has become more delicate and less controversial. Pohorly, whose tastes lean towards big wines, had crafted this French hybrid variety for dramatic fruitiness in both aroma and flavour. The result was a wine so distinctive that in one tasting, three tasters ranked it first among eight seyvals and five ranked it last.

Pohorly's penchant for fruity wines also led to the purchase of a large quantity of dutchess grapes, a North American hybrid rarely produced as a varietal. After tasting tank samples, however, Scholl & Hillebrand's technicians were less enthusiastic about the grape and have begun advising growers to switch to other white varieties, in particular such German whites as scheurebe, huxelrebe, kerner and ortega. The winery itself has planted experimental plots of kerner, bacchus, riesling, chardonnay, cabernet sauvignon and German clones of pinot blanc, pinot gris and pinot noir. Since many of these varieties are untried, the winery continues to work with experimental hybrids developed at Vineland which, Pohorly maintains, have been overlooked. Among them is the hardy white V64032 which he has taken to calling veebradt for his friend Ollie A. Bradt, Vineland's long-time grape breeder. A prolific variety with a thick, mildew-resistant skin, it is capable of producing a neutral white wine useful for blending.

One of Pohorly's personal challenges was making a quality cream sherry from that venerable but sometimes maligned North American grape, the agawam. The four hundred gallons he produced in 1982, in both the cream style and a medium-dry style, were available only in the winery's retail store. They were well enough accepted to remain in the Hillebrand line, fuelling its bid to market a full range of wines nationally. Hillebrand Estates can be expected to produce a champagne-style wine as well, since the parent company is associated with sparkling wine production. And in 1983 Hillebrand made from super-ripe vidal grapes a small but richly fruity quantity of the first commercially successful eiswein produced in Canada.

INNISKILLIN

ESTABLISHED 1974

COOPERAGE 200 000 gallons

TOURS & TASTINGS are held by arrangement. Tel. (416) 468-2187. Tastings only are available at the winery store west of Niagara-on-the-Lake. Exit from the Niagara Parkway at Service Road 66, and enter the winery from Line 3.

TASTER'S CHOICE features the ♀♀♀ chardonnay 1983 Seeger Vineyard, continuing a new style with more emphasis on oak-aging, and the champagne-style ♀♀♀ chardonnay blanc de blancs 1978, a memorable, yeasty sparkling wine. Excellent varietals include the ♀♀ maréchal foch, the best made in Canada, the fruity ♀♀ baco noir 1983, the full-bodied ♀♀♀ gewurztraminer 1983, the luscious ♀♀♀ riesling late harvest 1983, and the ♀ millot-chambourcin and ♀ chelois.

ALSO RECOMMENDED are the Brae blends, red and white, the Braeburn white, the gamay, the other rieslings, the vidals and the seyval blanc.

The almost instantaneous success of Inniskillin marks the major turning point in the modern story of Canadian wine. It was the first of the cottage wineries, effectively setting a new standard for the entire industry. The two-dollar winery licence issued to Donald Ziraldo in April 1974 was the first such licence awarded in Ontario since 1929, a breakthrough followed by market success that has encouraged more than a dozen other cottage, or estate, wineries to spring into being. Maj.-Gen. George Kitching, who was head of the Liquor Control Board of Ontario at the time and personally encouraged Ziraldo's application, has recalled that "nobody was praising Ontario wines." His memory was substantially accurate. Karl Kaiser, Inniskillin's Austrian-born winemaker, remembers that the first glass of Canadian wine he found acceptable was a white verdelet made at home by Irma Ziraldo, Donald's mother.

To the Ziraldo family, of northern Italian stock, wine and winemaking come as a natural heritage. Donald's father, after working in the Timmins gold mines, was a fruit farmer near St. Catharines when Donald and his younger brother, Robert, studied agriculture at the University of Guelph. The farm and nursery they then took over had been established in 1971, on a historic plot by the Niagara

Parkway, land originally granted to a British officer of the Royal Inniskillin Fusiliers that fought in the War of 1812, who named his farm for the regiment. Donald Ziraldo chose the name for his winery with encouragement from Kitching, who suggested that it would be "bloody nonsense" to give the winery a bogus European name instead of tapping a good regional one.

Although the Ziraldo family were all amateur winemakers, the event that sparked the setting up of a commercial winery was a 1971 confrontation between Donald Ziraldo and the blunt, opinionated Kaiser. The Austrian had come to the Ziraldo nursery to buy some French hybrid grape vines for his father-in-law's garden, and so disparaged Canadian wines in conversation that Ziraldo sprang angrily to their defence. Kaiser then produced a bottle of his own rosé, made in a classically dry European style from chelois grapes. From that tasting a friendship developed, and, ultimately, the partnership.

Kaiser, who was born in 1941, seven years earlier than Donald Ziraldo, had been introduced to viticulture when, in 1954, he entered a Cistercian monastery as a secondary-school student, staying on for a year as a novice, with duties that included working in the monastery's vineyards. Later, teaching economics in the grape-growing town of Zistersdorf, northeast of Vienna, he began helping at vintage with the grandfather of his future wife, Sylvia. The marriage led him to Canada when his wife's parents, living in St. Catharines, sent airline tickets for a 1968 Canadian vacation. The visit did not inspire him: "Everything was prohibited, like in the Middle Ages. The food was atrocious." And when, in 1969, he yielded to the entreaties of his wife and in-laws and emigrated, more of the unpleasant experiences which had marred the vacation now soured his new life. At that autumn's grape and wine festival in St. Catharines, he discovered that the wines of Canada suited him no better than the rest of the country. In the fall of 1970, he made a small quantity of wine from locally obtained grape juice, the variety of which was anonymous. But he was sufficiently pleased with it to find a grower the following year who sold him some chelois from which he made the rosé that impressed Ziraldo.

Ziraldo had begun early in 1973 to make tentative inquiries at the Liquor Control Board of Ontario about starting a new winery. His timing was fortunate, for relations between the LCBO's Kitching and Ontario grape growers were bitter. Born in China and educated in Britain, Kitching was less chauvinistic in his views than former heads of the LCBO. Shortly after his appointment, he was questioned by a reporter about his wine preferences. Naively, he replied he could think of nothing finer with roast beef than a good burgundy. When one of Ontario's leading grape growers took him to task, Kitching snapped, "Good God, you don't think you make a good burgundy!" During his five-year term, the LCBO was to list an additional thousand imported wines, exposing the Ontario product to fierce competition.

Kitching greeted the eventual Ziraldo application with support that included having the LCBO's accountants help draw up the cash-flow projections Ziraldo took to his bankers. Kitching also placed the board's support and distribution network behind Karl Podamer, whose champagne house got Ontario's second commercial cottage winery licence in the summer of 1975, a few weeks after Inniskillin's 1974 permit was upgraded to full commercial standing. Kitching, who had persuaded his political superiors to agree to liberalize retail operations by wineries, saw to it that the cottage winery products were placed in a number of LCBO stores. And his personal letters to store managers ensured that the products were featured. "I liked the look of Don," Kitching said later. "We wanted to make damn sure, if he was going to be first, that he wouldn't fall down."

Kitching saw Inniskillin's control of its own vineyards as one of Ziraldo's advantages. The original sixty-seven-acre vineyard was planted in 1974 chiefly to vinifera, including thirty acres of chardonnay, some johannisberg riesling and some gamay. When the winery moved in 1978 from the original old barn to its current modern quarters, Ziraldo raised some of the $2.5 million he needed by selling the vineyard to the Seeger family, German immigrants who had already been Inniskillin growers, with the winery retaining the rights to the grapes. In 1980 Ziraldo put together an Inniskillin-controlled partnership to acquire the nearby fifty-acre Montague vineyard, again already planted in vinifera grapes and premium hybrids. Another twenty acres around the winery itself contains research varieties ranging from cabernet sauvignon to some Russian vitis amurensis. Finally, Inniskillin has given fifteen-year contracts to several major growers whose vineyards are planted with vines developed at Ziraldo Farms & Nurseries, the family firm now managed by Robert.

The first Inniskillin wines, made by a frantically busy Karl Kaiser now working on a master's chemistry degree at Brock University, were well received. By 1977 the winery was selling all it could make, and at premium prices. Inniskillin's market debut, with wines crafted in the European table wine style, came just when the sales of imports overtook those of domestic products. Their price and style placed Inniskillin's among the imports.

So did the skill of their vintner. Inniskillin made its early reputation with maréchal foch, a temperamental red varietal attempted by a number of wineries following Chateau-Gai's much-publicized success of 1974. The results were so uneven that the market flinched, and today most of this widely planted grape goes into blended burgundies and clarets. Not so with Inniskillin's, where Kaiser's wide knowledge of chemistry comes into play. He theorizes that the grape is microbiologically unstable: while typically high in acidity at harvest, it also contains an alkaline substance – cream of tartar – which is freed during fermentation and can drop the acidity of the must so rapidly that the wine may be in danger of microbiological spoilage. Kaiser adds some fruit acid to the foch grapes during crush, protecting them through the early critical stages of fermentation until alcohol levels are high enough to ward off spoilage. Afterwards, a secondary, or malolactic, fermentation is induced, converting the wine's tart malic acid to smooth lactic acid.

Similar problems are presented by the léon millot grape, a hybrid related to foch which Inniskillin has vinified in limited quantities on its own or blended with the lighter-coloured chambourcin. Kaiser also makes a varietal red from the chelois grape, lighter than either the foch or the millot. All spend time in wood, and all respond well to aging. The well-made red hybrids appear to improve into the fifth

year after vintage, losing the bitter finish that typifies these varieties. Naturally, some peak much earlier than that, de chaunac being one that is ready within a year. Inniskillin has dropped de chaunac as a varietal – on its own, it is a rather ordinary wine – and uses it instead in its best-selling Brae Rouge blend.

The winery's name was made with reds, which still account for half its sales, but Kaiser's whites, notably the johannisberg riesling and chardonnay, rank consistently with the best of those varieties made in Canada. The chardonnays, which have made their way onto Air Canada's first-class menu and the boardroom wine list of the Royal Bank, are becoming more and more complex as the vines mature and Kaiser gains access to more French oak barrels. The rieslings are made in both the dry Alsatian and the slightly sweet German styles.

In a good vintage, Kaiser likes to leave some grapes on the vine well into late fall, maturing to a sweetness appropriate for a dessert wine. In the excellent 1982 vintage, the last variety harvested at Inniskillin was the vidal, a white hybrid normally made into an easy-drinking, fruity and early-maturing wine. In that harvest, however, the grapes stayed on the vines until the first week of November, achieving sugar levels of 26 to 28 degrees Brix, about 25 per cent sweeter than needed for a standard table wine. The result was a well-balanced, auslese-style dessert wine with the elegant aroma of the grape and 4 per cent residual sugar. Kaiser later regretted not leaving some fruit on the vine into December for a rich and syrupy "ice wine" made from very ripe grapes crushed when frozen. Such limited-quantity wines, while rarely commercial, attract a great deal of favourable attention. Inniskillin was alive to the promotional value of prestige offerings as long ago as 1978, when Kaiser put aside enough chardonnay for a five-thousand-bottle cuvée of sparkling wine to mark the winery's tenth anniversary. When this bottle-fermented bubbly was disgorged from the yeast in 1982, the result was an impressive blanc de blancs chardonnay, priced as high as French champagne. Also useful for prestige are the winery's numerous exclusive bottlings. For the Prince of Wales Hotel in Niagara-on-the-Lake, Inniskillin bottles a white varietal from the American dutchess hybrid, the name suited to the establishment's Edwardian character. Another white, the couderc muscat, is bottled exclusively for Toronto's noted Windsor Arms Hotel, and a 1978 gamay beaujolais was reserved for the Four Seasons Hotel in that city.

Ziraldo has also won high-profile export sales that include some Canadian diplomatic posts abroad. After one New York luncheon given by the Canadian consul-general, Ziraldo fielded telephone calls from several persons interested in representing his winery there. Perhaps his greatest coup has been the widely publicized 1982 order from the Burgundy shipper F. Chauvenet for Inniskillin's 1980 maréchal foch, the result of some prodding by Ontario's trade minister of visiting French officials. Announcement of the sale in the Ontario legislature soon cleared the rest of that vintage from the shelves.

Ironically, the order was then stalled in the politics which surrounds the wine trade between Canada and France. Before authorizing shipment, the French government asked that the Niagara Peninsula be designated as a wine-growing region so that the Inniskillin foch could be labelled in conformity with France's appellation of origin practice. This was resisted by the Canadian Wine Institute, which recognized that the French demand was considerably less innocent than it appeared on the surface: one of the arguments in the ongoing champagne case is that only sparkling wine made in that designated French wine district can be called champagne. The Chauvenet order has been delayed indefinitely. Other Inniskillin export sales have been shipped, however, including a small order for Japan's Seiyu department stores and another to the old British firm of wine merchants, Averys of Bristol.

MONTRAVIN

ESTABLISHED 1973

COOPERAGE 350 000 gallons

TOURS & TASTINGS are available Monday through Friday, 10 A.M. to 4 P.M.; after-hours tours are by appointment. Tel. (416) 563-5313. The winery is at 1233 Ontario Street; exit at Beamsville from the Queen Elizabeth Way.

TASTER'S CHOICE features the ❢❢❢ Podamer Blanc de Blancs Brut Canadian Champagne; well made are the ❢❢ Podamer Special Reserve and ❢ Podamer Brut.

ALSO RECOMMENDED are the ❢ Podamer Extra dry, the inexpensive ❢ Champagne Canadien Extra Dry and the ❢ maréchal foch.

The unexpected order for twenty-four cases of Podamer's expensive brut blanc de blancs champagne came as a tonic for Ernst Fischer's morale at a particularly critical time. The order emanated from the prime minister's office, and the wine, then selling for a little under fifteen dollars a bottle, was served at the state dinner for the Queen during her 1983 visit to Vancouver. The high-level recognition was comforting to the man who was struggling to salvage the troubled Podamer winery, since renamed Montravin Cellars.

Fischer, an Austrian-born enologist with experience on three continents, was a freelance winery consultant in the Niagara Peninsula when he was retained for the 1982 Podamer vintage. He stayed to take over both management and winemaking from Karl Podamer, whose lifelong career as a craftsman of champagne-style wines has been dogged by misfortune. Fischer found a superbly equipped winery in a building which looked, in Podamer's memorable phrase of the summer before, like "a bankrupt shopping centre." Podamer had excused the appearance by suggesting that it discouraged vandalism, a theory consistent with the fact that three earlier Podamer wineries had fallen victim to war or political unrest.

There was another explanation for the winery's delapidated quarters. Although Podamer's champagne-style products were competitive in quality, the company's still table wines were being ignored by consumers and even by vandals. Jack Couillard, the assistant general manager of the Liquor Control Board of Ontario, once described them as "a disaster." Fischer's new sales manager, Bruce Daigle, had been recruited from Andrés. When he tasted the Podamer inventory, he asked his former employer for a supply of table wines for personal consumption. The winery's reputation was clearly being devalued. Fischer moved quickly, clearing out inventory at fire-sale prices and replacing it with newly formulated blends in the new Montravin name.

The Podamer name remained, however, on the premium, champagne-style wines where the vintner's unquestionable talent was expressed. Born in Hungary in 1924, Karl Podamer is the third generation of his family to make what he has always insisted on calling champagne, since the wines are bottle-fermented just as they are in that French region. The family winery south of Budapest produced about a million bottles a year until it was destroyed by a 1944 bombing raid. The Podamers rebuilt only to be taken over in 1948 by the Hungarian government. Moving to Czechoslovakia, they saw their new winery nationalized in 1949. Soviet repression of the 1956 Hungarian uprising was the last straw for Karl Podamer, who fled eastern Europe to settle in Canada.

There was no opportunity at first to practise a craft that had been his passion since, at age nine, he began helping bottle the family's sparkling wines. His inquiries about starting a champagne cellar in Ontario were not going to be entertained until he became a Canadian citizen, a process which then took five years. He supported himself in the meantime by learning the butcher's trade and opening a delicatessen in Oshawa, all the while prodding the government for a winery licence. "I'm born and I die in the wine business," he vowed.

The breakthrough came after Maj.-Gen. George Kitching became head of the Ontario liquor board in 1970. Kitching, a more travelled man than his predecessors, believed that small, new wineries could push existing establishments towards better-quality wines. "We had some good Ontario champagnes," he said, "but here was a man who wanted to make nothing but champagne." In March 1973 the board gave Podamer the initial licence to produce samples, and, when these proved satisfactory, issued a full licence in mid-1975.

The new winery was backed by $750,000 from Podamer and fourteen other partners, all business people in the Niagara Peninsula. For his equipment, Podamer went to the same suppliers in Epernay, France, with whom his grandfather had dealt, reasoning that with first-class equipment he would be better able to make the top-quality wines he proposed to sell, over the liquor board's objections, at a considerable premium as compared with the domestic competition. Podamer, of course, did not see them as competition: "I don't make sparkling wines. I learned the so-called original French *méthode champenoise*. At that time, it was the only style." Kitching saw to it that Podamer got automatic listings in the LCBO's major stores, despite misgivings about price. Podamer's Special Reserve, which proved the winery's best seller, retailed at just over ten dollars. Its success undoubtedly encouraged him to produce the blanc de blancs served to the Queen, a cuvée made entirely from chardonnay grapes, the most costly currently being grown. His less expensive champagnes relied on such North American hybrid varieties as dutchess and delaware, grapes with the acidity and character to produce crisp and reasonably neutral bubblies.

By 1979, however, the winery was in financial trouble. The original shareholders sold the controlling interest to Sam Fuda, a Toronto real estate developer who was acting for investors in Italy as well as himself. The fresh capital enabled the winery to expand its product line to include six still table wines: four varietals – seyval blanc, muscat, de chaunac and foch – and two generics, Concerto white and red. It was the quality-control problems with these wines that finally led the Fuda group to buy Podamer out entirely and, in August 1982, install Fischer as general manager, with Podamer retained as a consultant.

Born in Vienna in 1936 and a graduate in viticulture and winemaking, Fischer had experience with sparkling wines. He had made them at two German wineries, in Turkey and New York State, and most recently at Chateau-Gai in Niagara Falls. One of the new products introduced under Fischer, in addition to the semi-dry Tassello Blanc, was Montravin Champagne Canadien, an inexpensive bubbly made by the Charmat process. With wines fermented in pressure tanks rather than individual bottles, this is a considerably

more economical way of making a bubbly, and it can make wines with a fresh fruitiness rather than the typical yeastiness of bottle-fermented champagne. Not that bottle-fermented sparkling wines are being dropped: a vintage champagne is planned, along with another based on riesling grapes. The immediate priority, however, has been to develop a broad new line of table wines, increasing the winery's economic base and also providing enough product to help get listings across Canada – Podamer champagne was sold only in Ontario. The only bubbly Fischer dropped was a sparkling red, undoubtedly the only bottle-fermented red made in Canada: for all its technical virtues, it was a wine for which there was almost no market.

The winery's appearance has been upgraded, too, with a large sign clearly visible from the nearby Queen Elizabeth Way. This new visibility can be expected to attract tours, particularly given the romantic aura surrounding champagne – though some wineries, Montravin included, prefer not to take visitors through the cool, dark cellars where fermenting bottles are stacked, because there is a real danger of bottles exploding. The pressure created by the fermentation of still wine with yeast and sugar can range from seventy to one hundred pounds per square inch, enough to shatter the occasional bottle with an undetected weakness. For its bottle-fermented products Montravin uses bottles molded to its own specifications, weighing a kilogram and costing about eighty cents each.

The sparkling wine may be allowed to rest for a year or more in contact with the dead yeast cells after fermentation is complete, picking up the complex toasted or yeasty flavours prized by champagne lovers. At the end of this period, the bottles are placed, neck down, in special racks where each is ''riddled''– given an eighth of a turn daily – until all the yeast sediment has been shaken onto the underside of the crown cap. At bottling, each of these riddled bottles has its neck immersed in a brine solution to freeze the sediment into a plug and then it is uncapped, the pressure expelling the plug. The bottle is topped up, sometimes with a sweet dose if the style of the champagne is meant to be off-dry, and sealed with the familiar champagne cork.

The time from the vintage of the wine in the bottle to its release as champagne can easily be three years. This time and the work involved, to say nothing of the price of premium-quality grapes, inevitably drive up the price. ''I realize our products are highly-priced,'' Fischer says, ''but they are made in the traditional French method.''

PELEE ISLAND

ESTABLISHED 1983

COOPERAGE 60 000 gallons

TOURS & TASTINGS are available at the winery on Highway 18, just east of Kingsville, Ontario. The vines are on Pelee Island.

TASTER'S CHOICE is the ♈ Vin Villa johannisberg riesling 1982, a fleshy, raisin-flavoured wine.

Pelee Island in Lake Erie, seen from the ferry docks at Kingsville on the Ontario mainland, lies low and indistinct on the horizon. About six miles long and four wide, the island has an average elevation of only fifteen feet above the lake. Its somewhat Mediterranean climate attracted Canada's first commercially important vineyard and winery in 1866, when a trio of American farmers planted grapes and built the Vin Villa winery, the foundations of which still remain. More than a century later, Austrian farmer Walter Strehn has revived viticulture

on the island, where the staple crop is soybeans, and revived Vin Villa.

Strehn was born in Vienna in 1949 and grew up at Deutschkreutz on the Austrian-Hungarian border, where his family has vineyards and a winery that sells in bulk to the Lenz Moser group. A graduate of the viticultural academy at Klosterneuburg in Austria, he first visited Canada in 1978, scouting opportunities for farm investment. He did not have grapes in mind – "All you hear in Europe about Canada is hunting, fishing and wheat" – but gravitated naturally to wine, particularly when he discovered a fellow Austrian vintner, Karl Kaiser of Inniskillin, already in Ontario. Immigrating the following year, Strehn immediately began a study of potential grape-growing areas. One of his future Canadian business partners, at a chance meeting in the Strehn winery in Austria, advised him to check out Pelee Island. When he did, Strehn learned not only that grapes had once flourished there but that, at $800 an acre, farmland was perhaps a fifth the cost of raw land in the Niagara Peninsula and even half that of farm acreage on the nearby mainland. In 1980 he began planting what grew to become a hundred-acre vineyard with vinifera varieties obtained from Europe, predominantly johannisberg riesling.

Pelee Island's original growers had planted chiefly delaware and catawba, North American varieties which once rivalled the labrusca varieties in the production of sweet and fortified wines. After the 1866 plantings, the island soon acquired several other vineyards and wineries, the most successful of which was the J. S. Hamilton company, purchased seventy-five years later by London Winery. These pioneer growers contended with humid heat in summer, which forces a virtual halt to field work in the middle of the day; even the night-time temperatures remain uncomfortably high. The grapes continue to mature to high sugar levels around the clock, but are also subject to diseases not easily controlled a century ago. The pioneers also had the obvious problem of transportation. Hamilton and other vintners were faced with barging casks of wines sixteen miles north to the Canadian mainland or twenty miles south to Sandusky, Ohio, itself a wine-growing area. Hamilton ultimately built a winery at Brantford, closer to his markets.

The main side-effect of the humid heat, aside from discomfort, was mildew, now easily fended off with chemicals. The transport problem remains, one reason land prices are still relatively low; the ferry that connects the island with Kingsville and with Leamington does not operate during the winter. Strehn may rebuild Vin Villa's fermenting capacity on the island, serving the tourist trade and summer cottagers, but his main 60 000-gallon winery was built in 1984 on a highway site near Kingsville on the mainland.

Midwinter ice has been known to form on the lake from the mainland to the island, an indication that grape growing there is not without its risks, despite the Mediterranean summers. Frost in the winter of 1981–82 decimated the vineyard's pinot noir, only 5 per cent of the total plantings but still the major red variety. Such other vinifera varieties as gewurztraminer suffered extensive bud damage, reducing Strehn's first commercial vintage. Further frost damage in the 1983–84 vintage showed that Strehn will have an ongoing problem on the island. The varieties or clones that best survived, including the riesling, have formed the basis for subsequent replantings. Strehn has also put in some reputedly winter-hardy European varieties that include an Austrian red called zweigeltrebe and a white called welschriesling, widely planted in eastern Europe and northern Italy and thought to be unrelated to the classic riesling family.

The winery and vineyards are solidly backed by Austrian investors, who have about 40 per cent, and Canadians, among them Kitchener businessman Donald Martin and Hungarian-born Karl

Gyaki, the Toronto-based wine merchant who handles Pelee's distribution. The Austrians include Strehn's family, and some of their support has been in kind: the large oak oval casks in the winery came from Deutschkreutz.

The winemaking style is traditional German-Austrian. The wines from Strehn's 1982 vintage, which earned him his licence, included some of the most attractive johannisberg rieslings ever made in Canada. The regular vintage riesling is full-bodied, even fleshy, with an enormous bouquet of ripe apricots. The late-harvest riesling, made from grapes picked in mid-November, is a soft, silky-textured, auslese-style wine with enough natural acidity to balance the sweetness. Strehn believes that Pelee Island's heavy and fertile soils, in addition to promoting comparatively high-tonnage harvests, keep grape acidity up despite the hot summers. The 1982 vintage also includes wines made from scheurebe and kerner, both white vinifera hybrids from Europe. The kerner in particular produces very full-bodied, fruity wines, good on their own and useful for blending with more neutral ones.

SUMAC RIDGE

ESTABLISHED 1980

COOPERAGE 40 000 gallons

TOURS & TASTINGS are available year-round from 10 A.M. to 6 P.M. and to 8 P.M. in summer; groups by appointment. Tel. (604) 494-0451. The winery, which has a full restaurant next to the tasting room, is 0.8 km (0.5 mi.) north of Summerland, British Columbia, on Highway 97.

TASTER'S CHOICE includes the ♈♈♈ perle of csaba 1983, a soft, sweet dessert wine, and the excellent varietals ♈♈ gewurztraminer 1983 and ♈♈ chancellor.

ALSO RECOMMENDED are chardonnay 1982, chenin blanc 1981, the ♈♈ 1983 gewurztraminer, the Okanagan riesling, Summerland Rosé, and ♈ verdelet.

The nine-hole course at Sumac Ridge once anchored a sleepy social club on the edge of the quiet Okanagan retirement town of Summerland (population 7500, half over age sixty-five). Since 1980, however, Harry McWatters and Lloyd Schmidt, who are significantly younger than the average Summerlander, have been lining the fairways with johannisberg riesling, chardonnay and gewurztraminer vines to develop the only Canadian winery with its own public golf course. And the combination works: while golfers swing, the clubhouse restaurant has become an effective showcase for Sumac Ridge and other local estate wines.

The bearded, convivial McWatters, born in Toronto in 1944, has been a salesman since he was eighteen. He grew up planning to follow his father, his grandfather and his great-grandfather into a career with the Toledo Scale Co., but when the company offered to enroll him in a management training course, he changed his mind and took a job instead as a salesman with a moving company. He showed his first somewhat serious interest in wine when he was sixteen by making a batch of potato champagne. It was unpalatable, but that failed to discourage him from pursuing the hobby – with fresh grapes – while his sales career progressed. In 1968 Casabello Wines, needing an aggressive salesman in the Vancouver area, offered what was a low-salaried job to McWatters. The winery's founder, Evans Lougheed, shrewdly invited the young salesman to the Penticton winery where McWatters took the job without even discussing salary. On his first payday he learned he was making only half as much at the winery as he'd earned at the moving company.

Lloyd Schmidt, as dour as McWatters is good-humoured, was born in 1940, son of Frank J. Schmidt, a vineyard foreman at Okanagan Mission for the pioneer grower J. W. Hughes who later bought what came to be known as the Beau Sejour vineyard, south of Kelowna on the east side of the lake. When Schmidt senior sold the vineyard in 1965 to Growers Wines, Lloyd stayed on as manager. He worked later as a viticulturist with the provincial government, and in 1979 joined Casabello, where he and McWatters became close friends and shared the desire to run their own winery.

Small estate or farm wineries became possible in British Columbia after 1977, when the provincial government decided to license what it then called cottage wineries, a California term. The government first proposed a maximum production of 20 000 gallons. McWatters and

Schmidt, after a serious feasibility study, concluded that at least 25 000 gallons were needed to support two families. They made the point to government, apparently with effect, for the maximum was raised to 30 000 gallons.

They began looking for a vineyard site in 1980. McWatters had decided that a highway location was vital, having seen how important

Casabello's Main Street location in Penticton was to that winery's success. The first choice was near Kaleden, south of Penticton, but not enough roadside acreage was available. Schmidt recalled an offer to sell that had reached Casabello some time before from the owners of the Sumac Ridge golf course. Casabello had not been interested, having sold its vineyard holdings several years earlier, but Schmidt and McWatters were. For $475,000, they bought thirty-eight of the sixty-two acres which comprised the original golf course. At $12,500, the per-acre cost was stiff for raw vineyard land, but the site was ideal. Jutting from the west shore of Okanagan Lake, the vineyard's microclimate benefits from reduced frost danger and receives the sun needed for maturing vinifera. Sumac Ridge has taken full advantage of this: the 1984 plantings even included two and a half acres of late-ripening cabernet sauvignon close to a south-facing rock bluff which, in most years, should radiate the additional heat needed to mature the vines. When Sumac Ridge opened its retail store in mid-1981, the wisdom of the highway location was evident immediately. "By September 1982 we had to serve coffee in our tasting room," recalled McWatters. "We didn't have a bottle of wine left to sell."

Estate wineries in British Columbia are required to have at least twenty acres of producing vineyard. McWatters and Schmidt persuaded the government to let them buy grapes from established growers, since the golf course vineyard would produce none until the 1983 vintage. At the same time, the winery negotiated a management lease for Guy Wilson's thirteen-acre vineyard at Naramata across the lake, on terms that give Sumac Ridge part ownership and nearly all the grapes, which include some of the best of the valley's Okanagan riesling.

In 1980 Sumac Ridge had its grapes crushed and its wines cellared at Casabello, while McWatters and Schmidt converted the clubhouse at Sumac Ridge into a winery for the 1981 vintage. From the first vintage of 1980, Sumac Ridge released only three wines, all made from hybrid grapes. The red came from the hardy seibel hybrid, chancellor, which has cabernet sauvignon in its ancestry. Although this grape is proving to be one of the best wine grapes among the red hybrids, only forty-five acres are grown in the valley, most of the tonnage going to Sumac Ridge or Calona. The two wineries have produced chancellor in somewhat different styles: Calona's 1981 vintage shows its nine months' oak-aging in an attractive finish, while Sumac Ridge, using stainless steel in its early vintages, made soft, fruity chancellors, suitable for early drinking. In 1983 the winery received its first small Limousin oak barrels, coopered in California under the watchful eye of the renowned vintner Joe Heitz, a friend of McWatters who also coached Lloyd's son, Alan, Sumac Ridge's developing young winemaker. Some barrels were intended for maturing the three hundred gallons of 1982 chardonnay Sumac Ridge made that year, but when the wine proved too delicate to be put into barrels, a portion of the chancellor was oak-aged.

The two whites released every year since 1980 have been the verdelet and Okanagan riesling. In both instances, the juice is separated from the skins immediately after pressing to produce light, delicate wines for early drinking. Best fresh and fruity, verdelet peaks after its second birthday. Okanagan riesling is a more difficult and challenging grape, with an assertive, pungent bouquet if the juice has had excessive contact with the skins. Sumac Ridge learned how to get a delicate wine, dry and crisp and best taken with food rather than as an aperitif. The 1984 vintage saw a change of style inspired by the Okanagan rieslings of Al Stratton at Mount Baker Vineyards, a new

Washington winery not far across the border from Abbotsford, British Columbia. Stratton leaves his juice on the skins for about twenty-four hours before fermentation begins, then centrifuges before inoculating it with yeast. After fermenting at 70°F for five or six days, the wine is centrifuged again. Stratton theorizes that Okanagan riesling is very susceptible to picking up what he calls the "cat pee" aroma from contact with the lees. Aggressive centrifuging removes yeast cells and other matter, leaving the wine clean and fresh. Lacking a centrifuge, Sumac Ridge attempts the same result by racking its wine aggressively.

Wines from vinifera have joined the winery's repertoire. The most extensively planted vinifera along its still-active fairways is the johannisberg riesling, followed by gewurztraminer and chardonnay. "We either own, contract or have a gentleman's agreement for about half the gewurztraminer in the valley," McWatters has said. "Lloyd thinks it is the best grape for the valley." The main contract grower for Sumac Ridge's gewurztraminer is Nick Broderson, who in 1980 meticulously planted a small vineyard with four-year-old vines at Kaleden. With his richly flavoured grapes, the wine, especially in an outstanding vintage such as 1983, is classic, spicy gewurztraminer. The winery's prime source for chardonnay has been the trio of so-called Basque vineyards established on the Thompson River near Ashcroft by Bill Drinkwater and his family. They are among the province's northernmost, but Drinkwater has been willing to protect his vinifera by burying them each fall. Sumac Ridge's 1982 chardonnay – only 123 cases were made – is from the first commercial harvest there: because the vines are so young, the wine is delicate and lacks the intensity of character to be expected as the vineyard matures.

Sumac Ridge has also produced two most interesting specialties. One is a soft, delicate, muscat-style wine from the Hungarian perle of csaba vinifera. "This is a wine we have a lot of emotional interest in," McWatters has said, explaining that in 1936 Lloyd Schmidt's father was given four vines of this early-maturing variety by a now forgotten source; they were planted and used in grape-breeding, but not propagated seriously until the late seventies. In the 1983 vintage, grower Douglas Sperling, who had propagated the vines, approached Sumac Ridge with five tons of perle of csaba that had ripened so early that Ste-Michelle, to which he is contracted, was not geared up to process them. Schmidt and McWatters eagerly accepted these grapes, and their light dessert wine was ready for consumption by the end of January. Even rarer is a sauternes-style chenin blanc made in 1982 from grapes in Oliver grower Joe Petronio's vineyard, which had been touched by botrytis cinerea. This fungus, rare in the Okanagan but common in Sauternes in France, dehydrates and shrivels the berries, concentrating both sugar and flavour. Petronio harvested with a Brix reading of 32 degrees, at least 50 per cent sweeter than needed for ordinary dry table wine. When natural fermentation stopped, the resulting wine still remained sweet and had the rich, honeyed aroma and texture of a botrytised wine. Only twenty gallons were made, destined to be sold, if at all, in premium-priced half-bottles. Some will be used as treats for close friends and some, perhaps, will be set aside for succeeding anniversaries at Sumac Ridge.

UNIACKE

ESTABLISHED 1980

COOPERAGE 17 000 gallons

TOURS & TASTINGS are available Monday through Saturday 10 A.M. to 6 P.M.; groups by appointment. Tel. (604) 764-8866. Drive east on Pandosy Street from its intersection with Highway 97 in Kelowna, and stay with it when it becomes Lakeshore Road. Watch for the sign.

TASTER'S CHOICE includes the very dry ▼ Chasselas, the award-winning ▼ Okanagan riesling and the dry chelois rosé.

Richard John Uniacke has become a footnote in Canadian history, memorialized by Mount Uniacke in Nova Scotia, where he was the first attorney-general. The family name, which can be traced to fourteenth-century Ireland, had otherwise vanished in Canada through a lack of male descendants until the Kelowna grape grower David Mitchell, a descendant through his mother, adopted the name and family crest for his new estate winery. In Latin, the crest announces, "This is unique," certainly the objective of Mitchell and his wife, Susan. It also reminds them of their Nova Scotia heritage.

Mitchell is a farmer by avocation. A geology graduate of Halifax's Dalhousie University, he worked in Rhodesia, where he nearly bought a farm in 1969, and then moved to Calgary to pursue a

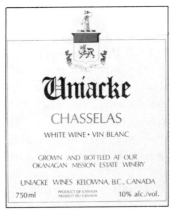

geology career he found increasingly less absorbing. Early in 1974, during a skiing vacation to the Okanagan, the Mitchells wandered into a local real estate office and ended up buying a fifteen-acre vineyard near Kelowna. Susan Mitchell has remembered: "We knew absolutely nothing about growing anything. David didn't even know how to start the tractor." The vineyard proved to be too small, too vulnerable to frost and too committed to grape varieties Mitchell considered undesirable. In 1978 they moved to 180 acres on the precipitous eastern shore of Okanagan Lake, the site of some of the valley's earliest and best vineyards. The upper slopes, unsuited to cultivation, were resold for real estate development. On the remainder, Mitchell already had forty acres in grapes, apples and pears, with another thirty to be cleared and planted to grapes over the next five years.

Mitchell planted his newly cleared acreage largely in such white vinifera as gewurztraminer (six acres) and johannisberg riesling (five acres). He sells most of the grapes along with his inherited de chaunac production to Mission Hill, where he has contracted the tonnage not committed to Uniacke. Small 1978 plantings of merlot and pinot noir, which yielded promising red wines in the 1981 and 1982 vintages, had been expanded by 1983 to two-acre plots of each. The Mitchell vineyard also includes two acres of chardonnay and one of semillon. Chasselas is now planned, since a white made from purchased grapes of that variety has become Uniacke's most popular wine.

Mitchell has planted many of his vinifera directly on their own roots rather than on grafted roots resistant to the root louse phylloxera. Grafting is time-consuming and expensive, and Mitchell was in a hurry. Impulsiveness also characterized his sudden entry into the winery business. When two Edmonton lawyers offered help in financing a winery, the Mitchells aired the idea with a fellow Maritimer, David Newman-Bennett, an architectural draftsman from Sackville, New Brunswick, who had become a Kelowna builder and happened to be renovating their home. Newman-Bennett turned out to be interested himself, and a partnership was struck. "We just felt," Susan Mitchell has said, "that we would be more comfortable getting into the winery business with somebody we knew than with two high-powered lawyers."

Newman-Bennett, who left the partnership in 1983 to pursue other interests, designed the Mediterranean-style winery on a hillside overlooking the vineyards and Okanagan Lake. At the time of the first crush in the fall of 1980, however, the partners had just had time to dig the cellars, a hillside bunker for tanks and barrels, crudely covered to keep out the weather. With consulting help from John Bremmer and Lynn Stark of Bright's, Uniacke in 1980 made about nine thousand bottles of wine. Most were whites, including a johannisberg riesling and an Okanagan riesling; the red was a chelois, a French hybrid grape that produces wines of good character but so light in colour as to verge on rosé. For the 1981 vintage the consulting winemaker was Don Allen, a retired naval captain and vineyardist at Westbank who pioneered the winery's pinot noir and merlot, the latter being the first commercial merlot made from Okanagan-grown grapes. The fifty cases released at Christmas 1982 sold quickly at the winery's retail store.

For its third vintage, Uniacke changed winemakers again, this time employing twenty-one-year-old Tilman Hainle, whose German-born father is developing a vineyard and winery at Peachland across the lake. Despite his youth, Hainle had already graduated at the top of his class from the Weinsberg Institute in Germany. He also had some actual winemaking experience at the Claremont winery and with his father, who had been making remarkable wines for home consumption since 1973. Hainle's winemaking confirms the direction Uniacke has been taking: wines are usually dry, with the exception of the award-winning Okanagan riesling, which is sweetened with some reserved grape juice.

As the winery grew towards a planned production of ten thousand gallons a year, the partners learned what a burden it is to market even that comparatively small quantity. Uniacke was unknown and, with only two wines listed, had limited exposure in British Columbia liquor stores. The Mitchells were haunted by bank problems, and in early 1983 even considered selling. Instead, however, along with Claremont and Gray Monk, they signed a marketing agreement with Estate Wines, a new Kelowna firm of wine agents. Within months, Estate Wines had sold most of the 1982 vintage before it was even in bottles. That vintage consisted of chasselas, johannisberg riesling, gewurztraminer, Okanagan riesling and chelois, plus small quantities of pinot noir and merlot, wines that will continue to be sold primarily through the winery store run with hospitality by Susan Mitchell.

PART III

PLONK: THE LEGACY OF PROHIBITION

The stubborn challenge Canadian wineries have had to overcome is represented by the career of the late Col. Donald McGugan, chairman of the British Columbia liquor board from 1951 until his retirement in 1969 at age seventy-nine. British Columbia in 1921 had been one of the first provinces after Quebec to legislate a government monopoly on the sale of alcohol as prohibition laws were repealed. Invariably, the men called to head these new provincial monopolies were heavy-handed autocrats: many came from military backgrounds and many, too, were abstainers. McGugan fitted the mold perfectly, except in this last respect. He came from the other school of Canadian drinking, which likes strong drink and plenty of it, though not at the dinner table. It was, and to some extent still is, the classic pattern identified by J. V. McAree in the *Toronto Mail & Empire* in 1932: "The drinking habits of Canadians are, unfortunately, more like those of Americans than Englishmen. They do not habitually drink with their meals. They habitually drink before meals or some hours later. Prohibition undoubtedly did much to strengthen this habit if it was not the original cause. Drinking was more or less furtive. People drank when they had the opportunity."

Like the early chairmen of other liquor boards, McGugan viewed the sale of liquor for profit as a distinctly secondary intent of the law under which he worked. "As far as I am concerned," he told a 1969 inquiry, "the act was only for control." Born in Strathroy, Ontario, McGugan had gone to Victoria to article as a lawyer, and interrupted his career for wartime service with B.C.'s notable Seaforth Highlanders. He joined the new liquor board as a legal advisor in 1923. Many of the liquor controls were of his devising, though his practice departed from his preaching, as wine industry sales executives often discovered. McGugan, who never accepted hospitality from the wineries, always took his guests to lunch at Victoria's Union Club, where he lived. Andrew Peller, the founder of Andrés Wines and one such guest, has described the experience in his autobiography: "The meal was always preceded by at least six strong martinis which had no visible effect on him but which left me decidedly stupid, even though I managed to refuse a couple." Meredith F. Jones, then president of Bright's, staggered to a hotel bed from his first lunch with the colonel, waking up only the next morning.

This taste for intemperate drinking has dogged Canada's social development since Bishop Laval first excommunicated the liquor traffickers of New France. Early Canadian farmers exchanged rye for whisky at the local still as readily as they exchanged wheat for flour at the grist mill. And they learned to drink with gusto. Historian Ruth Spence, whose father, Frank, was a leading turn-of-the-century prohibitionist, has noted: "In many families whisky was served to each member of the household in the morning. It was considered to be a precaution against colds and to enable one to do hardy work." Drinks were commonly taken later in the day as well. At the time of Confederation, the legal stills in Ontario were producing about two gallons of spirits a year for every inhabitant.

The hard drinking of spirits and beer led to the temperance movement that emerged in the early nineteenth century. Ruth Spence has pointed out that "there was at first no suggestion of abstinence from wine, ale or beer; in fact, the use of these was encouraged, in the supposed interest of true temperance." By mid-century, however, fuelled by evidence of social dislocation and their own growing respectability, the temperance crusaders had become prohibitionists in full cry. One of them, Leonard Tilley, was among the Fathers of Confederation, and his province, New Brunswick, was, in 1855, the first to prohibit the sale of alcohol. A Fredericton liquor dealer challenged the law all the way to the Privy Council in London, which, to the prohibitionists' delight, ruled the Temperance Act was constitutional. The New Brunswick experiment eventually degenerated into chaos, but the neighbouring state of Maine made prohibition stick in 1858. Gen. Neil Dow, a dry politician in Portland, Maine, urged it on an 1859 committee of the Upper Canada legislature, writing that: "Pauperism in this city has fallen off thirty-seven per cent, and drunkenness more than one half . . . and the same results are observed throughout the state."

With such examples, Canadian prohibitionists gained ground. Beginning in 1864, laws authorized local option, and some sixty-five counties and municipalities took advantage of these provisions to vote themselves dry. The women's suffrage movement lined up strongly for temperance. By 1887 the Dominion Alliance, a new coalition of the anti-drink groups, was threatening to form a new political party for women's suffrage and temperance. Prohibition had become such an issue that in the 1896 federal election, Liberal leader Sir Wilfrid Laurier promised, if he won, to hold a national referendum and to abide by the results. When the referendum was held two years later, prohibition was carried nationally by a paper-thin margin of 13 000, with every province save Quebec providing a dry majority; Quebec, where the Church had a winemaking tradition of some antiquity, voted four to one against going dry. Prime Minister Laurier, a Quebecker, wriggled from his embarrassing promise by telling the Dominion Alliance that since only 44 per cent of the eligible voters had even taken part in the referendum, ''no good purpose would be served by forcing upon the people a measure which is shown by vote to have the support of less than twenty-three per cent of the electorate.''

The Alliance responded with campaigns in the provinces. Prince Edward Island was the first, in 1901, to go dry, and in 1948 it was the last province to repeal that law. When World War I broke out, prohibitionists quickly and successfully made going dry a patriotic gesture until, in December 1917, Sir Robert Borden's Union government made prohibition national. A new era began, and as good a sign of it as any was the two-year bootlegging sentence handed out to the senior British Columbia civil servant in charge of enforcing the prohibition law. Defiant Quebeckers and many other Canadians skirted the dry laws. Liquor boards, pioneered by Quebec in 1921, finally provided the answer: since people were going to drink anyway, they might as well do so – in moderation, of course – under government supervision. Zealous prohibitionists were bitterly disappointed, noting that distillers also favoured the boards, but for quite another reason: they provided a safe, secure marketing channel.

The 1927 arrival of safe, secure liquor store marketing exposed the wineries to competition for the first time in a decade. During Prohibition, they enjoyed the unparalleled boom because the Niagara grape growers, when Ontario went dry in 1917, persuaded the United

Farmers government to exempt wine and thus ensure a continued market for the grape crop. The government tried silencing protests from the abstainers by legislating naive marketing restrictions for wine. The wineries, for instance, could sell to the public only at the winery and only in mimimum quantities of five-gallon containers or twelve-bottle cases, a restriction meant to make purchases costly enough to discourage drinking. Also allowed was the production of medicinal wines, obtainable by prescription at drug stores. There was an astonishing demand for these wines, of course: in 1924, the province's four thousand doctors issued 739 855 prescriptions for tonic wines. These dubious products were, by law, laced with enough herbs that overindulgence caused vomiting. Naturally, some wineries kept such herbs to a minimum. The government righteously certified twenty-three of these – with names such as Dr. Coventry's Invalid Port and Dr. J. O. Lambert's Elixir Tonic Wines – as unsuitable for sale.

Predictably, the demand for wine, the only legal alcoholic beverage, was so enormous that forty new wineries were licensed in Ontario during Prohibition, with the number swelling to fifty-two by 1927. They not only bought the entire grape crop but imported half as much again from the United States. In the eight years following 1921, production of Canadian wine soared from less than half a million gallons to six million gallons. People were drinking everything in sight, provided it contained alcohol.

Ontario's wineries emerged from Prohibition as little more than opportunistic factories making flavoured alcohol. Gone was the competence shown as early as 1867, when the wines of Clair House Vineyards of Cooksville were, at a Paris wine exposition, compared favourably to French beaujolais. Ontario's new liquor control board, set up in 1927, had A. R. Bonham, chemist for the provincial health department, evaluate the wines then in storage: he condemned thousands of gallons. Veteran winemaker Edwin Haynes, then Bonham's assistant, suggested that many wineries "probably were producing more vinegar than wine." Even K. H. Smith, the president of the company that became Chateau-Gai, admitted in 1931 that, "from the standpoint of world standards for wine, the Canadian wine industry is not a 'wine' industry at all but rather an industry for the manufacture of a cheap alcoholic beverage from grapes, sugar and water." Wineries had so little credibility that they could not prevent

Prime Minister R. B. Bennett from cutting by two-thirds the tariff against French wines. Dismissing their protests, Bennett snapped: ''Go home and learn how to make wine.'' Consumption of Canadian wine, after soaring in the twenties, peaked in 1932 and then plunged, recovering slowly only after the war and not regaining its lost ground until 1962. The wineries would have been no worse off had they been closed entirely by Prohibition and then made a fresh start.

Prohibition, obviously, had serious negative impacts on Canadian wine. Growers lost the incentive to improve their grape varieties so long as they could sell everything. Wineries, because they, too, could sell everything, lost the incentive to produce quality wines; in fact, they could legally disguise winemaking errors in strong-tasting medicinal wines. The generation of consumers that suffered through Prohibition turned to soundly made whisky and beer – when these were available. They handed down no wine-drinking tradition to the next generation, which then educated itself with a succession of faddish pop wines, the popularity and profitability of which distracted the wineries from developing high-quality table wines until the seventies. Finally, the new liquor boards isolated Canadian wineries and consumers from what was happening in the rest of the wine world. Either administrators like the martini-drinking McGugan were disinterested in wine and did not trouble to make available many imports, or they were excessively protective. When the French launched a suit against Canadian champagnes in 1964, for example, G. H. Sheppard, then the chief of the Ontario board, seriously considered a retaliatory ban against French champagnes.

Within this sheltered environment, many in the industry failed to appreciate how far their wines lagged behind world standards. In a devastating 1965 critique, the noted British wine writer Cyril Ray suggested the British would prefer almost any cheap vinifera from Europe or South America to a range of Chateau-Gai wines. ''His remarks don't mean a damn thing,'' snapped Canadian Wine Institute president Philip Torno. ''He is making a comparison of Ontario wines with wines of other countries, which is not really fair, and there is nothing wrong with the quality of our wines.'' It took imported wines just twelve years to capture half the Canadian wine market and force the domestic wineries to undertake quality improvements.

THE WINEMAKERS: DECATHLON STARS

When the chemist Edwin Haynes started a long winemaking career in 1938 with Chateau-Gai, he faced with his colleagues the daunting task of producing a full range of wines from four grape varieties – the concord, niagara, catawba and delaware – none of them desirable wine grapes. By the time of his retirement from Andrés's Winona, Ontario, winery in 1980, though, he had at least forty grape varieties to cope with, including French hybrids and vinifera. "If you can't make good wine with that selection, there's something the matter with you," he commented.

Haynes, born in 1913, graduated in chemistry from a Toronto technical school and began working as a junior assistant in the Ontario Department of Public Health laboratory set up by A.R. Bonham just after Prohibition. It was Bonham's job to test Ontario-made wines and prevent unpalatable products from reaching the liquor stores. In 1938 Alex Sampson, the new president of Canadian Wineries, later named Chateau-Gai, asked Bonham to recommend a young chemist to run the winery's several laboratories. Haynes got the job and worked with the tempestuous and ill-tempered Sampson until 1960, except for a five-year stint as winemaker at London Wines and a two-year period as the operator of his own private dairy products laboratory. Haynes then moved to the United States, first to the St. Julian winery in Paw Paw, Michigan, and then to Widmer's Wine Cellars, an upstate New York firm which has been in operation since 1888. At both American wineries, Haynes continued to vinify the same labrusca varieties he had used in Ontario, though by the time he returned to Canada in 1975 to join Andrés, New York wineries such as Widmer's had made significant plantings of hybrids and vinifera.

Having spent much of his career working with labrusca grapes,

Haynes has been reluctant to denigrate them. At Widmer's, a varietal called Lake Niagara, made entirely from the niagara grape, was once that winery's best-selling wine, well enough made to please even an experienced taster like wine writer Leon Adams, who wrote: "To my taste it has been the ideal blend of the grapy labrusca flavour in a tart medium-sweet wine." Haynes strongly believes there is a place for those wines. Indeed, consumers accustomed to such strongly flavoured wines find them quite acceptable, as Haynes learned when he first encountered California wines and found them somewhat insipid compared with his own Ontario wines. The marketplace would prove Haynes correct, for concord-flavoured wines and sweet red wines still sell in major quantities. A medium-sweet red from Calona, which sells about 400 000 gallons a year, is the biggest-selling domestic red in Canada.

Haynes was not always able to convince his various employers to have faith in sweet red wines. Once, he made a sweet concord wine and proposed that Chateau-Gai, for whom he then worked, release it bearing the name Canasta, after the popular card game. Sampson turned it down, losing – in Haynes's view – the chance to market a wine similar to the kosher wines, Manischewitz and Mogen David, which became widely popular in the United States and appealed to a clientele far beyond the Orthodox Jewish community. But while the market for such wines has been vast and continues to be important, it is also slowly declining, as North American palates have largely converted to European-style wines.

The winemaker who had more to do than any of his peers with moving Canadian wines towards this European style was one of Haynes's closest friends, Adhémar de Chaunac, a French-born chemist who made wine at Bright's from 1933 until he retired in 1966. Bright's chairman, W. D. Hatch, whose father recruited de Chaunac, contended that de Chaunac was by far the best enologist in Canada during his time. William Anderson of Jordan & Ste-Michelle, a founding member with de Chaunac of the Canadian Society of Enologists, has said: "I found him very, very gruff, rather outspoken and with definite opinions. But I enjoyed the man. He was good for the Canadian wine industry." De Chaunac, a count who had served in the French army during World War I, was as demanding and eccentric as Haynes was easygoing. "He didn't walk . . . he stalked," a colleague later recalled. De Chaunac persuaded Bright's to import hybrid and vinifera vines from France, vines capable of making dry table wines with which he had grown up. He was early to recognize that the shortcomings of Canadian wines were due ultimately to the inadequate grapes available to winemakers, since even a moderately skilled amateur, given good grapes, can produce sound table wines. His work with vinifera in North America – chardonnay and pinot noir – preceded the better known efforts of Dr. Konstantin Frank in New York State. However, de Chaunac's chief impact was through the red table wines marketed by Bright's from the hybrid varieties. Haynes recalled that de Chaunac especially preferred the wines made from the chelois grape, the basis for Bright's Manor St. Davids claret. The contribution of the Bright's winemaker was memorialized in 1972, when the hybrid Seibel 9549 was named for him at a black-tie dinner at the exclusive Niagara Falls Club. Only one other Canadian was invited to the dinner: Edwin Haynes.

William Anderson, chief enologist at Jordan & Ste-Michelle Cellars in St. Catharines, was born in Guelph and graduated as a University of Guelph microbiologist in 1950. Immediately, he joined the Jordan & Ste-Michelle winery. During his lifetime career, he has become perhaps the finest vintner of sherries and ports in Canada. But, like Haynes, he has had to be flexible. He recalls his early career: "I was the chemist, I was the production manager, I fermented the wines, I did monthly inventories. You did everything but sweep the floor, and sometimes you swept the floor. You grew up with the business."

Anderson became Jordan's chief winemaker so quickly because, six months after he joined the winery, the enologist with the associated Danforth winery, Ralph Crowther, resigned to become a scientist at the Vineland experimental station. With J.H.L. Truscott, Crowther later developed an accelerated method for making flor sherry that has been widely adopted by wineries. The Canadian wine consumer, during the first decade or so of Anderson's career, primarily bought fortified wines – port- and sherry-type wines made chiefly from three native grape varieties, the concord, niagara and agawam. "You could produce with those varieties excellent sherries and ports if you processed them properly, put them into small forty-gallon oak barrels at the proper time," Anderson learned. "You had to know what you were doing, but if you did it right and got it out of the wood at the right time and aged it six or seven years, you could produce excellent sherries and ports.'' At one time, Jordan had between twelve and thirteen thousand oak barrels for aging fortified wines. Most of them had come from a Seagram distillery where they had been used for aging spirits. Today, the winery in St. Catharines has only about a thousand barrels for aging fortified wine, an indication of how far the demand for those wines has dropped. The winery's premium port no longer has a general listing in liquor stores; the premium cream sherry, however, is still selling reasonably well, and is still made in the classic way, by blending sherries up to eight years old. One of Anderson's finest achievements is the winery's Reserve Rare Canadian Sherry, a creamy wine based on de chaunac grapes and blended from vintages ranging from 1967 to 1980.

Like Haynes, Anderson also had to be a versatile winemaker. In 1953 the winery decided to upgrade its carbonated sparkling wine and produce instead a bottle-fermented champagne, blended from catawba and delaware grapes. This was released both in a pink and a white version, and for a long time the pink outsold the white. The owners of the winery at that time, the Torno family, asked Anderson to produce a dry Brut champagne. It was way ahead of most consumers, and didn't sell. ''The Tornos drank it with their friends,'' Anderson said. In the early sixties, Anderson made a crackling rosé that for a time was one of Jordan's best-selling wines. He remembers it for another reason: he was rewarded $100 for suggesting the name – Valley Crackling Rosé – inspired by the nearby Jordan Valley.

Canadian-born winemakers such as Edwin Haynes and William Anderson remain in the minority in the Canadian wine industry. There are only a few other active Canadian-born winemakers. Edward Arnold, who later became the president of Bright's, has a food science degree from the University of British Columbia. Robert Claremont, who made wine at the St. Julian winery and at Calona before buying his own estate winery, is a microbiologist from the University of Guelph. Their small numbers reflect both the short wine tradition of this country and the lack of a school of enology. Typically, Canadians working as winemakers have been trained as chemists, as in Haynes's case, microbiologists, as in Anderson's, or food technologists. The tradition has persisted, with the chemistry department at Brock University in St. Catharines graduating several of the more recent winemakers, among them Inniskillin's Austrian-born Karl Kaiser and Chateau-Gai's Polish-born Mira Ananicz. These days, however, the net is being cast wider. Almost the entire winemaking team at Andrés in Winona comes from the Univeristy of California's renowned enology school at Davis. Nearly all the winemakers at Jordan & Ste-Michelle Cellars have graduated from German enology schools, usually the one at Geisenheim. Walter Gehringer, for several years assistant winemaker at Andrés in British Columbia, was the first Canadian-born student to graduate from Geisenheim, an achievement all the more impressive because he had a poor command of written German when he began his studies.

There are comparatively few French-trained winemakers working in Canada, though one of them, Paul Bosc of Chateau des Charmes, is among the most exciting winemakers in the country today. Italian-schooled winemakers are found in the Quebec wineries; as well, Colio Wines at Harrow, in southwestern Ontario, has Carlo Negri, whose competent wines have beome prize winners and who has even made a good wine with the reviled concord grape. And one South American is making wine in the Canadian industry today: Chilean Hernan Gras, winemaker at Bright's since 1973. He was born in Chile in 1946, the son and grandson of grape growers. He majored in enology at the University of Chile, but political instability in his homeland in the early seventies led him to cut short a winemaking career and immigrate to Canada, where, he has admitted, "I didn't even know they produced wine." Early in 1973, Gras was interviewed by Bright's shrewd veteran director of research, George Hostetter. Although Bright's then had no need for a winemaker, Hostetter was impressed by Gras's willingness, and moreso by his training: Gras's university thesis had been on malolactic fermentation, a technique for reducing acidity in wines and thus a most useful skill in a Canadian winery. Gras spent five years in viticultural research at Bright's until he was promoted to winemaker in 1978.

Gras believes winemaking is a mix of technology and artistic expression. The challenge of winemaking is particularly involved at a large, old winery such as Bright's, where a large part of the cooperage still is wood. It is not easy to maintain wooden tanks, Gras agrees, "but if you want to produce good wine, you have to have some wood. It's part of the life of a wine." Wood cooperage, usually made either from oak or redwood, is used almost exclusively for red wines, which are mellowed as they mature because of the minimal exchange of air through the pores of the wood.

Other winemakers do not share Gras's traditional view, however. Those at the large Andrés winery at Winona, for example, keep nearly all their wines, except sherries, in stainless steel tanks. These are easier to sterilize, and wines can be produced in a fresher, fruitier style because the tanks, which do not "breathe" as wood does, nearly eliminate exposure of wines to air. The wineries of Quebec also are committed almost totally to stainless steel or fibreglass tanks that make wines for early consumption, using oak chips when wood flavour is required. Small oak barrels, about fifty gallons in capacity, are used for maturing premium table wines, such as the chardonnays made by Paul Bosc and Karl Kaiser. The subtle flavour of oak, carefully modulated, adds considerable complexity to such wines.

What sets a Canadian winemaker apart is the remarkable versatility demanded of him. "You name it, we produce it," Gras has said. Several examples display the breadth of winemaking skill required of Gras. In 1980 the winery claimed to be the first in Canada to employ commercially the technique of carbonic maceration used in Burgundy to make, among other wines, the beaujolais nouveau, which can be consumed within six weeks of the vintage. The winemaker, rather than crushing the grapes, puts them whole in an enclosed tank and then crushes them only after they have begun to ferment. The Bright's gamay nouveau, a soft and very grapy wine not unlike a young beaujolais, is the result: a wine meant to be consumed within a few months. At least four other Canadian wineries have since produced similar wines.

The second example is a wine with only 5 per cent alcohol, Club Spritz, produced in 1982 in response to the growing interest in so-called light, or low-calorie, wines. Club Spritz is a blend of white wine and effervescent mineral water, a deceptively difficult technical achievement, since the winemaker at vintage must be certain to produce a wine sufficiently flavourful to allow it to be diluted.

As well, Gras and Hostetter have together resolved one of the more vexing problems facing Canadian vineyards: how to use the surplus production of red grapes when consumer demand has swung to white wines. At Bright's, red-skinned and red-fleshed de chaunac grapes are crushed, and the liquid passed through activated carbon filters, yielding a juice with only the slightest blush. As much as 50 000 gallons a year are produced, serving as a blending base for Bright's highly successful House Wine, a generic in which Gras takes particular pride. His personal favourites among his wines include a dry red table wine, baco noir, made from a clone of that hybrid grape selected specially by Hostetter in 1955, and arguably the best red Bright's offers. "We have the resources," Gras says. "If we don't produce good wine, it's our fault."

If any winery has the resources, it is Andrés. Edwin Haynes, when he joined the winery near the end of his career, was impressed that there were no "hidebound" notions among the youthful team. David Hojnoski, the winery manager at Winona since 1979, agrees with Haynes's assessment. "When I came to Andrés, I found there was not much tradition but a unique and different approach to the market." Hojnoski previously spent fourteen years at Gold Seal, a New York winery founded in 1865 and for most of its history run by French-born and trained enologists; Hojnoski was its first American-born winemaker.

Andrés held more than a few surprises for Hojnoski, one of them being the production of wines with less than 7 per cent alcohol, such as Baby Duck. Hojnoski thought it was risky, and he was right. First, alcohol levels of about 9 or 10 per cent inhibit bacterial spoilage, whereas there are many hardy spoilage organisms capable of functioning at lower levels, expecially if the wines are nourishingly sweet. Second, low-alcohol wines are inherently unstable, since alcohol is an important part of a wine's skeleton, keeping it fresh and clean-tasting. These risks are overcome at Andrés – and other modern wineries – by maintaining the cleanliness standards of a medical ward. As soon as fermentation ends, the young wines are "cleaned up" – passed through centrifuges and filters to remove unwanted solid matter and remaining yeast cells – and then kept under aseptic conditions in stainless steel tanks. Just before bottling, they are filtered through ultrafine membranes to eliminate any microbes or yeast cells that might still remain. In traditional winemaking, the wines clarify naturally by gravity over a matter of months, assisted only by gentle fining or by filtration. This is, as Hojnoski and fellow vintner Barry Poag recognize, a period of risk which they prefer to eliminate by cleaning the wines quickly. Theirs is state-of-the-art winemaking.

Winemakers have other methods of ensuring that their products remain stable on liquor store shelves. At the small but modern Corelli winery near Montreal, Carmine Saccareccia sends his wines through a pasteurizing cycle, relying on heat to kill microbes and yeast. Other wineries add the chemical potassium sorbate to inhibit spoilage. The stakes are high: Inniskillin once had to refilter and rebottle an entire vintage of seyval blanc when proteins in the wine began casting a harmless but cloudy sediment. All methods to combat spoilage are effective, but Hojnoski argues that Andrés's cold sterile bottling best preserves fresh, clean flavours. Andrés has also led in the application of technology to cold stabilization, a process that corrects a problem peculiar to high-acid wines: their tendency to precipitate some of that acidity as harmless crystals of tartrate, sometimes called "wine diamonds" and frequently mistaken by consumers for either undissolved sugar or, worse, glass fragments. These crystals are perhaps the most common cause for the return of wines from consumers and liquor boards, which is why wineries prefer to eliminate them before they occur. One solution is to induce the tartrates to change chemically from potassium tartrate to sodium tartrate, the latter remaining dissolved in the wine. But this also increases the sodium content of wines to a level unacceptable to sodium-sensitive consumers. The preferred method, most commonly used in Canadian wineries, is to chill the wines to slightly below the freezing point: the tartrate then crystallizes and falls to the bottom of the storage tank. Cold stabilization, as this method is called, can be done as simply as leaving the winery's cellar doors open during a typical Canadian winter, letting nature do the freezing. The equipment at Andrés, said to be the first such installation in North America, chills the wines until crystals of ice form. The tartrates are then removed by centrifuges. The whole operation takes ninety minutes and assures that no wine diamonds will appear in a bottle.

Large Canadian wineries – and this also is true of large wineries anywhere – are "market driven," a phrase coined by Dr. Allan Jackson, director of technical services for Chateau-Gai. The wines they produce are those that they believe to be in demand by consumers, rather than wines that are the personal statements of their winemakers. While every winery does produce limited quantities and sometimes large quantities of distinctive "personal statement" wines, winemakers for the most part devote enormous effort to the art of blending the finished wines until they are acceptable to the market.

Blending is perhaps the real art in a large commercial winery. At the big Andrés winery in Winona, winemaker Barry Poag, a University of Guelph microbiologist, stores separately the wines made from each of the grape varieties with which he works: each generic brand is produced by blending various wines chosen from this inventory, with a fresh lot of a particular brand blended every three or four months. This blending strategy allows the winery to respond flexibly to changes in consumer demand. Perhaps more importantly, it is easier for the blender to achieve a consistent character in a generic wine by making several fresh lots throughout the year, rather than producing the entire year's supply at once. All wines change character as they mature: to compensate for such changes among the various wines, the blender must vary the proportions of wines in a blend each time a new one is made up, but always with the aim of a consistent final product. Since wines made from the elvira grape, for example, become heavier in flavour as they mature, the winemaker will likely add less to blends as his stock of elvira ages. In any event, most of the popular blends sold by Canadian wineries have not been produced for aging, since they are generally consumed within months of being released from the wineries.

Vintners at the major wineries spend so much time blending proprietary wines that their handiwork with specialty wines frequently is overlooked. Andrés's Barry Poag is pleased "to be able to show the consumer that a large commercial enterprise has the ability to produce high quality wines." Indeed, some such wines are never sold: Andrés produced a 1979 chardonnay blanc de blancs sparkling wine served only on special occasions in the winery and to winery guests.

TRIAL AND ERROR:
VITICULTURE IN CANADA

In 1860 Count J. M. De Courtenay sought the government of Lower Canada's support for ambitious trials both of grapes and silk-growing near Quebec City; he was rejected, but he was, perhaps, the country's first grape grower to request a subsidy. The French-born nobleman then moved to Cooksville, in Upper Canada, and established his forty-acre Clair House vineyard, where he wrote his pamphlet *The Canada Vine Grower: How every farmer in Canada may plant a vineyard and make his own wine.* The count, whose Clair House claret was compared favourably to beaujolais at an 1867 Paris wine exposition, was also one of the first to warn growers against planting native North American labrusca, for they produced a wine "of a very disagreeable flavour."

Perhaps because his winery failed, his advice was ignored. In 1927 the Horticultural Research Institute of Ontario at Vineland, Canada's leading grape breeding station, was only recommending three labrusca grapes – concord, niagara and worden – and kept them on the recommended list until 1963. As recently as 1979, when the more daring growers already were planting vinifera, or European, grape varieties, an HRIO pamphlet for growers, *The Grape in Ontario,* barely mentioned them. There never has been any doubt that vinifera, though challenging to grow, produce superior table wines. But the conservative government grape specialists always have hesitated to advise equally conservative farmers to risk their vineyards and their livelihoods on vinifera. John Vielvoye, a viticulturist with the British Columbia government, has argued: "The industry experience on vinifera has been mixed, to say the least. It is an area where some growers are taking an enormous risk."

The risk became apparent to the vinifera growers in the Niagara Peninsula in 1980. That fall, they had harvested 884 tons of grapes, double the previous year's vinifera vintage, and a further increase was expected the next vintage. However, on Christmas Eve the temperature snapped from safely above freezing to damage levels: −26°C at the Vineland station. Temperatures during the following three weeks continued to roller-coaster between thawing and freezing. In the 1981 vintage the vinifera growers considered themselves lucky to harvest 793 tons: they had expected a bigger setback.

Neither Vineland's grape expert, Dr. Helen Fisher, nor her retired predecessor, Ollie Bradt, were surprised at such setbacks, for the scientists always have been cautious about vinifera, even those that flourish in German winters almost as cold. Since 1913 Vineland has sought to breed varieties that combine the winter-hardy and disease-resistant qualities of native varieties with the winemaking qualities of classic European grapes. The Summerland research station in British Columbia recently has striven for the same objective. Canada's new group of European-trained winemakers have chafed at the challenge of making world-class table wines with grape varieties more noted for their growth habits than for the wines they produce. However, most growers, and for good reason, also prefer vineyards planted to low-risk vines. Christmas Eve 1980 was not an isolated incident.

The Horticultural Research Institute of Ontario started in 1906 at the aptly named postal station of Vineland on a farm donated by a wealthy native son, M. F. Rittenhouse. The initial grape program aimed at producing tough-skinned table grapes, capable of being shipped by rail to the prairies and by sea to Britain and arriving in sound condition. The research changed direction during Ontario's Prohibition when, because wine was the only legal alcoholic beverage, growers clamoured for wine grape varieties for their doubling vineyard acreage until wine demand and grape prices collapsed in the thirties. It is difficult to produce successful new varieties: HRIO made 57 000 crosses during its first thirteen years of grape-breeding and ultimately disposed of every one of the plants. The more modest second phase during the next eight years saw only 2119 crosses made, of which 131 were evaluated for a further period until, in 1961, one – a port and sherry grape called Veeport – was released for commerical planting.

In the years between the wars, the conservative Vineland scientists were constantly under pressure from amateur horticulturists to test new vinifera varieties. One such gadfly was the Reverend Paul Crath who, in 1925, brought cuttings back to Canada from the Ukraine. Included was a black grape called the Vatican. The cuttings were from the vineyard of an Italian prisoner of war who had laboured in the Papal gardens and, on repatriation, took home two vines. The Reverend, who cultivated his vines in Toronto, urged Vineland in 1938 to import for trials a number of hardy plants from the Ukraine, including grapes and walnuts. Another pair who prodded Vineland were Italian-born St. Catharines grape grower Joe Violante and his Bulgarian partner, Constantine Styanoff Kerimoff. They made such extravagant claims for their Bulgarian vines that the Ontario minister of agriculture referred the matter to E. Frank Palmer, director of the HRIO from 1916 to 1957. Although Palmer had earlier told Crath that of the forty vinifera varieties Vineland had previously tested, none was found commercially viable, he did agree to test the Bulgarian vines, but, clearly exasperated, warned his minister there was "no particular reason to believe that this further attempt to grow vinifera grapes in eastern North America would be any more successful than the many attempts of the past 300 years. However, this is an experimental station ..."

Vineland's research was set back by World War II, during which delivery of hybrid vines from French breeders was prevented. When these vines again began arriving after the war, research work was assigned to Ollie Bradt, a 1938 graduate of the Guelph agricultural college, and the son of a respected St. Catharines agricultural field man for the province. In short order, he set the station's breeding program on the course it was to follow beyond his 1978 retirement: sparing use of vinifera, but considerable breeding among the French hybrids and in combination with HRIO's hardy 1929–37 crosses. With the single exception of Veeport, the result of a 1929 cross, every one of the eight varieties, including three table grapes, released commercially by Vineland has had at least one French hybrid vine in its parentage.

Since 1913 Vineland has tested perhaps 100 000 seedlings to yield these commercial varieties, demonstrating the difficulty of creating acceptable new grapes. Some of those crosses continue to be evaluated, either by Vineland or by stubborn growers such as Hillebrand Estates's Joe Pohorly, who is propagating one white variety which he proposes be named Veebradt in honour of the scientist. (All

Vineland's commercially released crosses, as a matter of policy, have the prefix Vee in their names.)

The research station's progress has, however, been hindered by abrupt changes in the wine market. Prior to the mid-sixties, most domestic wines were sweet or fortified, styles which demanded little of the grape varieties beyond productivity. Next there was a thirst for table wines: first for reds and then, when Canadian vineyards were committed chiefly to red grapes, for whites. Wineries and growers scrambled to keep pace with consumer tastes. Not surprisingly, Vineland's first commercial release, the Veeport, was aimed at port production while the next release, the Vincent, was a red wine grape. But the three wine grapes released in the late seventies all have been white varieties.

Bradt was trying to keep up, not only with his crosses but also with his test plots. A fifty-vine mother block of seyval blanc was first planted at Vineland's thirty-five acre vineyard in 1950, but there was no significant demand for the vines for another twenty years. Then, almost overnight, this French hybrid variety, distantly related to the classic chardonnay grape, became the most rapidly planted new white grape variety in Ontario and a leading grape in the revival of south-western Ontario's historic vineyards.

This region's first commercial vineyard was planted in 1866 on Pelee Island in Lake Erie. Within two years, the growers had formed the original Vin Villa Vineyards winery and began making award-winning wines which encouraged an industry to develop in south-western Ontario. By 1900 Essex County, with more than 1700 acres under vine, was the province's third most important grape-growing county after Lincoln and Wentworth in the Niagara. Ontario had thirty-five operating wineries at the turn of the century, twenty-three of them in the southwest. Then, in 1897, tariffs against imported raw tobacco sparked a boom in tobacco farming in southwest Ontario; less-profitable grapes were quickly pushed aside. By 1914 fewer than three hundred acres of vineyard remained, and a decade later, when U.S. Prohibition had wiped out the export market for southwestern Ontario wines, only fifty acres remained.

The revival came only in 1973. Attracted by the southwest's longer growing season, Grimsby grower Ronald Moyer planted eighty acres, mostly to French hybrids. Alan Eastman, a third-generation fruit farmer at Blenheim, began converting his farm to grapes, again mostly hybrids, and eventually opened the Charal winery. Subsequently, Austrian-born Walter Strehn re-established plantings on Pelee Island, a flat and fertile expanse given over mostly to soybeans. At the University of Guelph, a report of the land resource science department surveys other potential vineyard sites. The revival has been given a further push both by Bright's decision to open an experimental plot in the southwest and by the employment of a professional viticulturist at the federal research station at Harrow.

In British Columbia, the pioneer of commercial wine grapes was a Kelowna rose-grower named Jesse Willard Hughes, who in 1926 planted a vineyard at Okanagan Mission, on the east side of Okanagan Lake and still one of the valley's best sites. He contracted his grapes to Growers Wines of Victoria for a reported $100 a ton. In 1932 he sent a trial shipment to the Jordan winery in Ontario, which was pleased with the higher sugar levels of the western fruit, but preferred to buy grapes in Ontario for $40 a ton. Hughes's varieties included a blue labrusca hybrid, the bath, cuttings for which came from the New York State experimental station at Geneva. The bath, which matures to higher sugars than the concord, was once the Okanagan's second most widely planted red variety after de chaunac. Since the labrusca flavours make it suitable primarily for sweet reds and fortified wines, it is no longer in favour.

While Hughes was playing it safe with labrusca vines, the case for vinifera was made by two Hungarian brothers who had arrived in the Okanagan in the early twenties. Dr. Eugene Rittich, later the winemaker at Growers from 1935 to 1957, and his brother, Virgil, both had European vineyard experience. Their first vineyard site in 1930 at Black Mountain, north of Kelowna, was at two-thousand-feet elevation and prone to frost. However, the frost helped single out the hardier of their fifty European vines, which they later planted in their commercial plot at Ellison, also north of Kelowna. Among these varieties were müller-thurgau, sylvaner, chardonnay, chasselas, two muscats and two Hungarian varieties, the excellent and the perle of csaba, all whites; there was one promising red, the blauburgunder, a German variant on pinot noir. The brothers believed the trick to growing vinifera successfully in the Okanagan was to bury them each fall beneath a protective covering of earth. The practice, still in occasional use in Canadian vineyards, is effective but troublesome and expensive.

In 1940, when it became known that both Vineland and New York's Geneva Park station intended to import hybrid vines from France, Virgil Rittich argued that these varieties already were known in France as producers of "disappointing" wines, and reiterated his belief that "the Okanagan Valley is not only perfectly suitable for European grape growing, but its climate is in many respects superior to most of the vine-growing countries of middle Europe."

Like Vineland, the Summerland research station north of Penticton, which was established in 1905, has had trial grape plots that include vinifera. A test with about 150 varieties, which started in 1931, was wound up in frustration in 1945. A decade later, Dr. Donald Fisher, then Summerland superintendent, acquired seventy new test varieties, including hybrids and such vinifera as gamay, pinot noir and pinot blanc. The hybrids – among them foch, de chaunac and verdelet – proved to be much more productive and disease-resistant, and the wineries began to recommend them. They flourished alongside the locally developed Okanagan riesling, which is now the best-adapted and most widely planted white in British Columbia.

The Okanagan riesling is seldom a winemaker's favourite grape: Karl Kaiser of Ontario's Inniskillin sneers that "it stinks." But its productive reliability was a boon to the Okanagan wineries when, in the late seventies, a consumer demand for white wines exploded. A decade earlier, the growers, on the advice of wineries and government, had committed their vineyards to two-thirds red grapes, one-third white, and nearly all of them indifferent hybrids. Now the industry needed the reverse ratio, along with better quality hybrids and certainly vinifera as well. The Okanagan had only to look two hundred miles south to Washington's vinifera vineyards to see how far British Columbia was lagging. In 1974 the provincial Department of Agriculture – prodded by earlier vinifera trials at Casabello – secured from Washington four thousand cuttings, comprising eight different vinifera varieties. The survivors of the bitter winter of 1978–79 were johannisberg riesling, chenin blanc and gewurztraminer.

What may be a turning point in Okanagan grape growing occurred in 1976. Dr. Helmut Becker, long-time director of grape research at the Geisenheim Institute on the Rhine, detoured through the valley after a consultation in Washington. Fond of saying that Winnipeg lies on the same latitude as Geisenheim, Becker assured his Canadian hosts that German grapes would flourish in the Okanagan, and offered grower George Heiss a test selection. Heiss, who was planning the Gray Monk winery, turned the offer over to the entire industry. So began an eight-year trial of Geisenheim vinifera grapes in test plots in both the north and south ends of the hundred-mile-long Okanagan Valley. Among those varieties which now show most promise are three white grapes, the scheurebe, ehrenfelser and kerner. A host of other vinifera are under test, either as extensions of the Becker project or in daring private ventures. For example, Indian-owned Inkameep Vineyards at Oliver has plots of at least a dozen obscure varieties, including a temperamental Russian vine called matsvani. Serious commercial winemaking tests with those grapes were begun during the 1982 vintage by John Bremmer of Bright's, with as few as one hundred bottles produced of some varieties.

Clearly, vinifera will grow in Canada. The various plant diseases and the insects which previously devastated the plantings today can be controlled, and the most winter-hardy have been identified – the johannisberg riesling is perhaps the most hardy, one reason why it is more widely planted than any other vinifera in Canada. The meticulous growers have begun to succeed with other such vinifera as chardonnay and gewurztraminer. No red vinifera has yet shown much promise, though there is some hope for the pinot noir and its tougher genetic cousins from Germany. But in the main, the Canadian vineyards are given over to French hybrid grapes. The hybrids invariably give a higher per-acre yield than the vinifera and are more reliable producers generally. In their own sensible interests, growers prefer the comparative security of hybrids to the perceived risk of vinifera. Some hybrids, as Rittich observed, do make disappointing wine, but others – notably seyval blanc, vidal and verdelet among the whites, and chancellor and baco noir among the reds – can make satisfying, even excellent wines. Because the hybrids are generally not vinified as varietals anywhere else in the world, except in the eastern United States, the wines have novel flavours that reward serious exploration by the student and drinker of wine.

PART IV

PART IV
WINE GUIDE

TO THE READER

Recommending wines for an audience one has not met is at least as difficult as picking neckties for other people. The reader should always remember that these notes are not graven in stone: it is the right of any individual, and indeed it is his duty, to drink what most pleases him.

Your favourite wine may not be on this list. While this usually means it was not one of the author's favourites, there are other reasons for omission. The least expensive generic blends are often part of a family of blends from a winery, having a package or a name in common and little to distinguish them beyond degree of sweetness. There comes a point at which the palate tires. This has been especially so in my case with the inexpensive, sweet red table wines, cloying to the regular wine consumer's palate and declining in market share. Although these have generally not been tasted, I recognize that they still bring pleasure to thousands.

Many of the best wines are available only in the province of production. Although most provincial liquor boards are prepared to order case lots from other provinces, the cost can be discouraging.

The wines are ranked. Any wine receiving at least *one glass* is sufficiently interesting to be singled out from the crowd; *two-glass* wines have begun to combine quality and good value, and those marked with *three glasses* are exceptional achievements. These rankings, of course, are subjective, a matter of personal choice with which there can certainly be disagreement.

Finally, it is as well to remember that wines are not scored against any particular set of imports. They are ranked as Canadian wines, not as Montrachets or Moselles: the soils, climates, grapes and wineries here combine to produce wines that are distinctive and on occasion distinguished in character, but they are not European wines.

Included immediately below is a list of the principal wine grapes used in Canada. Most commercial table wines are simply generic or brand-name blends from a variety of grapes, designed to be consistent over time in taste and quality. But when a bottle of Canadian wine bears on its label the name of the predominant grape from which it is made – such as vidal or chardonnay or de chaunac – it may well be of better than average quality. More to the point, the varietal name on the label is a helpful guide to consumers. The alert wine drinker soon discovers that all well-made johannisberg rieslings have a lovely floral aroma and a fresh, fruity character, qualities derived from the grape itself. If that character becomes a consumer's favourite, he soon learns to seek out such wines. Much of the needless confusion about wine drinking disappears once a consumer begins noting which grapes he prefers consistently and which he does not.

THE GRAPES

Agawam

An American hybrid once common in Ontario vineyards, now being replaced, used primarily in sweet whites, where its high degree of fruitiness is desirable.

Aurore

An early-maturing vine planted in Ontario and New York, somewhat neutral in flavour, and used in dry and medium-dry white blends. A good example is Charal's Chandelle Blanc, a blend of aurore and french colombard.

Auxerrois

A vinifera variant of pinot blanc that makes crisp, dry white wines with attractive, fruity bouquets. Good examples are made by Chateau des Charmes in Ontario and Gray Monk (as pinot auxerrois) in British Columbia.

Bacchus

A German vinifera cross that powerfully expresses the muscat characteristics of its ancestry; used in German-style dessert wines. A good example is made by Gray Monk.

Baco Noir

This French hybrid was one of the first planted on a commercial scale in Canada; it yields full-bodied, robust, dry red wines that age well, perhaps because there is cabernet sauvignon in its background. A good example is made by Bright's from grapes grown from a clone specially selected in 1955 by George Hostetter, the winery's research chief.

Cabernet Sauvignon

A late-maturing, red vinifera that produces some of the world's greatest wines. The Canadian climate is unkind to it: Bright's re-planted its Niagara-region cabernet vines three times in twelve years because of frost. Sumac Ridge in British Columbia has a small plot growing carefully next to a heat-reflective rock face, and even then expects the fruit to ripen adequately only one year in three.

Catawba

A variety native to eastern North America, it was important fifty years ago when its strong, grapy flavours were well suited for fortified wines and medicinal, Prohibition-era wines.

Chancellor

A Seibel hybrid brought to New York from France in 1939, but propagated only modestly in Canada, where it has proved too suscep- tible to mildew for Niagara but does well in the drier Okanagan. Its genealogy includes cabernet and alicante, and the wines are claret- style reds with modest aging potential. Good examples are Calona's richly-oaked vintages and the lighter vintages from Sumac Ridge and Chateau-Gai.

Chardonnay

One of the world's outstanding white wine grapes. Vines are moder- ately hardy, light producers and subject to mildew, but the wines are elegant and dry, and capable of gaining power with three or four years' bottle-aging. Bright's 1955 pinot champagne and 1956 pinot chardon- nay (as the grape sometimes is called) were the first commercial vinifera from a major Canadian winery. Notable examples are made by Chateau des Charmes, Inniskillin, Bright's, Charal, Chateau-Gai, Casabello and Sumac Ridge. The grape is also used in champagne- style wines: examples include Inniskillin blanc de blancs, Podamer blanc de blancs and Bright's brut.

Chasselas

A high-yielding, early-maturing white grape notable for low acidity and common in Swiss vineyards; the wine is relatively neutral and easy to drink. Uniacke's style is dry and nutty.

Chelois (Seibel 10878)

Phillip Wagner has suggested that the reds from this hybrid hint of Burgundy. Grapes are grown both in Ontario and British Columbia, and the wines are usually medium-bodied with a slightly bitter finish; those made in B.C. are lighter in style. There are good examples from Inniskillin, Uniacke, Pandosy Cellers and Andrés (B.C.).

Chenin Blanc

A white vinifera made in a host of styles from dry and elegant to fruity. The variety shows promise in the Okanagan. Examples are from

Sumac Ridge, Casabello, Mission Hill, Calona, Bright's and Ste-Michelle.

Le Commandant
A dark-red grape grown chiefly to be blended for its colour.

Concord
A dark, blue-skinned labrusca grape developed in Concord, Mass., about 1849, and once the leading commercial grape in the eastern U.S. and Ontario; it is suitable only for sweet and fortified wines, never for dry table wines. An example is Colio's Fragolino, an unusual, sweet red table wine.

De Chaunac
Originally the Seibel 9549 and renamed in 1972 for the late Adhémar de Chaunac, winemaker at Bright's, this prolific red grape makes sound but, unless blended, seldom remarkable table wines. Several wineries also make a white blending wine with it. Good examples are Andrés (Ontario) de Chaunac Blanc and (B.C.) Similkameen Superior, and from Inniskillin, London and Pandosy Cellars.

Delaware
A labrusca hybrid usually used in blends and sparkling wines. A varietal example is made by London.

Dutchess
An American hybrid grape, with a genealogy that includes concord and delaware, producing fruity white, and best when young; it is also used in sparkling wines. Examples come from Inniskillin and Charal. The grape's name is not a misspelling of the title of nobility: introduced to the American Pomological Society in 1881, it was named for the New York county where it originated.

Ehrenfelser
A German hybrid cross of riesling and sylvaner that makes full-flavoured wine of lovely bouquet. Examples come from Andrés (B.C.) and Gray Monk.

Gamay
A vinifera relative of pinot noir, and *the* grape in Beaujolais country, it makes soft, fruity reds and good nouveau wines. Examples are from Inniskillin, Bright's, Chateau des Charmes and (a rosé) Chateau-Gai.

Gewurztraminer

"Gewurz" means spicy in German, and typical wines are golden-hued with a lovely spiciness in the finish; this is the wine for Chinese food. Good examples are made by Inniskillin, Mission Hill, Gray Monk, Uniacke, Calona, Bright's, Hillebrand, Sumac Ridge and Claremont.

Léon millot

A French hybrid making inky-red wines that are comparable to, but heavier than, foch. Inniskillin does a good one.

Johannisberg Riesling

A classic German vinifera, and likely the most widely planted in Canada. The best Canadian examples are slightly off-dry whites, or dessert-style wines loaded with flavour. Examples are made by Inniskillin, Chateau des Charmes, Chateau-Gai, Bright's, Barnes, Jordan & Ste-Michelle, Andrés, Uniacke, Gray Monk, Pelee Island, Calona, Charal, Vineland and Colio.

Kerner

A German vinifera hybrid making fruity white wines. Examples come from Gray Monk and Pelee Island.

Maréchal Foch

A red French hybrid, the second most widely planted in Canada; its wines are dark, with a vegetal aroma, their flavour recalling chocolate, and usually high in acid. Examples are made by Inniskillin, Grand Pré, Calona, Pandosy Cellars (Foch Nouveau) and Colio (Rosso Riserva).

Merlot

A red vinifera making soft, flavourful, dry reds, sometimes light in colour. Good examples come from Chateau-Gai and Uniacke.

Okanagan Riesling

A hybrid white of unknown ancestry, most widely planted white in B.C.; it usually makes undistinguished wines unless carefully blended or vintaged by an exceptional winemaker. Made by Sumac Ridge, Uniacke,Claremont and Pandosy Cellars (Mission Hill) as a varietal, and blended in Calona's Schloss Laderheim and Casabello's Fleur de Blanc.

Pinot Blanc

A white vinifera producing full-bodied, dry wines. Examples come from Claremont and Divino.

Pinot Gris

A vinifera producing elegantly dry whites. Gray Monk offers a good one, while Divino makes it into a rosé.

Pinot Noir

This red vinifera yields light-bodied wines capable of elegance. Examples come from Uniacke, Casabello, Mission Hill, Chateau des Charmes, Pelee Island and Inniskillin.

Rougeon

A late-maturing, red hybrid making a medium-bodied wine with spicy aroma and high acidity. Calona and Claremont offer examples.

Siegfried Rebe

A German vinifera cross, full-flavoured, with a dramatic bouquet. Reif makes a good one.

Scheurebe

A riesling-sylvaner cross producing full-flavoured, fruity whites. Andrés (B.C.) and Pelee Island have good examples.

Seyval Blanc

A white French hybrid with some chardonnay in it, and, since 1977, the most widely planted white hybrid in Ontario; the wines range from dull and heavy to crisply fresh. The best examples are made by Chateau des Charmes and Colio; others come from Inniskillin, Andrés (1982), Bright's, Montravin and Charal.

Verdelet

A late-maturing, heavy-yielding, white French hybrid widely planted in B.C. A good blender, dry, crisp and neutral on its own. Andrés and Sumac Ridge make examples.

Vidal

A white hybrid said to have trebbiano and ugni blanc in its ancestry; a good, fruity and aromatic blender and fine dessert wine. Good examples are made by Inniskillin (1983 Late Harvest Vidal), Bright's, Reif, London and Colio.

Villard Noir

A red French hybrid of minor importance; the grapes usually go into blends.

White Diamond

A labrusca hybrid used for sweet whites and fortified wines.

RED WINES

L'Acadie Rouge (Grand Pré)
> A light-textured blend of de chaunac and foch with lots of wood.
> The winemaker calls this a "spaghetti wine."

Alpenweiss Red (Chateau-Gai)
> Emulates the soft, slightly sweet, German style reds.

Auberge Red (Andrés)
> Everyday blend.

Bacaro (Divino)
> A light-bodied, dry blend. A sturdy, everyday wine.

Baco Noir 1982 Vintage Selection (Bright's Ontario)
> ♥♥ Dark red with a smoky aroma, good body, and full fruity
> flavours; finished with a clean bitter bite. The best Canadian
> example from this grape variety.

Baco Noir 1982 Late Harvest Vintage Selection (Bright's Ontario)
> ♥ Dark red wine with an intense, toasty aroma. A lower acidity
> makes it seem lighter in structure. Dry. Potential to mature
> to ♥♥.

Baco Noir 1982 (Bright's Vaseaux Cellars, B.C.)
> Ruby red, fruity, and medium-bodied: light in character.

Baco Noir (Charal)
> ♥♥ A lively colour, a complex aroma, showing some wood and
> recalling pinot noir, and a flavour that balances wood and fruit:
> good finish.

Baco Noir 1983 (Hillebrand)
> ♥ Dark red, with a smoky aroma and good fruit, but tart in the
> finish.

Baco Noir 1982 (Hillebrand)
> Ruby red, with a smoky aroma and good fruit, but tart in the
> finish.

Baco Noir 1983 (Inniskillin)

　♟♟　Dark red with a fresh, berry-like fruit which will appeal to beaujolais fanciers.

Baco Noir 1983 (London)

　♟♟　A dark-red wine with an attractive aroma that recalls cinnamon: will develop well with three or four years' cellar-aging.

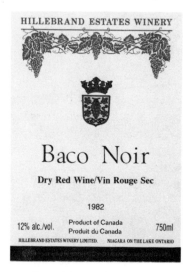

Baco Noir 1981 (London)

An award-winner for London in a U.S. competition, this ruby red has a grassy bouquet: light-bodied and dry, with the typically bitter hybrid finish.

Le Baron Rouge (Hillebrand)

A bright red blend of foch, de chaunac, le commandant, and villard noir, loaded with fruit flavours: soft and well-balanced.

Bellevista de Chaunac (London)

A dry, light-bodied red.

Brae Rouge (Inniskillin)

　♟　A mellow generic blend, based on de chaunac, and known formerly as Vin Nouveau.

Burgon Rouge (Casabello)

A blend of B.C. and Washington grapes: medium dry.

Burgonay (Casabello)
> The bone-dry version of this winery's Burgon.

Burgundy (Mission Hill)
> Ruby red, this wine is an effective blend of young and mature wines, soft on the palate and dry.

Caberneaux (Geloso)
> A medium-bodied dry wine of attractive, bright ruby colour and clean aroma, which Geloso has listed in several western provinces.

Cabernet/foch (Beaupré)
> A medium-bodied, light red wine with the aroma of the foch grape but a smooth finish: the cabernet in the blend is wine from South America.

Cabernet non-vintage (Divino)
> Light red in colour and light-bodied, this dry wine has a slightly musty aroma.

Cabernet Nouveau (Divino)
> Dark rose in colour, this is fresh and fruity without being as cloyingly grapy as most nouveau wines: flavour is attractively spicy.

Cabernet sauvignon 1983 (Mission Hill)
> A barrel sample reveals a dark red wine, intensely fruity and very tannic. Potential to mature to ♟♟♟ .

Cabernet sauvignon 1981 (Mission Hill)
> ♟♟♟   Dark red, with rich, vanilla-like aroma, and intensely fruity: long finish, and dry. Still slightly tannic, this wine will continue improving in the bottle to the end of the decade.

Cabernet (Andrew Wolf)
> Ruby red in colour, with a sweet, candied aroma: dry, light-bodied, and easy to drink.

Canadian Burgundy (Andrew Wolf)
> Deep red, short on aroma, but soft and full-bodied.

Canadian Burgundy (Casabello)

Based on foch grapes, this dark red is light in body with an astringent finish.

Castel 1983 (Bright's Ontario)

  ♈♈ So dark in colour that it stains the glass, this is a full, gutsy wine with a smoky aroma, a spicy note to the flavour and a long finish.

Castelnovo (Corelli)

Sold in a barolo bottle, this wine, blended from cabernet sauvignon and montepulciano musts, has been matured over oak chips to add to its bouquet and complexity: medium-bodied, with a soft finish.

Cavallo Rosso (Chateau-Gai)

Made with de chaunac grapes, this emulates the slightly astringent, Italian-style reds.

Cellar Cask Dry (Andrés)

A dry, everyday blend.

Cellar Cask Medium Dry Red (Andrés)

Sweet and grapy with a pronounced concord flavour. A big seller in Ontario.

ANDRÉS

Cellar Cask
RED WINE/VIN ROUGE

Andrés Cellar Cask Medium Dry Red Wine is a light-bodied red table wine blended from premium grapes and is the perfect wine to complement any occasion. Serve at room temperature or slightly chilled.

PRODUCT OF CANADA   Andrés Wines Ltd., Winona, Canada   PRODUIT DU CANADA

11.5% alc./vol.   2L

Chambord (Secrestat)

Dry, full-bodied, with a nutty aroma, and the slightly caramelized flavours typical of wines from concentrates.

Chambourcin 1983 (Andrés Ontario)

Dark red, full-bodied wine with an aroma recalling tobacco; intensely fruity and well-balanced. A potential ♟♟ if released by the winery.

Chancellor 1982 (Calona)

♟♟♟ A dark red of richly fruity aroma: full-bodied, the wood well balanced by the wine's intense brambleberry flavour, and with a lingering finish. Outstanding.

Chancellor 1981 (Calona)

♟♟♟ A well-balanced, lean and elegant wine, with enough wood-aging to add complexity.

Chancellor 1983 (Casabello)

Light red in colour, this is a light-bodied, fresh and dry wine, lacking in complexity.

Chancellor 1982 (Chateau-Gai Lincoln County)

♟♟ Dark with a complex, somewhat grassy aroma, this wine still is young, tannic and developing in the bottle: begin opening after 1986.

Chancellor (Sumac Ridge)

♟♟ Dry and soft in texture. Future vintages may have some time in oak, and be more complex.

Chandelle Rouge (Charal)

Light-bodied, dry and fruity: blended from de chaunac and villard noir.

Chateau de Lyons Red (Montravin)

Comparable to **Concerto Red**.

Chelois 1983 (Andrés Ontario)

♟ A dark red, robust flavour, with a smoky aroma.

Chelois 1981 (Inniskillin)

    ❦   Light in colour and light in texture: tart, with a bitter finish. This wine needs three or four years' bottle-aging to develop.

Chelois (Jordan & Ste-Michelle Ontario)

    Dry and typically light in colour, with a musty overtone to the flavour.

Chelois (Mission Hill/Pandosy)

    Light red, with a delicate, fruity aroma: soft and round in texture.

Chevalier Rouge 1981 (Hillebrand)

    ❦   Made primarily from foch, this dark wine, full-bodied with an attractive aroma, has the slightly bitter finish typical of the varietal.

Concerto Red (Montravin)

    A dark-red, somewhat neutral wine with a crisp, astringent finish in the Italian style.

Cour Rouge (Chateau des Charmes)

    ❦   Dark red, robust and dry.

Cuvée d'Amour (Grand Pré)

   ♟♟♟   A dark, tannic wine with great potential, recalling a good Italian barolo, but made from the Russian michurnitz grape.

Cuvée des Moines de l'Abbaye (Verdi)

   A fruity wine with 10 per cent alcohol, based on the grenache grape: a lively red colour, and chillable.

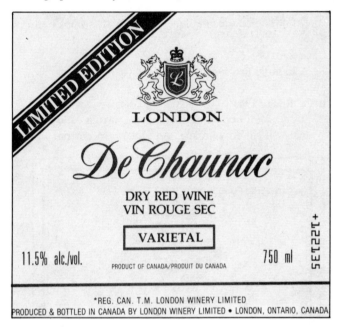

De chaunac 1983 Limited Edition (Barnes)

   ♟♟   A dark red wine with a dramatic, fruity aroma, soft texture and long, lingering taste.

De chaunac 1982 Vintage Selection (Bright's)

   A fresh, fruity, ruby-red wine, dry but slightly tart in the finish.

De chaunac 1983 (London)

   ♟   A dark and full-bodied dry red wine with an interesting smoky aroma and rich fruit flavours.

De chaunac (Mission Hill/Pandosy)

   ♟   Bright red, with a jammy aroma and medium body: fruity but with a firm finish, and dry.

Domaine D'Or Red (Andrés)
>Light-bodied, fruity and sharp.

Dry Red (Mission Hill)
>Dark ruby red, this is a simple, clean red blend based on the foch grape: the finish is a bit tart.

Durnford House Red (Charal)
>A full-bodied, deep-coloured wine with a smoky aroma.

L'Entre Cote Red (Bright's)
>A light-bodied foch blend, somewhat tart.

Etienne Brûlé Rouge 1983 (Hillebrand)
>❦ A dark, full-bodied red with fruity flavours and a bitter finish that will soften with age. An Ontario bicentennial blend.

Fragolino 1980 (Colio)
>❦ A sweet, slightly crackling red made entirely from concord grapes. Not to everyone's taste, but a remarkably well-made example of a labrusca wine.

Gala Italian Red (Casabello)
>The bone-dry member of the Gala family.

Gala Red Medium (Casabello)
>A medium all-purpose blend.

Gala Rich Red (Casabello)
>A sweet red blend.

Gamay beaujolais 1982 (Chateau des Charmes)
>A lively red colour, medium-bodied, but tart.

Gamay beaujolais 1981 (Chateau des Charmes)
>A soft, fruity, orange-tinted wine. Easy drinking.

Gamay Noir (Inniskillin)
>♟ A light, fresh, fruity red, enjoyable when young. It mellows with age, but should not generally be cellared for more than five years.

Gamay nouveau (Chateau des Charmes)
>♟ A soft and very fruity red, released about forty-five days after the vintage each November and meant to be consumed within the next few weeks. Admirers of the nouveau style find that Chateau des Charmes does a good example.

Haut Villages Dry Red (Calona)
>Light in colour, with a jammy aroma and a dominant, fruity foch flavour: dry and slightly tannic.

Heritage Estates Canadian Burgundy (Barnes)
>Blended from de chaunac and petite sirah, this wine is comparable to the winery's claret, with slightly more body.

Heritage Estates Canadian Claret (Barnes)
>♟ Its blend of 70 per cent foch and 30 per cent California petite sirah yields an honest, medium-bodied red: good value.

House Red (Andrés)
>Called Dinner Wine in Ontario, this is a slightly sweet, everyday red.

Interlude Red (Jordan & Ste-Michelle)
>Dark red, this grapy, soft-textured wine is clean, simple and easy to drink.

Jordan Valley Canadian Burgundy (Jordan)

A thin, dry, brick-hued wine whose flavours seem to have dried out.

Lake Country Red (Andrés)

Ruby red with a candy aroma, medium body, and slightly sweet finish.

Lasalle Notre Vin Maison Rouge (Bright's)

The Quebec blend of the winery's popular dry House Wine, this was the third largest-selling domestic red in 1982.

Léon Millot 1982 (Charal)

♀   An inky red aged in new American oak, which blends with the fruit for a complex bouquet: full-bodied and dry.

Léon Millot (Inniskillin)

♀♀   A dark, full-bodied red.

Maréchal Foch (Charal)

A dark red, with a plum-like aroma, soft and full bodied. This wine will benefit from two to three years' bottle-aging.

Maréchal Foch 1981 (Colio)

♀♀   A dark-red, dry wine with berry-like flavours and a nutty, bitter finish.

Maréchal Foch 1980 (Grand Pré)

Dark, with lots of oak character, and an astringent backbone.

Maréchal Foch (Gray Monk)

The winery's first red, this is a light-bodied, adequate, but not distinguished example of the varietal.

Maréchal Foch (Inniskillin)

♀♀   Dark, full-bodied, with a complex aroma of grapes and oak, this is a big, chewy wine and, in most vintages, the best-made varietal foch in Canada.

Maréchal Foch (Jordan & Ste-Michelle Ontario)

Dark, medium-bodied, somewhat sharp.

Maréchal Foch 1983 (London)

   ♟   A big, purple, fruity wine from a good vintage. A couple of years' bottle-aging will mute the bitter finish.

Maréchal Foch 1981 (London)

   ♟   Ruby red: a lighter, fresher and fruitier approach to this grape than most have taken.

Maréchal Foch (Mission Hill/Pandosy)

        Dark red, with a jammy but fresh aroma: a fruity, Beaujolais-style wine.

Maréchal Foch (Montravin)

   ♟   This vastly improved foch, compared with the early release under the Podamer label, is full-bodied, richly oaked, and has a long, pleasant finish.

Maréchal Foch 1983 Limited Edition (Barnes)

        Light red, fruity and tart, but capable of mellowing with age.

Maréchal Foch 1981 (Calona)

  ♟♟   Brick-red with a subtle aroma blend of fruit and vanilla: medium body, fruity flavour, and a crisp, dry finish.

Maria Christina (Jordan & Ste-Michelle)

        This blend bears a family resemblance to Toscano from the same winery, but it is noticeably sweeter and fuller-bodied. The light (low-alcohol) version is soft and medium dry and can be chilled.

Merlot 1980 (Chateau-Gai Lincoln County)

        Short on colour, this could be taken for a rosé, but it is soft, dry and fruity.

Merlot 1980 (Inniskillin)

   ♟   Light ruby colour with a strawberry aroma: dry and light in texture but with good fruit.

Merlot 1983 (Mission Hill)

        A barrel sample reveals a purple wine, intensely fruity and very tannic. Potential to mature to ♟♟♟ .

Millot-Chambourcin 1980 (Inniskillin)

❦   A dark, full-bodied wine with a blend that gives it a bit more complexity.

Mission Hill Burgundy 1981

❦   Dark, grapy in aroma, and full-bodied, with adequate fruit: dry.

Mission Ridge Premium Dry Red

Bright in colour, with a fruity, jammy aroma: medium-bodied, full-flavoured, well-balanced and dry.

Mon Village Red (Bright's)

Light red in colour, this is a medium-bodied, somewhat neutral, dry, claret-style wine.

Mountain Red (Calona)

Everyday red.

La Nuit d'Amour (Verdi)

A pleasantly soft-textured dry wine of good fruitiness.

La Nuit Volage (Lubec)

A dry red.

Pinot Noir 1982 (Casabello)

Made from Washington State grapes, with typical pinot noir lightness in colour and texture, but subtle, fruity bouquet.

Pinot Noir 1978 (Casabello)

Light in colour and body, this red made from Washington State grapes is now past maturity.

Pinot Noir 1982 (Chateau des Charmes)

ΥΥΥ   A surprising, dark red colour, and good minty/oaky nose and flavours: well-balanced. This wine will develop well in the bottle.

Pinot Noir 1981 (Mission Hill)

ΥΥΥ   Unusually dark for the variety, with a rich, toasty aroma: soft, full-bodied and fruity.

Pinot Noir 1981 (Uniacke)

Υ   Almost as light in colour as a rosé, this soft, fresh wine has a kiss of oak. Future vintages are worth looking for.

Plaisir Divin (Bright's Quebec)

A light-bodied, dry, ruby-red wine with a jammy aroma: for everyday drinking.

Première Rouge (Charal)
> This is a medium-bodied, dry commercial blend of foch and de chaunac.

Primeur Rouge 1982 (Chateau des Charmes)
> Blended from gamay, villard noir and pinot noir, this is a lively, fruity wine somewhat in the Beaujolais style.

Princière Rouge (Chateau-Gai)
> Very dry, ruby-coloured and light-bodied: blended primarily from French hybrids.

Red Dry (Calona)
> Everyday red.

Red Wine (Beaupré)
> Bright red with a clean foch aroma, this is a soft and fruity dry red.

Réserve à Vincent (Geloso)
> Its somewhat jammy aroma and fruitiness give this wine a slightly sweet finish, though it is reasonably dry.

Réserve du Patrimoine (Geloso)
> Orange tints suggest a mature wine, and the aroma recalls the sangiovese grape: soft, full-bodied, and one of this winery's best.

Riserva Rosso 1982 (Colio)
> ♛♛♛ Purple; complex aroma: full-bodied and fruity. Dry.

Riserva Rosso 1981 (Colio)
> ♛♛♛ Dark red, full-bodied and fruity, with a complex bouquet, blended primarily from foch, with some chelois and cabernet sauvignon. A personal favourite of the winemaker.

La Romaine Rouge (Geloso)
> A full-bodied, dry wine, and the fourth largest-selling domestic red.

Rosengarten 1983 (Reif)
> Ruby-red, this vintage is fresh, fruity and balanced.

Rosengarten 1982 (Reif)

A blend of villard noir, de chaunac and foch, this is a purple wine, with good fruit but a tart, bitter finish.

Rossini (Chantecler)

Dry, and packaged attractively in a straw-covered, Chianti-type bottle.

Rosso (Colio)

A light-bodied, simple table wine for those who prefer reds tending to the medium dry.

Rougeon 1981 (Calona)

❦❦ A dramatic, spicy, orange-peel aroma in a full-flavoured, wood-aged wine, with a crisp, slightly acidic edge. For hearty dishes.

Rougeon (Claremont)

Robust and medium-bodied, with a dramatic, spicy aroma. Aged two years in oak, this variety often benefits from being cellared in the bottle until it is five years old.

Royal Red Medium (Calona)

A medium-sweet with a labrusca tone, smooth, sweet and grapy. The top-selling Canadian red, showing the national sweet tooth.

Ste-Michelle Grande Cuvée (Jordan & Ste-Michelle)

A medium-bodied, brick-hued wine with a bitter finish.

Sentinel Rouge 1982 (Chateau des Charmes)

❦ Purple and full-bodied with a fruity bouquet, this wine is a blend of hybrids and vinifera, happily without the bitter finish typical of the red hybrid grapes.

Servino (Secrestat)

A dry red.

Severnyi (Grand Pré)

❦❦❦ Huge, dark fruity red recalling a zinfandel.

Similkameen Superior Red (Andrés B.C.)

A dry and well-made de chaunac: best when young and fresh.

Sommet Rouge (Calona)

🍷 A bright red de chaunac, with foch and some California red in the blend: aroma toasty from barrel-aging, medium-bodied, but full-flavoured and dry.

Table Ronde (Chantecler)

A semi-dry, good-selling red.

Tiffany Red (Calona)

A low-alcohol wine meant to be chilled, less interesting than its white counterpart.

Toscano Rosso (Jordan & Ste-Michelle)

Dry, and robust. The Ontario version, blended from foch, de chaunac and baco noir, is dark, somewhat light-bodied and acidic. Blended from foch, de chaunac and California vinifera, the B.C. version is softer and medium-bodied.

Tournefête Vin Rouge (Lubec)

A dry red.

Valdessa Rouge (Charal)

A dry oak-matured blend, simple and straightforward.

Vaseaux Cellars Premium Red (Bright's B.C.)

A dark red foch blend, dry and somewhat astringent.

Le Vieux Manoir (Verdi)

The same varieties blended for this winery's La Nuit – carignane, alicante, grenache and ruby cabernet – are used here to achieve a somewhat fuller-bodied dry result.

Villard Noir 1982 (Chateau-Gai Lincoln County)

🍷 Ruby red, with a smoky aroma: youthful tannins still mask the fruit. Open after 1986.

WHITE WINES

L'Acadie Blanc (Grand Pré)

❦❦❦ An outstanding white made from a Vineland-bred hybrid: gold in colour, its complex bouquet giving a hint of pineapple and new oak, and dry and tart. A wine for food.

Adagio (Barnes)

A light, fruity wine with a muscat note.

Aligoté 1983 (Bright's)

❦❦❦ Pale green with a complex, nutty aroma, this is a flinty, sophisticated wine that demands a dozen oysters to go with it.

Aligoté 1981 (Chateau des Charmes)

❦ A pale, delicate wine with a kiss of oak: dry and crisp.

Alpenweiss (Chateau-Gai)

A German-style white designed fresh and fruity, and meant to be drunk young.

Auberge White (Andrés)

Medium-bodied, sweet and grapy.

Aurore 1982 (Andrés Ontario)

❦ Glints of green, grapefruit aroma: soft and off-dry.

Aurore 1983 (Andrés Ontario)

❦ A gold-coloured wine with a dramatic, strawberry-like aroma: fruity and off-dry.

Auxerrois 1983 (Andrés B.C.)

❦❦ Greenish glints, delicate aroma: a soft, fruity white with a touch of sweetness.

Auxerrois 1981 (Chateau des Charmes)

❦❦ Pale, with an attractive bouquet of fresh hay, and herbaceous flavours: full-bodied, soft and dry, with a lingering finish.

Bacchus (Gray Monk)

♥♥   An aromatic wine from the muscat family, best sipped on its own or with a simple dessert.

Le Baron Blanc (Hillebrand)

A blend of dutchess, vidal and riesling: pale, dry and crisp.

Bianco Secco 1982 (Colio)

♥   A pale, fresh wine with a nutty finish, recalling Italian whites, even though the winemaker was working largely with de-coloured de chaunac juice.

Blanc de Blancs (Beaupré)

Pale and dry, with a fruity aroma but neutral in flavour.

Botticelli White (Andrés)

Bold, soft, sweet, 9 per cent alcohol wine: flavours are like a basket full of fresh labrusca grapes.

Brae Blanc (Inniskillin)

♥   A fruity but crisply dry blend of dutchess and premium hybrids.

Braeburn (Inniskillin)

♥   Pale, with greenish glints, this fresh, fruity wine with a flowery aroma proclaims itself dry but finishes just a touch off-dry.

Canadian Rhine Castle (Jordan & Ste-Michelle B.C.)

Slightly sweet, with a muscat aroma. The Ontario version is sugary and flabby. The winery originally wanted to label this as "liebfraumilch," but were dissuaded by German objections.

Canadian Riesling (Beaupré)

Pale, medium-dry example of Okanagan riesling, light in character.

Canadian Sauternes (Chateau-Gai)

A straw-coloured, sweet white, made with labrusca grapes, that has the typical grapy flavours and bouquet of these varieties.

Capistro (Chateau-Gai)

The first of the specially designed Canadian-made light wines, and still one of the best: fresh, fruity and a shade off-dry.

Castini Bianco (London)

> An off-dry wine, dominated by the labrusca flavour of the elvira grape.

Cellar Cask White (Andrés)

> Simple, everyday wine in a bag-in-box. **Cellar Cask Reserve** is somewhat drier.

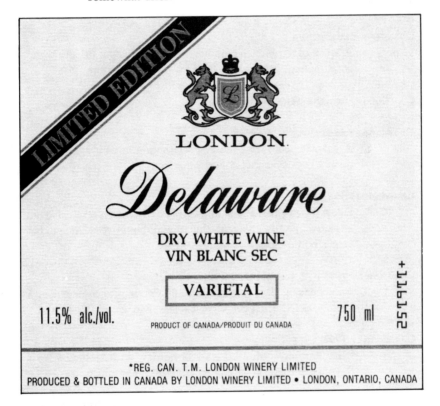

Chablis (Beaupré)

> Pale and full-bodied; clean, but somewhat less dry than a chablis should be.

Chablis (London)

> A dry blend of seyval blanc, delaware, elvira and emerald riesling, the latter from California.

Chablis 1981 (Mission Hill)

> Pale, with a delicate, fruity nose, medium-bodied and fruity in flavour: finished with a hint of residual sweetness.

Chablis (Mission Hill)

> This pale, greenish wine with the delicate aroma of new hay is somewhat fatter and slightly sweeter than one expects in a chablis, but still is attractive.

Chandelle Blanc (Charal)

> A touch of the French colombard grape gives this off-dry white an attractive, grassy aroma and a soft, full texture.

Chardonnay See also **pinot chardonnay**

Chardonnay 1983 (Andrés Ontario)

> A pale, delicate wine, somewhat lacking in fruit intensity but crisply dry. Potential ☂ when mature.

Chardonnay 1983 (Bright's B.C.)

> ☂☂ Pale with greenish glints, this crisply dry wine has an elusive but attractive perfume, suggesting it will improve with another year's bottle-aging.

Chardonnay 1983 (Casabello)

> ☂ Another lean, dry wine but with more complex aromas and a kiss of oak to flesh it out. Give it at least two years in the bottle.

Chardonnay 1982 (Casabello)

> Pale, lemony-coloured and bone-dry with delicate fruit flavours: the grassy aroma recalls sauvignon blanc.

Chardonnay 1982 (Charal)

> ☂ Pale, with a flowery bouquet and delicate in flavour: crisp and dry.

Chardonnay 1982 (Chateau des Charmes black label)

> ☂☂☂ Crisp and dry in the Burgundy style, this wine derives its complex aroma and flavours from oak maturing. The winery also releases less intense chardonnays with gold and white labels. All are elegant examples of the best chardonnay-making in Canada.

Chardonnay 1982 (Chateau-Gai Lincoln County appellation)

Gold, with a subdued personality which should mature with bottle age: dry and austere.

Chardonnay non-vintage (Divino)

A pale, lean, bone-dry wine with a faintly musty aroma.

Chardonnay Private Reserve 1979 (Divino)

Gold and full-bodied, this is an austere example of the variety.

Chardonnay 1982 (Hillebrand)

Pale and dry, but still developing character.

Chardonnay 1983 (Inniskillin)

♟♟. Pale gold, crisp and dry, this is an attractive French-style wine with a toasty flavour and ripening aroma. About 30 per cent of it was first oak-aged and then blended with unoaked wine.

Chardonnay 1983 Montagu Vineyard (Inniskillin)

♟♟ Pale gold, this has been aged totally in French oak, developing a rich, toasty flavour.

Chardonnay 1983 Seeger Vineyard (Inniskillin)

♟♟♟ Pale gold, with a rich, toasty flavour, this has an intense aroma and potential to mature to a fine, buttery chardonnay.

Chardonnay 1982 (Inniskillin)

♟♟ This vintage was the first to get more oak-aging to balance, and add complexity to, the fruit: a good burgundian style has emerged.

Chardonnay 1983 (Mission Hill)

♟♟ Light gold with a delicate buttery aroma, full-bodied and intensely fruity.

Chardonnay 1983 (Reif)

A very pale, delicate wine, cleanly made but lacking intensity.

Chardonnay 1982 (Sumac Ridge)

Pale, with light glints of green, and a bouquet that recalls truffles: light, delicate and dry.

Chasselas 1983 (Mission Hill)

🍷 Pale, with delicate aroma, this is a crisp, dry, light-bodied wine.

Chasselas 1983 (Uniacke)

🍷 Pale with a fruity aroma: dry and slightly tart.

Chasselas 1982 (Uniacke)

🍷 Very dry and light in body, with a slightly nutty flavour. The grape is popular in Switzerland and other cold-climate regions because it is mature by midseason, prolific, and low in acidity.

Chateau de Lyons White (Montravin)

A blend made for Les Lyons Imports of Markham, Ont., this is a fruity, Germanic-style white.

Chenin Blanc 1982 (Bright's Vaseaux Cellars, B.C.)

🍷🍷 This vintage is sold out, but its quality makes future vintages worth searching for. It was a lush, fruity wine, like biting into a ripe peach.

Chenin Blanc 1981 (Calona)

🍷🍷 A charming, full-bodied wine with green glints and ripe, lush bouquet and flavour.

Chenin Blanc 1982 (Casabello)

🍷 A well-balanced, crisp white with good body, almost a nutty flavour, and an apple-like aroma.

Chenin Blanc 1981 (Mission Hill)

🍷 Greenish glints and a perfumed aroma: fuller in body, less crisp than this winery's Private Reserve, and dry.

Chenin Blanc 1981 Private Reserve (Mission Hill)

🍷🍷 Greenish glints and an elegantly perfumed aroma: full-flavoured but with a crisp acid backbone, and dry.

Chenin Blanc 1981 (Mission Hill/Pandosy)

Delicate aroma and flavours, crisp and dry.

Chenin Blanc 1981 (Sumac Ridge)

A pale white with a delicate bouquet and relatively high acidity that will appeal to some.

Concerto White (Montravin)
> This gold-coloured wine has 30 per cent Italian trebianno wine in the blend, resulting in an almond aroma and a dry, nutty flavour.

Cour Blanc (Chateau des Charmes)
> ♥ A crisp, fruity white now being finished nearly dry.

Cuvée Blanc (Charal)
> A crisp blend of siegfried rebe and riesling: fruity but dry.

Cuvée Blanc (Geloso)
> The top-selling Quebec white, made in a style the winery calls "amiably dry."

Cuvée Val-Jalbert (Julac)
> A dry white.

Delaware 1982 Limited Edition (London)
> ♥♥ A pale, straw-coloured wine with a flowery aroma and intense grape flavours that linger on the palate: dry, but the fruit makes it a sipping wine.

Domaine d'Or White (Andrés)
> Delicate, fruity, off-dry, with a California character.

Dry White non-vintage (Mission Hill)
> ♥ A fresh, clean and dry generic, delicate of aroma and somewhat neutral in flavour: aims at the style of Bordeaux.

Durnford House White (Charal)
> A fresh, fruity blend, just slightly off-dry, for everyday consumption.

Dutchess (Charal)
> Dry and fruity, with a herbal aroma: best consumed young.

Dutchess 1983 (Jordan & Ste-Michelle Ontario)
> Straw-coloured, with a delicate flowery aroma and pleasant, if subdued, fruit: dry.

Dutchess 1982 (Jordan & Ste-Michelle Ontario)
Delicate herbal aroma, dry and crisp.

Eagle Ridge Mountain White (Andrés Ontario)
Made largely from labrusca grapes, this is nevertheless acceptably clean, fresh and grapy in aroma, and slightly sweet in the finish.

Edelwein (Chateau-Gai)
A German-style white, somewhat heavier in texture than Alpenweiss.

Ehrenfelser 1983 (Andrés B.C.)
♈♈♈ Light gold with a complex aroma hinting of fruit and herbs: fuller-bodied and sweeter than the 1982, with natural sweetness balancing the wine's cleansing tartness.

Ehrenfelser 1982 (Andrés B.C.)
♈♈♈ Pale gold colour, intense aroma: a full-bodied white with lovely fruity flavours and an off-dry finish.

Ehrenfelser 1983 (Gray Monk)
♈♈♈ Lovely ripe aroma with intense, mouth-filling fruit. The full flavour gives the impression that this dry wine is just slightly off-dry.

Eiswein 1983 (Hillebrand)
♈♈ This specialty wine is available in very small quantities: made from vidal grapes harvested early in December, it is sweet and rich, with intense strawberry-like flavours.

L'Entre Cote White (Bright's)
A seyval blanc blend – dry, crisp and clean.

Entre Deux Pays (Corelli)
Verduzzo grapes dominate this full-bodied wine, dry in the Italian style. Let it breathe to dissipate a slight sulphurous odour.

Entre Lacs (Bright's)
An austerely dry wine, straw-coloured and medium-bodied.

Entre Nous (Chateau des Charmes)
> Pale and dry, this wine has a delicate fruity aroma and clean, fresh flavours, but not much character.

Etienne Brûlé Blanc (Hillebrand)
> Specially blended from seyval blanc and vidal for the Ontario bicentennial in 1984, this wine, with hints of green in the colour, is flowery in aroma and dry in finish.

Falkenberg (Jordan & Ste-Michelle B.C.)
> A soft, fresh, full-bodied wine with 20 per cent chenin blanc in a blend of B.C. grapes.

Falkenberg (Jordan & Ste-Michelle Ontario)
> Brilliant, straw-coloured wine with a subdued aroma and an uncomplicated fruitiness.

Fleur de Blanc (Casabello)
> This was once the best of the Okanagan riesling wines: the blend has changed in recent years to replace some of the Okanagan riesling with vinifera to the wine's benefit.

Franciscan Canadian Chablis (Andrés)
> Green glints in the colour – a fruity, medium-dry white with a delicate floral aroma. The blend has been improved since the 1983 vintage with the addition of ehrenfelser grapes.

Fumé Blanc 1983 Private Reserve (Mission Hill)
> ♀♀ This dry wine has the typical so-called grassy aroma of the sauvignon blanc grape, with a fruity flavour recalling kiwi fruit.

Furmint 1983 (Bright's B.C.)
> ♀ One of the experimental varieties available only at the winery store, this pale greenish wine shows a ripe, herbaceous aroma but somewhat less fruit in the mouth: dry.

Gala Keg Dry White (Casabello)
> An everyday white sold in a convenient bag-in-box as well as a two-litre bottle.

Gala Keg Medium Dry (Casabello)
> Similar to but significantly sweeter than its dry companion.

Gala Mini-keg Dry White (Chateau-Gai)

Dry simple, grapy wine packaged in a one-litre box; designed for picnics and similar rustic occasions.

Gamay beaujolais Blanc de Noir 1981 (Chateau des Charmes)

Pale, thin, and somewhat neutral in character.

Gamay Blanc 1983 (Inniskillin)

🍷 Pale with a blush of orange, this is a nutty, full-bodied white with character.

Gewurztraminer 1983 (Bright's)

A golden-hued white: may ripen, after two years bottle age, but now lacks spice.

Gewurztraminer 1982 (Bright's)

Gold, with a subdued aroma and flavour.

Gewurztraminer 1981 (Calona)

🍷 Green glints, attractive, herbaceous aroma, and soft texture: lacks the spiciness expected in this variety.

Gewurztraminer 1983 (Casabello)

Pale with just a blush of pink colour, this wine has delicate aromas and a subdued character which should emerge with bottle age: off-dry.

Gewurztraminer 1982 (Casabello)

Gold in colour, subtle and restrained in character, and off-dry. This has replaced the 1978 vintage that has matured past its prime in the bottle.

Gewurztraminer 1983 (Claremont)

Medium-bodied dry wine with a sweet candy-like aroma. Subdued fruit flavours.

Gewurztraminer 1982 (Gray Monk)

🍷🍷 Golden-hued, with the spiciness this grape should produce: dry.

Gewurztraminer 1983 (Hillebrand)

🍷🍷 With its fine, spicy aroma and a peppery finish, this dry, Alsatian-style wine has potential to become more intense in the bottle.

Gewurztraminer 1982 (Hillebrand)

♟♟ Pale gold in colour, dry, with good body and excellent, spicy aroma and flavours. Older vintages have developed a bouquet of honey and apricots.

Gewurztraminer 1983 (Inniskillin)

♟♟♟ A full-bodied wine, with a good spicy aroma and character; crisp and spicy flavours.

PRIVATE RESERVE

Gewürztraminer
1981

This wine has been selected by our winemaker for limited bottling as his PRIVATE RESERVE. Only varietal wines of outstanding character and vintage merit this recognition.

This bottle is Private Reserve

Mission Hill Vineyards Inc., Westbank, British Columbia

750 ml.   11% alc. / vol.   White Wine   Vin Blanc

MISSION HILL VINEYARDS INC.

Gewurztraminer 1981 Private Reserve (Mission Hill)

♟♟ Gold, with a lovely lichee-nut aroma, soft and full-bodied: a long, lingering, dry finish.

Gewurztraminer 1981 (Mission Hill)

♟ Pale gold with greenish glints and a delicate, spicy aroma, soft, fruity flavours, medium-bodied: a slight residual sweetness in the finish.

Gewurztraminer 1983 (Reif)

♟♟ Gold, with an elegantly spicy aroma and delicate flavours.

Gewurztraminer 1982 (Sumac Ridge)

    ♟   Pale, with green glints, and a fine, spicy bouquet: light in body, almost dry, leaning towards the Alsatian style.

Gewurztraminer 1983 (Sumac Ridge)

    ♟♟   A lemon-coloured, fat, richly flavoured wine, almost dry: much more intense than the 1982.

Gewurztraminer 1982 (Uniacke)

    A pale gold, crisply dry wine with a flowery nose and somewhat lacking in the spice usually associated with this grape.

Gold Shield (Andrés)

    A well-made, German-style white with a muscat aroma and fruity flavours.

Grüner Veltliner 1983 (Inniskillin)

    ♟   A pale, greenish-hued wine with a very delicate aroma, but full and fruity like a fresh melon.

Haut Villages Dry White (Calona)

    ♟   Green glints and a ripe, intensely fruity aroma: soft in texture with good body, finishes dry. Very much a California-style wine.

Heritage Estates Canadian Chablis (Barnes)

    A crisp, clean, dry table wine.

Heritage Estates Canadian Rhine Wine (Barnes)

    A blend of seyval blanc, dutchess, ventura and emerald riesling: soft and off-dry, aiming at a simple German style.

Hochtaler (Andrés)

    Light wine with a perfumed bouquet, modelled on the medium-dry German whites.

House Wine (Andrés)

    Known as Dinner Wine in Ontario, this one is simple and fruity.

House Wine (Bright's)

    This well-made, medium-dry white was the fourth largest-selling domestic white by 1982, when a dry version was added. In Quebec comparable blends are sold as **Notre Vin Maison**.

Interlude (Jordan & Ste-Michelle)
A German-style, medium-dry wine made in Ontario with elvira subconcentrate, and full of grapy flavours; the B.C. version is slightly less fruity.

Johannisberg riesling See also **riesling**

Johannisberg riesling 1983 (Andrés B.C.)
♙♙ Light gold, with an attractive floral aroma typical of the variety: fruity and off-dry, with a tart finish recalling Rhine wines.

Johannisberg riesling 1982 (Andrés Ontario)
♙ Pale gold with an attractive floral aroma, soft in texture: well balanced.

Johannisberg riesling 1983 (Barnes)
♙♙♙ Full bodied, with a touch of sweetness: attractive floral aroma and ripe peach flavour.

Johannisberg riesling 1983 (Bright's)
♙♙ A green-gold wine with a delicate flowery aroma, subdued fruit and a dry finish.

Johannisberg riesling 1981 (Bright's)
Gold colour and nutty aroma signals that the vintage is past its peak.

Johannisberg riesling 1983 (Calona)
Pale gold, with a full, flowery aroma. A potential **♙♙** wine with a year's bottle-aging.

Johannisberg riesling 1982 (Calona)
♙♙ Straw-coloured with a delicate, flowery aroma and clean, delicate fruit flavours: a slight touch of residual sweetness.

Johannisberg riesling 1983 (Casabello)
A wine with greenish hues, flowery aroma, and a touch of residual sweetness to bring out the charm of the variety.

Johannisberg riesling 1982 (Casabello)
Pale, almost dry; its bouquet and fruit flavours become complex as this wine matures.

Johannisberg riesling 1982 (Charal)

🍷 Pale, with a flowery nose, and crisp.

Johannisberg riesling 1983 black label dry (Chateau des Charmes)

🍷🍷🍷 Light gold, with a dramatically flowery aroma and full body, but crisply dry.

Johannisberg riesling 1983 black label late harvest (Chateau des Charmes)

🍷🍷🍷 A very elegant dessert wine, intensely fruity in aroma and flavour, and silky on the tongue.

Johannisberg riesling 1982 white label (Chateau des Charmes)

🍷 Gold, intensely fruity aroma, good body, yet crisp and dry in the Alsatian style.

Johannisberg riesling 1982 (Chateau-Gai Lincoln County appelation)

🍷🍷 Straw-gold, with a delicate, flowery nose and a fruitiness of medium intensity: just a hint of sweetness gives it charm.

Johannisberg riesling 1981 (Chateau-Gai Lincoln County)

Slightly softer and with more fruit than the 1980 version, but still a good varietal wine.

Johannisberg riesling 1980 (Chateau-Gai Lincoln County appelation)

A pale gold wine with a honey-like character in old age.

Johannisberg riesling 1983 (Colio)

🍷🍷 An elegant, flowery wine with so much fruitiness in the flavour that it seems sweeter than is indicated by its sugar code of one.

Johannisberg riesling 1982 (Colio)

🍷🍷 Pale gold in colour, very delicate, with an elegant, flowery aroma: slightly and refreshingly tart.

Johannisberg riesling (Hillebrand)

🍷 Both 1982 and 1983 vintages have flowery aromas and are just sweet enough to bring out charm.

Johannisberg riesling 60th Anniversary Special Reserve (Jordan & Ste-Michelle B.C.)

🍷🍷🍷 Fat, fleshy wine with a lingering finish from the 1983 vintage.

Johannisberg riesling Special Reserve 1983 (Jordan & Ste-Michelle Ontario)

    ❢❢❢   Gold in colour, this intensely fruity wine is silky and elegant in the classic late-harvest German style.

Johannisberg riesling Special Reserve 1982 (Jordan & Ste-Michelle Ontario)

    ❢❢   A ripe, fruity wine with a lovely apricot aroma.

Johannisberg riesling 1983 (Mission Hill)

    ❢❢❢   Pale, and a ripe aroma of peaches: intensely fruity, with a crisp, slightly tart finish.

Johannisberg riesling 1982 Late Harvest (Pelee)

    ❢   Golden-hued, with a bouquet of ripe apricots: sweet and full-bodied, lingering flavours, in something like the German auslese style.

Vin Villa Johannisberg riesling 1982 (Pelee)

    ❢❢   Pale, with a subdued aroma, but raisiny flavours and a fleshy texture: off-dry.

Johannisberg riesling 1983 (Reif)

    ❢❢   Flowery, full and fruity. The previous vintage was the first sold out after the winery opened.

Johannisberg riesling 1982 (Uniacke)

    🍷   A tart, fruity wine with an aroma recalling peaches.

Johannisberg riesling 1983 Late Harvest (Vineland/St. Urban's)

    🍷🍷   Complex, full-bodied, and intense. This impressive first release from the winery bodes well for planned 1984 vintage releases of bacchus, chardonnay, seyval blanc and vidal as well as riesling.

Kerner (Gray Monk)

    🍷🍷   The dramatic bouquet recalls lichee nuts: dry but full-bodied, almost fat in texture, its finish long and lingering. A good wine with cheese or pâté.

Kerner 1983 (Inniskillin)

    🍷   Pale, delicate, subdued fruitiness: dry.

Lasalle Notre Vin Maison Blanc (Bright's Quebec)

     A medium-dry table wine.

Maria Christina (Jordan & Ste-Michelle)

     This blend bears a family resemblance to Toscano from the same winery, but it is noticeably less dry and fuller-bodied. The light (low-alcohol) version is fresh and fruity.

Matsvani 1982 (Bright's B.C.)

    🍷   Pale green with complex fruit flavours and dry finish. This vintage was experimental: later vintages are available in commercial quantity.

Matsvani 1983 (Bright's B.C.)

    🍷🍷   A real charmer, this flavoursome wine from a Russian grape variety has an attractive muscat aroma. It is just slightly off-dry.

Mission Ridge Premium Dry White

    🍷   Pale, with greenish glints, a flowery aroma and fruity flavours: medium-bodied, crisp and dry.

Mon Village (Bright's)

     Crisp, and dry in the Bordeaux style: blended from Ontario and French white wines.

Mountain Sauterne (Calona)

     An off-dry blend including Okanagan riesling.

Nietzscheim (Charal)

This winery's entry into the German taste-alike league is a delicate blend of seyval blanc and riesling.

Novembrino 1983 (Colio)

❦ This white, nouveau-style wine is a real novelty, worth looking for in future years. This version, a blend of seyval blanc and 15 per cent riesling, was as delightful as biting into a cool, fresh muscat grape.

Okanagan riesling 1983 (Mission Hill/Pandosy)

Pale, its musty aroma typical of the variety: lean and light-bodied, with just enough residual sweetness to take the edge off its acidity.

Okanagan riesling (Sumac Ridge)

The winery's original style was dry and delicate: with the 1983 vintage, its wine was finished with just a hint of sweetness.

Okanagan riesling 1982 (Uniacke)

Pale, with a flowery aroma; well-balanced.

Orfée Blanc (Geloso)

Dry and crisp in the Italian style.

Perla 1980 (Colio)

🍷 A sweet, fruity white made from niagara, another labrusca, and handled well.

Perle of Csaba 1983 (Sumac Ridge)

🍷🍷🍷 Pale, with green glints and a lovely muscat bouquet: a soft, fruity and slightly low-alcohol sweet dessert wine, with a lingering finish, sold only in half bottles. Drink young.

Pinot Auxerrois (Gray Monk)

🍷🍷🍷 This clean, fresh white, its delicate bouquet recalling apples, is made from grapes propagated from Alsatian cuttings. Greenish-gold, full-bodied, even fleshy, with good balance and long finish: dry without being austere.

Pinot Bianco non-vintage (Divino)

🍷 A pale straw-coloured wine with a subdued, fruity aroma and good fruity flavours, though slightly tart: crisp and dry.

Pinot Bianco Private Reserve 1980 (Divino)

Gold with a subdued aroma, this crisply dry wine has complex herbal flavours.

Pinot Blanc 1983 (Claremont)

Straw-coloured, this full, fleshy wine is so fruity that, while the label says dry, the impression it leaves is off-dry.

Pinot chardonnay See also **chardonnay**

Pinot chardonnay 1983 Limited Edition (Barnes)

🍷🍷 Straw-coloured, delicate and full-bodied, worth cellaring for two years.

Pinot chardonnay 1982 (Bright's)

🍷 The winery has released this variety since 1956, invariably in a steely, austere style. Still to come is the 1983 vintage, which includes some oak-matured chardonnay: it should be softer in texture.

Pinot chardonnay 1983 (Jordan & Ste-Michelle)

A pale wine with a delicate, herbal aroma and subdued fruit: dry. Potential to mature to 🍷.

Pinot chardonnay 1982 (Jordan & Ste-Michelle Ontario)

🍷🍷 Richly gold like a sauterne, with an unusual, buttery aroma: flavour is ripe and finish dry. A controversial wine.

Pinot gris 1982 (Claremont)

A delicate bouquet, but good body and balance, finished with a touch of residual sugar, leaving it charmingly off-dry.

Pinot gris (Gray Monk)

🍷🍷🍷 This grape, which inspired the winery's name, is also from Alsace: the straw-coloured wine is dry, but soft and full-bodied, with a delicate, fruity bouquet.

Princière Blanc (Chateau-Gai)

A very dry, crisp white that compares well with Bordeaux in its price range: blended from chardonnay, French hybrids and California varieties.

Rêve d'Eté (Chantecler)

A medium-dry wine made primarily from the California emerald riesling grape.

Rheingold 1982 (Reif)

    Pale, with a flowery aroma, this is a complex, somewhat sub-dued blend of white hybrids: just a whisper of sweetness.

La Rienha 1983 (Bright's B.C.)

    A light, crisply dry white with an interesting peppery note in both the aroma and the flavour.

Riesling See also **johannisberg riesling**

Riesling (Andrew Wolf)

A golden, full-bodied white, soft in texture, and showing the complexity of maturing in wood.

Riesling 1983 (Claremont)

Greenish in colour with a fruity aroma, this is a soft, slightly off-dry wine, a nice example of Okanagan riesling.

Riesling 1983 (Inniskillin)

    Pale greenish hue, with a developing flowery nose, good fruit, and balance: dry. The winemaker considers this the best standard-grade riesling he has made.

Riesling 1983 Late Harvest (Inniskillin)

    Brilliant silvery green hues which will become gold with age. This wine has an aroma of honey and apricots, rich fruity flavours and a long, lingering finish: sweet and with a touch of botrytis.

Riesling 1982 (Inniskillin)

    A delicate floral aroma, and dry.

Riesling 1983 (Mission Hill)

    This pale, dry wine has a delicate flowery aroma but con-siderably more fruit in the flavour than the nose suggests.

Rinegarten (Casabello)

Emulating a German-style white, this is a blend of Okanagan riesling and muscat, dry but fruity.

Riserva Bianco 1981 (Colio)

    A straw-coloured wine, made predominantly from seyval blanc, with a ripe, fruity bouquet, clean flavours and good finish: dry.

Rkatsiteli 1983 (Bright's B.C.)

A pale, fresh fruity wine with a delicately flowery aroma, but the flavour is tart.

Royal White (Calona)

The sweet companion to Royal Red.

Ste-Michelle Grande Cuvée (Jordan & Ste-Michelle)

A pale, crisply dry Bordeaux-style wine, neutral in character: good with shellfish.

Sauvignon (Fumé) Blanc 1983 (Claremont)

ΥΥ   Pale, with greenish glints, this has a lovely flowery aroma and is full-flavoured and fruity: slightly off-dry.

Sauvignon Blanc 1982 (Claremont)

Greenish glints, full-bodied, with the typical, attractive, grassy aroma and flavours of this grape. Enough character to be served with veal and roast fowl.

Sauvignon Blanc 1983 (Mission Hill/Pandosy)

ΥΥ   Pale, greenish glint and a ripe, grassy aroma, true to the variety: intensely fruity with a long finish, and dry.

Scheurebe 1983 (Andrés B.C.)

ΥΥΥ   Light gold, with a lovely, fruity aroma: a soft, fleshy wine with a long finish. Slightly sweeter in style than the 1982.

Scheurebe 1982 (Andrés B.C.)

ΥΥ   Pale, with a haunting aroma of new-mown hay: good fruit flavours, and crisp in the finish.

Schloss Hillebrand (Hillebrand)

ΥΥ   Full-bodied, medium dry, with a silky texture and a dramatic, spicy bouquet that comes from the German morio-muskat grape in this blend of seyval blanc and other hybrids. The best of the pseudo-German whites made in Canada.

Schloss Laderheim (Calona)

Υ   Patterned after best-selling German whites, this complex blend is based on Okanagan riesling. Light straw colour and fruity aroma: soft in texture, and just off-dry.

Selected riesling 1983 (Jordan & Ste-Michelle Ontario)
A clean, fresh, uncomplicated riesling, fruity and just off-dry.

Selected riesling 1982 (Jordan & Ste-Michelle Ontario)
This is Jordan's johannisberg riesling for general distribution: delicate, flowery aroma, light in body and fruity.

Semillon 1983 (Mission Hill)
Pale, with a delicate herbal aroma and flavours, tart and dry. Potential to mature to at least ▼.

Sentinel Blanc 1982 (Chateau des Charmes)
▼   A crisp, dry, Bordeaux-style wine.

Serekseya Rozovaya 1983 (Bright's B.C.)
Pale, with a melony aroma, this is a tart, fruity wine from a Russian grape variety.

Servino (Secrestat)
A light-bodied dry white.

Seyval Blanc 1982 (Andrés Ontario)
▼   Pale and intensely fruity, with a powerful aroma, soft and off-dry: a lovely sipping wine.

Seyval Blanc 1980 (Andrés Ontario)
Pale, with a delicate aroma: fresh and fruity, but tart in finish.

Seyval Blanc 1983 (Barnes)
▼▼   Pale gold, with a fruity nose and crisp, nutty finish.

Seyval Blanc (Charal)
▼▼   Pale gold, with an aroma and flavours reminiscent of apples: full-bodied, and finished with a touch of residual sugar.

Seyval Blanc (Chateau des Charmes)
▼▼   Clean, pale, crisp and dry. One of the best wines from this grape.

Seyval Blanc 1983 (Colio)
▼▼   Pale, fresh and dry. Colio examples develop complexity with a year or two bottle age.

Seyval Blanc 1982 (Colio)

🍷🍷 Pale, with a lovely floral bouquet, crisp and dry.

Seyval Blanc 1983 (Hillebrand)

🍷 The style has changed: the wine is drier, crisper and more delicate.

Seyval Blanc 1982 (Hillebrand)

The winery set out to make really big seyvals, with plenty of skin contact, and the result has been a controversial wine, with an aroma and flavours pleasantly recalling rhubarb.

Seyval Blanc (Inniskillin)

🍷 Clean and fruity is this winery's style. The 1983 is clean, dry and subdued in the style of the 1981. The 1982 vintage encouraged an off-dry wine with a big, fruity aroma.

Seyval Blanc 1983 (Jordan & Ste-Michelle Ontario)

Straw-coloured wine with intense fruit in the aroma and flavour, but a bitter finish.

Seyval Blanc 1982 (Jordan & Ste-Michelle Ontario)

🍷 Soft and fruity, with a flowery aroma: off-dry.

Seyval Blanc 1982 Limited Edition (London)

A lean and somewhat neutral white, slightly bitter in the finish.

Seyval Blanc 1983 (Mission Hill/Pandosy)

    ❢   Dry, fruity wine with a ripe apricot aroma.

Seyval Blanc (Montravin)

        Pale, dry, delicate, and somewhat neutral in flavour.

Seyval Blanc 1982 (Reif)

        A clean, crisp, greenish-hued wine, somewhat neutral in fruitiness.

Seyve Villard 1983 (Andrés Ontario)

    ❢   Light gold, with a nutty aroma and an interesting, if tart, melon-like flavour.

Siegfried Rebe 1983 (Bright's B.C.)

        This experimental variety is thin, too acidic, and has an unusual aroma, unlike wines from the same grape grown in Ontario.

Siegfried Rebe 1982 (Charal)

    ❢   A fleshy wine with a complex, fruity aroma; sometimes the winery blends it with dutchess.

Siegfried Rebe 1983 (Reif)

    ❢❢   A fresh and elegantly perfumed wine, with good fruit and a tart finish.

Sommet Blanc (Calona)

    ❢   Pale straw colour, fruity aroma, light-bodied, delicate and dry: based on verdelet.

Tassello Blanc (Montravin)

Pale, with greenish glints; refreshing, fruity and slightly tart.

Tiffany White (Calona)

A pale green wine with a California aroma, just off-dry; one of the best of the light (8 per cent alcohol) wines.

Toscano Bianco (Jordan & Ste-Michelle)

Dry, with a flowery aroma. The Ontario version is 60 per cent elvira, but the labrusca character has been overcome successfully by a concentrator that drives off the aroma. The B. C. wine is slightly fuller bodied.

Toscano Light (Jordan & Ste-Michelle)

Low-alcohol (7.9 per cent) slightly grapy in aroma, but otherwise neutral and dry.

Tourbillon d'Automne (Verdi)

A dry wine based on California-grown ugni blanc grapes, which make clean, fresh wines there and in Italy, where the grape originates.

Valdessa Blanc (Charal)

A dry white blend which endeavours, with some success, to compete with inexpensive dry whites from France.

Vaseaux Cellars Premium White (Bright's B.C.)

♥   A fruity, California-style wine with an attractive aroma reminiscent of grapefruit: flinty dry finish.

Verdelet 1983 (Andrés B.C.)

♥   Pale with green glints and a forceful, flowery aroma: medium-bodied and slightly off-dry, tart in finish.

Verdelet 1982 (Andrés B.C.)

♥   Delicate, flowery nose with a crisp, apple-like finish in the mouth: dry.

Verdelet 1983 (Casabello)

Greenish-hued, delicate in aroma and character, and a touch tart: off-dry.

Verdelet 1983 (Mission Hill/Pandosy)
>Greenish glints, and a ripe, rhubarb-like aroma: fruity and tart.

Verdelet (Sumac Ridge)
>♥ A dry white of delicate bouquet that is best drunk young, perhaps fifteen months after vintage.

Vidal 1982 (Charal)
>♥♥ Greenish gold, with fruity aroma and flavours: very German in style.

Vidal 1983 (Hillebrand)
>♥ Full-bodied and fruity, this has just enough sweetness to balance the natural acidity, leaving a crisp finish.

Vidal 1983 (Inniskillin)
>♥ Pale, with a flowery nose and a silky texture: fruity with an off-dry finish.

Vidal 1983 Late Harvest (Inniskillin)
>♥♥ Pale, with a flowery aroma: fruity, with a tartness that lets this wine finish freshly and cleanly.

Vidal 1982 (Inniskillin)
>Very aromatic and dry.

Vidal 1982 Late Harvest (Inniskillin)
>♥♥ A lovely, fat wine, with a flowery bouquet and the long, sweet finish of an auslese-style German white.

Vidal 1983 (Jordan & Ste-Michelle Ontario)
>♥♥ Straw-gold, with a delicate aroma, but good fruity flavours and a cleansing tart finish: slightly off-dry.

Vidal 1982 (Jordan & Ste-Michelle Ontario)
>♥ Lemony gold in colour with an aroma of lichee nuts: slightly off-dry.

Vidal 1983 (Reif)
>♥♥ This vintage shows a flowery aroma, intense fruit and a silky finish: off-dry.

Vidal 1982 (Reif)

    ♀   A silky-textured wine with a nutty bouquet and grapy flavours recalling muscat: off-dry.

Vin Blanc (Claremont)

    A dry but full-flavoured blend of verdelet, chenin blanc and semillon: popular in seafood restaurants.

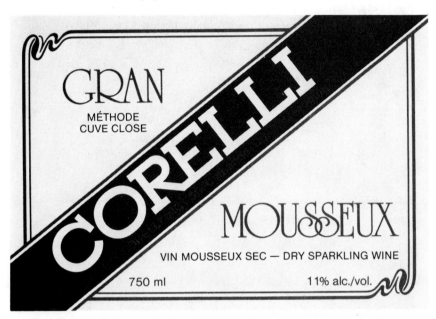

Vin Villa Johannisberg riesling 1982 (Pelee)

    ♀♀   Pale, with a subdued aroma, but raisiny flavours and a fleshy texture: off-dry.

Weinfest (Barnes)

    A blend, soft and fruity in a German style.

Weiss Burgunder 1983 (Bright's B.C.)

    ♀♀   An attractive pale straw-coloured wine with a complex aroma, good fruit and good balance, with the potential to age well in the bottle.

Welschriesling 1983 (Inniskillin)

    A very delicate, almost neutral wine: dry.

White Dry (Calona)
>   Everyday white.

White Wine (Beaupré)
>   Pale, with a fruity aroma, this is a straightforward, medium-dry wine aimed at the Canadian sweet tooth.

Wintergarten (Andrés)
>   Slightly sweeter than Hochtaler from the same winery.

SPARKLING AND ROSÉ WINES

Alpenweiss Sparkling (Chateau-Gai)

A straw-coloured, carbonated sparkler: fruity, and finishes slightly sweet.

Baby Duck (Andrés)

Sweet, sparkling red with a labrusca character.

Canada Cooler (Chateau-Gai)

Low alcohol (4.5 per cent), citrus-flavoured, carbonated beverage using a base of neutral white wine: refreshing on a hot day.

Champagne Canadien Extra Dry (Montravin)

♥ This winery's first bulk-fermented sparkling wine is clean, fruity and slightly sweet in the style of German bubblies, and inexpensive.

Chandelle Rosé (Charal)

Soft, fruity and medium dry, with a muscat spiciness in the aroma.

Chardonnay Blanc de Blancs 1978 (Inniskillin)

♥♥♥ The winery's first bottle-fermented, champagne-style wine, this is a fine, complex, yeasty sparkler, very dry and altogether memorable.

Club Spritz (Bright's)

With 5 per cent alcohol, this light wine mixed with sparkling mineral water is a refreshing, inexpensive hot-weather poolside drink. Comes in both red and white.

Coola Bianco (Jordan & Ste-Michelle)

This tart, lime-flavoured beverage is another of the citrus fad wines recently on the market.

Cuvée Blanc (Calona)

A straightforward, carbonated sparkler: bubbles are short-lived.

Dry Rosé (Mission Hill)

   ♥♥   This salmon pink, medium-bodied, dry rosé is crisp, fresh and appealing.

Gamay Rosé 1980 (Chateau-Gai)

      An attractive, dry rosé, with a pleasantly fruity bouquet.

Gramma Mary's Honey Wine (Andrew Wolf)

      An interesting rosé made with grenache grapes and the lightest touch of fermented honey wine. Available only at the winery, it is named for the vintner's mother-in-law.

Grand Mousseaux (Corelli)

      A sparkling bubbly with a fresh, fruity bouquet: this wine seems almost to foam on the palate.

Imperial Dry (Chateau-Gai)

   ♥   Chateau-Gai was the first North American winery to secure rights to the Charmat process for bubblies: this example, from French hybrid and catawba grapes, is slightly sweeter than the winery's **Imperial Brut**. Both are fruity like German sekts.

Kurhauser Trocken Sekt (Andrés)

      A sparkling wine competing with the popular German import: crisp but not too dry, and bubbles are short-lived.

Lonesome Charlie (Jordan & Ste-Michelle)
A sweet, blueberry-flavoured pop beverage.

M. Lamont Brut (Chateau-Gai)
A pleasantly inoffensive carbonated sparkling wine, just off-dry.

Pinot Gris Private Reserve 1979 (Divino)
❡ Orange-tinged rosé from a grape usually used for whites: this dry wine has an unusual taste and note of pepper.

Pinot Noir Rosé 1983 (Mission Hill)
Salmon pink, with a fruity aroma and a hint of residual sugar: astringent alcoholic finish.

Podamer Blanc de Blancs Brut Canadian Champagne (Montravin)
❡❡❡ A dry, bottle-fermented chardonnay, with long-lasting bubbles, toasty aroma and a fine, complex, yeasty character.

Podamer Brut (Montravin)
❡ A somewhat drier bottle-fermented bubbly, fruity but crisp.

Podamer Extra Dry (Montravin)
❡ In the tradition of champagne, extra dry really means medium dry: a grapy blend based on seyval blanc and dutchess.

Podamer Special Reserve (Montravin)
❡❡ A medium dry, bottle-fermented blend of hybrids and vinifera with a nutty, yeasty flavour.

President Extra Dry (Bright's)
❡ A classic, bottle-fermented bubbly, yeasty and with long-lasting bubbles, first released in 1949; the more recently released ❡ Brut is flinty and drier.

Pronto (Jordan & Ste-Michelle)
A sweet, cola-flavoured pop beverage sold only in Jordan's Ontario wine store.

Richelieu Canadian Champagne (Andrés)
Straw-coloured, with long-lasting bubbles and a good yeasty aroma: full-bodied, fruity flavours: dry.

Rosata (Colio)

A good, crackling, orange-coloured dry rosé from de chaunac.

Rosé (Montravin)

A clean, fruity de chaunac rosé, with just a touch of sweetness.

Serekseya Chornaya 1983 (Bright's B.C.)

A light, dry rosé with a fruity aroma and a lively peppery note to the taste. Another experimental wine.

Sparkling Alpenweiss (Chateau-Gai)

A carbonated white.

Spumante Bambino (Jordan & Ste-Michelle)

A sweet, carbonated, muscat-flavoured wine for those who enjoy the better-made but more costly muscat-flavoured spumante wines from Italy. Spumante Gold is a drier version of this product.

Spumante Bambino Gold (Jordan & Ste-Michelle)

A simple, grapy sparkler with large, lazy bubbles, a label that says dry and a taste that says sweet.

Summerland Rosé 1982 (Sumac Ridge)

Salmon-coloured, with a jammy nose, this unique blend of Okanagan riesling and chancellor is dry, but has just enough acid to give it backbone.

Vaseaux Cellars Premier Brut (Bright's B.C.)

This sparkler has tiny bubbles, a hint of muscat in the taste, and is sweeter than a brut should be.

FORTIFIED AND SWEET WINES

1966 Reserve Rare Canadian Sherry (Jordan & Ste-Michelle)

ɣɣɣ Creamy, amber-coloured: complex in flavour, lingering in finish.

Ancient Mead (London)

ɣ In Canada, only London makes mead, a rich, sweet honey wine.

Apricot (Mission Hill)

ɣ Clear and full-flavoured: an aroma of ripe apricots and almonds in this eau de vie.

Bartlett Pear (Mission Hill)

ɣɣ Clear and dramatic eau de vie, with a lovely aroma of fresh pears and a delicate pear flavour.

Cream Sherry (London)

ɣɣɣ Amber, with a grapy aroma and a rich, nutty flavour that lingers on the palate: sweet, but not heavy.

Double Six (Chantecler)

The company's leading apple cider.

Dry Flor Sherry (London)

ɣɣ Pale and crisp, for sophisticated sherry drinkers.

Dubleuet (Julac)

This sweet, fortified, blueberry-based aperitif is a subtle blend of the berry's flavour and aromas of various herbs. A distinctive product. The SAQ in one of its price lists offers a fanciful sangria recipe using this wine: three ounces each of Dubleuet and red wine, four ounces of vodka, eight ounces of ginger ale, and ice cubes.

Golden Cream Sherry (Andrés)

ɣɣ Amber; nutty aroma, full, smooth and lingering flavours.

Grappa (Mission Hill)

Clear, with a delicate, grapy aroma. A rounded, smooth example of a distilled beverage that can sometimes be fiery.

Hallmark Dry Sherry (Chateau-Gai)

🍷🍷🍷 A smooth and richly satisfying golden amber sherry with a nutty aroma.

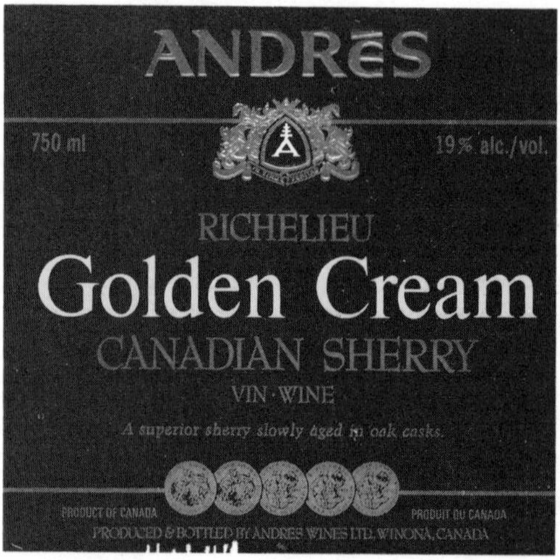

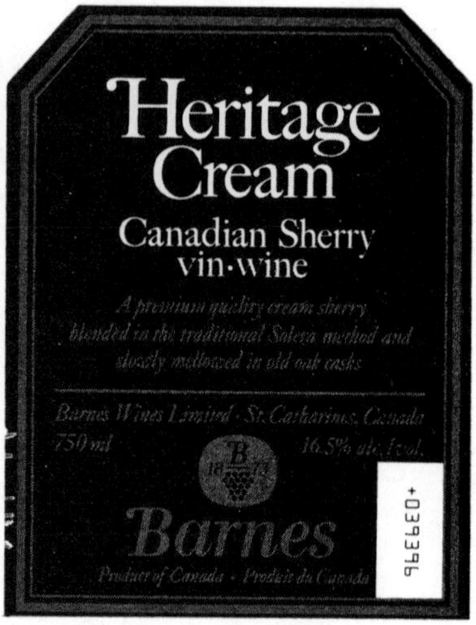

Hallmark Cream Sherry (Chateau-Gai)

Very sweet, caramel-coloured sherry with a subdued aroma.

Hallmark Oloroso Sherry (Chateau-Gai)

Sweet and grapy in flavour, this is somewhat clumsy in texture.

Heritage Cream Sherry (Barnes)

🍷🍷 Medium sweet sherry whose fruit flavours are still fresh.

Heritage Dry Sherry (Barnes)

Amber-coloured, nutty, and just off dry.

Heritage Ruby Canadian Port (Barnes)

🍷🍷🍷 Barnes made its reputation in fortified wines: this full-flavoured, oak-matured example is a newly blended premium product that shows its winemakers haven't lost the art.

Heritage Very Pale Dry Sherry (Barnes)
Ⳇ   Austerely dry golden sherry with a fine nutty aroma.

Kirsch (Mission Hill)
Clear and subdued, with a clean cherry aroma and flavour.

Light-n-Easy Sparkling Cider (Andrés Ontario)
A crisp, clean and refreshing apple-flavoured beverage.

Maximum Mousseaux Extra (Bright's Quebec)
A Charmat-process sparkling apple cider with 4.5 per cent alcohol: refreshing and inexpensive.

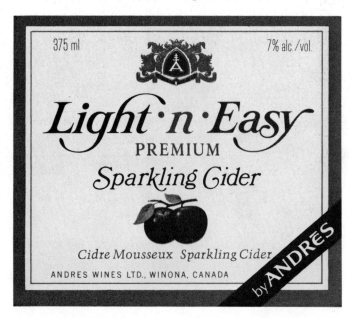

Mission Hill Aperitif (Mission Hill)
ⳆⳆ   An unusual aperitif wine, made by blending the juices of foch and riesling grapes and fortifying to 18 per cent with wine alcohol. Pink, full-bodied, richly flavoured: sweet in taste, but crisp and clean in finish.

410 Port (London)
Ⳇ   Medium-bodied ruby port, fresh and smooth.

Port (Mission Hill)

    ❦❦   A full-bodied, dark red, with a rich aroma of fruit and wood, and smooth, lingering flavours.

Private Stock Port (Chateau-Gai)

    Amber-coloured and very sweet.

Private Stock Sherry (Chateau-Gai)

    A sweet, nutty-flavoured sherry.

Sherry (Mission Hill)

    ❦❦   A dry, nutty, lemon-coloured sherry with a long finish.

INDEX